CASH CASH CASH

The Three Principles
of Business Survival and Success

Leslie N. Masonson

HARPER BUSINESS

A Division of Harper & Row Publishers, New York

Grand Rapids, Philadelphia, St. Louis, San Francisco
London, Singapore, Sydney, Tokyo, Toronto

Neither the author nor the publisher is engaged in rendering financial, legal, or accounting services to the reader through the sale of this book. Individual situations do vary, so the reader should consult a competent professional on questions specific to the individual.

The author and the publisher disclaim any liability or loss incurred, directly or indirectly, as a consequence of the use and application of any information contained in this book.

International Standard Book Number: 0-88730-410-9

Library of Congress Catalog Card Number: 90-4460

Printed in the United States of America

Library of Congress Cataloging-in-Publication Data

Masonson, Leslie N.
    Cash, cash, cash: the three principles of business survival and
success / Leslie N. Masonson.
        p.   cm.
    ISBN 0-88730-410-9
    1. Cash management.   2. Cash flow.   3. Success in business.
I. Title.
    HG4028.C45M2275 1990   90-4460
    658.15′244—dc20   CIP

90 91 92 93 HC 9 8 7 6 5 4 3 2 1

To my lovely and loving wife Marilyn,
my terrific son Dan,
and my delightful daughter Amy

Contents

Preface

Why I Wrote This Book

I have written this book to help you maximize your company's cash flow. That means getting the money from your customers sooner, paying your bills the last possible moment, concentrating your money to a single bank account, using the latest cash management techniques and information systems, managing your accounts payable, accounts receivable, and inventory more effectively, and knowing how to deal with your banks to squeeze every penny out of your daily business into an increased cash flow position. In today's uncertain and fast-changing world, you need all the help you can get to manage your company's cash effectively or you'll end up in bankruptcy.

If you have just started a business, are a small business owner, or are a financial manager or owner of a middle-sized company, then this book is for you. It will provide you with hundreds of tips on improving your cash flow by making simple changes to the way you manage your cash and your bank relationships.

This Book Contains Hundreds of Money-Saving Ideas

This book is divided into 14 information-packed chapters on improving your cash flow. Here is a brief description.

Chapter 1 covers the major reasons why businesses fail and why managing your cash is the most critical job you have. It offers a ten-question quiz to determine if you have cash management savvy.

After completing Chapter 2, you will understand the five key cash management objectives, the financial value of a day's lost interest resulting from delays in your billing and disbursing functions, and the reasons cash is a liability if you waste it instead of earning interest on it. You will also realize why banks have not been providing you with the specific services you need.

In Chapter 3 you get step-by-step guidelines on handling your accounts receivable, inventory, and accounts payable. These 59 specific recommendations will save you money.

Chapter 4 tells you everything you always wanted to know about how banks process and clear checks. And more importantly, it will teach you how to get the fastest availability on your money and how to interpret bank availability schedules to benefit you.

After completing this last chapter, you'll be ready to tackle the first key cash management objective—collecting your money faster than a speeding bullet. Chapter 5 covers the six types of remittances you can receive, the four types of check float you should master, the benefits and workings of two types of lockbox plans, and the additional benefits attainable using lockbox networks that speed your customer checks into available funds even while you're office is closed.

Chapter 6 focuses on the second objective—cash concentration. It shows you three ways to move your money from multiple banks to a central bank account for more productive use. Also included are three case studies to illustrate the best approach for you to use.

Disbursing your money slowly is the third objective and is covered in Chapter 7. Here the three types of disbursement accounts are explained, and the best one to use in your case is clearly illustrated by realistic examples. This chapter also covers ways to pay vendors, employees, and shareholders, using electronic funds transfer alternatives. Bank account reconcilement services, unique drafts, corporate trade payments, and electronic data interchange are all discussed.

Chapter 8 provides you with insight into methods for getting daily information—the last cash management objective—on your bank balances and deposits. Bank and third-party service providers are reviewed, and the benefits of treasury work-stations are explained.

After understanding the latest cash management techniques, you are ready to assess the effectiveness of your cash management practices. By using the CASH MAP in Chapter 9 you can diagnose your system and compare it to a state-of-the-art cash management system. You can now take the appropriate steps to change your system to maximize your cash flow.

Negotiate, negotiate, negotiate. That's the focus of Chapter 10. In dealing with your banks you need to know how to evaluate your banking relationships, how to manage them, and how to compensate your banks. This chapter covers these areas in detail. You will no longer have to feel uneasy and less than knowledgeable when dealing with your bankers. Moreover, once you obtain and review the bank's account analysis statement for your account, you will be in a much better negotiating position.

Chapter 11 provides you with specific information on the cash management services offered to small and middle-sized firms by 52 banks that I surveyed. It also provides the average pricing for 25 bank services in four geographic regions so that you can compare bank prices.

To provide you with additional insights on bank cash management services and bank calling officer effectiveness for small and middle-sized firms, I included six surveys that covered these areas. These surveys are found in Chapter 12.

The varying viewpoints of three experienced bankers across the country are provided in Chapter 13. These bankers discuss their views on the small and middle-sized business cash management marketplace. You'll find their insights very informative.

Finally, I present my view of the future in Chapter 14. I cover areas that you should be getting ready for, including banking deregulation, interstate banking, technological advances, and the use of expert systems.

Last but not least are thirteen information-packed appendixes that will provide you with additional resources to manage your cash.

How to Maximize Your Cash Flow
Using This Book

If you plan to read this book once and put it on your bookshelf, then you won't benefit from the many cash flow opportunities available to you. Read key chapters two or three times until you squeeze out all the money-making ideas. This book, unlike many that you have read, contains hundreds of cash management nuggets that are waiting for you to "mine" them. Keep a pen and pad handy. Make notes in the book's margin and make longer notations on your pad. Rearrange your notes into a list of priorities—items that will save you the biggest bucks— and then take action. It takes time to make changes, but you must start today. Don't forget, one-time improvements will provide long-term benefits.

You may become annoyed at the amount of detail that I present. I don't apologize for that because you need specific details to take action. Any good consultant would do the same for you. My objective is to motivate you to take action now.

Why I'm Qualified to Write
This Book

By profession I'm a cash management consultant. Over the last dozen years I've performed cash management studies for hundreds of firms in many industries with annual sales ranging from $25 million to $50 billion. I've identified over $50 million in savings for these firms by analyzing their cash management systems. My consulting experience spans three years as head of my own firm, nine years at Citibank/Citicorp and Bank of America NT & SA, coupled with seven years of bank operations management experience at Irving Trust Company.

For the past six years, I've been editor of the *Cash Management Digest & Analysis* newsletter that is published by Warren, Gorham & Lamont. I've also trained thousands of financial executives in cash management techniques over the past dozen years. I've also created the first video cash management training course, entitled "Managing Corporate Cash," which was produced by the Center for Video Education, Inc.

Contact Me after You've Read This Book

My purpose in writing *Cash Cash Cash* is to offer my expertise to firms like yours which desperately need cash management help—most firms do, whether they admit it or not. Unfortunately, there are few, if any, ways for you to get the detailed information you need to maximize your cash flow.

I invite each of you to contact me with any comments—both positive and negative—on this book. Furthermore, if you need guidance or encouragement in implementing any of the steps mentioned in this book, call or write. Our relationship does not have to end once you put this book down. I'd love to hear about your successes or difficulties in improving your cash management system or in dealing with your banks. Send me your comments and questions. The ball is in your court.

I look forward to hearing from each of you soon. Write or call. Have a great year and persevere!

Leslie N. Masonson, CCM
President
Cash Management Resources
20 McGarrah Road
Monroe, NY 10950
(914) 783-1231

Acknowledgments

First and foremost, I thank my family—Marilyn, Dan, and Amy—for their patience and understanding during the many lost weekends and for putting up with my occasionally "strange" behavior during the winter of '89 as I was completing this book.

I also want to thank Dr. Bernell K. Stone, Harold R. Silver Professor of Finance at Brigham Young University Graduate School of Management, for his time and effort in reviewing the manuscript. His numerous comments were perceptive, precise and extremely helpful. The editorial assistance, support, and dedication provided by Martha Jewett, Executive Editor at Harper Business, and Publication Services were superb. Publisher Mark Greenberg's constant encouragement and positive comments were appreciated. And to all the other professionals at Harper Business, thanks for your top-notch work. All these individuals played a part in turning this manuscript into a well-tuned, easy-to-read book.

The following individuals and organizations were gracious in providing their survey resources for use in the book: Beth A. Ritchey, Research Associate, Trans Data Corporation; Terry Hill, Manager, National Media Relations, National Federation of Independent Business; and Arthur J. L. Lucey, President, Alexander Lucey, Inc.

Additionally, I thank the 52 banks that provided information on their cash management services and pricing and National Bank of Detroit, Security Pacific National Bank, Digital Design, Inc., and Gelco Payment Systems, Inc. for permission to use certain printed material as exhibits. Special appreciation goes to three bankers who agreed to provide candid interviews that were presented in Chapter 13. These individuals were Keith D. Kulper, Vice President of Midlantic National Bank; Karl Ostby, Vice President of Norwest Bank Minneapolis; and the anonymous West Coast banker.

1

"Happiness Is Positive Cash Flow"

Frederick Adler

Without Cash Your Company Can't Survive

Good cash management is practiced by few and misunderstood by many . . . it should be practiced on a daily basis . . . it should be a way of life. —Edwin Lederman, Partner, Laventhol & Horwath

Cash is king; without it your company can't survive. Remember the three most important criteria in buying real estate: *location, location, location.* The same concept applies in running a business, except the three keys are *cash, cash, cash.*

Cash is the most precious commodity. Lack of cash is the primary reason for business failures. Let's look at some facts. In 1989 about 690,000 new businesses incorporated, 500,000 self-employed businesses formed, and 100,000 partnerships occurred. Sixty-three percent of them probably won't survive six years. According to a 1989 study by the National Federation of Independent Business' research foundation and American Express, 19 percent of nearly 3,000 firms surveyed didn't survive three years. (*New Business in America: A Three Year Study of Small Businesses and Their Owners*)

Business Failures Due to Cash Flow Problems

Earlier studies found that 27 percent of new businesses failed within two years, 51 percent within four years. Many reasons are given for this high failure rate. Let's look at a some statistics.

BDO Seidman, the national accounting and consulting firm, surveyed 1,873 business owners in 1989 in four industry groups and with annual revenues ranging from $2 million to $100 million. When asked, "What is the biggest concern for your business?" the business owners named:

- Cash flow (21%)
- Increasing sales volume (21%)
- Managing rising overhead (16%)
- Affordable employee benefits (14%)
- Availability of qualified labor and management (13%)
- Managing growth (12%)
- Foreign competition (3%)

According to 1989 business failure statistics from Dun & Bradstreet, there were 47,719 business failures compared to 57,099 in 1988—a drop of 12.9 percent.

A 1985 study of 203 firms by the Comprehensive Accounting Corporation cited the following reasons for business failure, as reported in *USA Today*, June 5, 1985:

Reason	Percentage
Bad management	33%
Inadequate capital	21
Lack of experience	16
Owner not dedicated	16
Economic circumstances	13
Poor cash management	11
High interest rates	7
Overspending	5
Other	18

In summary 32 percent of the failures were due to capital or cash shortfalls, and 20 percent were due to a combination of economic reasons and high interest, which can also affect a firm's cash position.

A 1975 study by Dun & Bradstreet found that *one-third* of business failures resulted from cash flow problems.

Poor Cash Management: An Overwhelming Reason for Business Failure

These independent studies indicated that the key concern or reason for business failure was *poor cash management*. If you do not pay attention to your actual daily cash flow, you face the threat of imminent financial extinction.

The Twin Evils

. . . most business failures are due to the twin evils of under-capitalization and inadequate cash flow. The name of the game, particularly for new and small firms, is cash flow management.

Source: Oliver L. "Bo" Hagan, Herzog professor in free enterprise, Baldwin Wallace College, quoted in Richard J. Maturi, "Staying Afloat," *Entrepreneur,* January 1989, p. 100.

Whom Is *Cash Cash Cash* Aimed at?

Cash Cash Cash was written for a very select audience:

- individuals starting a home-based or other type of business
- current owners of small businesses and the owners and financial managers of middle-market firms
- bankers who sell cash management services to these firms

The most common definition of a small business used by bankers is a firm with annual sales up to $10 million. Middle-market firms are defined by bankers as having annual sales up to $250 million. Although these definitions are arbitrary, they are as good as any. The Small Business Administration defines a small business as a firm employing from one to 500 persons, depending on the industry classification. By that definition *99 percent of all businesses in the United States are considered small.*

Cash Cash Cash has been written for two primary reasons—to help *you* stay in business and improve your firm's bottom line. It will also help you manage your accounts receivable, accounts payable, and inventory.

If you're not an expert in managing your firm's cash and handling your banking relationships, this book is for you. No matter whether your firm is a sole proprietorship, partnership, or corporation or whether it is for-profit or nonprofit, your firm needs cash to survive. Cash, not the goods or services you produce, is the ultimate end-product of your business. Without suffient cash coming through the front door, there is little hope that your business will survive.

Cash Cash Cash Concentrates on Day-to-Day Activities

Hundreds of books have been written on running small businesses, but they have not devoted more than a few pages, if any, to explaining practical cash management techniques. Even books focusing on cash flow or financial management from the perspective of small to middle-size firms have concentrated only on the accounting or financial statement aspects of cash, rather than the day-to-day operational and banking aspects. My objective is to fill this information void.

Cash Cash Cash will help you through the confusing and often mystifying subject of cash management and bank cash management products for your business. The subject matter is explained from the hands-on perspective of a cash management practitioner, not from an accountant's perspective and not through the use of arcane formulas and concepts.

Don't Be Naive about the Importance of Cash Flow

Every businessperson has a different opinion on the importance of managing cash and managing a businesss. I've heard some strange statements about cash flow and the economy. Here are a few paraphrased samples:

I don't pay too much attention to my day-to-day finances. My accounting records indicate that I'm doing fine. If I sell more of my products, my cash flow will take care of itself.

My company is very profitable. I have no cash flow problems.

I never plan for an unexpected business downturn, since it may never happen.

Do any of these statements sound familiar? Businesses run by people with these opinions may be prime candidates for bankruptcy. Let's review some actual quotes from more perceptive sources.

Cash inefficiencies in small companies can often reduce cash flow by 25% to 30%. More entrepreneurs are concerned with deals than with cash efficiency. (Udayan Gupta, "Locating Those Costly Leaks," *Venture*, December 1985, p. 118.)

Most modest-size companies like to think they're doing a good job of managing their most liquid asset—cash—but most don't. (Nathaniel Gilbert, "How Banks Look at Your Assets," *D&B Reports*, May/June 1986, p. 31.)

. . . [many small business owners] wake up one day to find that the price of success is no cash on hand. They don't understand that if they're successful, inventory and receivables will increase faster than profits can fund them. (John Sloan [President, National Federation of Independent Businesses], "Big Ideas for Your Small Business," *Changing Times*, November 1989, pp. 57–58.)

. . . Know where your money is . . . . That means getting a grip on simple but critical numbers like cash on hand, accounts payable and receivable, inventory, debt, overhead expense and available capital, including lines of credit. ("Big Ideas for Your Small Business," *Changing Times*, November 1989, pp. 57–58.)

It seems axiomatic that business assets should earn their keep all the time, cash no less than equipment. But it is astonishing how many executives who fret over idle equipment pay little attention to idle cash. (Anthony T. Bray, "Financial Planning for Principals of Privately Held Corporations," *Inc.*, March 1985, p. 116.)

Are You Cash Management Savvy?

Take This 10-Question Quiz

As the owner or financial manager of your company, how much knowledge of cash management practices and bank cash management products do you have? Ask yourself the following questions (be honest, now).

1. How current is your cash management knowledge? Are you aware of the revolution in electronic funds transfer (EFT) and electronic data interchange (EDI)? Are you aware of personal computer (PC)-based software that can save you time and money?

2. Do you have effective cash management practices to collect, disburse, and concentrate your cash?

3. Do your banks offer you competitively priced cash management products? How do you know?

4. Are you receiving the fastest availability on your deposited checks? If you're not sure, how do you find out?

5. Does your primary bank send a calling officer to see you on a periodic basis. If not, why not?

6. Do you use the same bank account for deposits and disbursements? (If so, you're not operating effectively.)

7. Are you receiving daily information on your deposits and balances via a PC? If not, why not?

8. Do you receive a monthly account analysis statement from your bank? If you don't, do you know how to get one? It is not a bank statement.

9. Do you know the financial condition of your banks? If not, do you know where to get the information?

10. Do you know where to find the resources you need to automate your cash management practices and procedures?

Not having the answers to these question is an excellent reason to keep reading this book.

Cash Cash Cash **Is Easy to Read**

This book is written in an easy-to-read style. It contains check-lists, tables, charts, quotes, and anecdotes. *Cash Cash Cash* is also easy to understand. It provides specific information that can be put to immediate use. Here's a sampling of what's ahead in upcoming chapters:

- Latest techniques available to manage your cash effectively
- Guidelines to develop your own effective cash management system
- Methodology to evaluate your existing cash managment system, to identify bottlenecks, and to make improvements
- Knowledge you need to talk intelligently with your existing or prospective bankers
- Ways to deal with banks to obtain the necessary services at a competitive price
- Instructions for using an account analysis statement to uncover unnecessary bank services and excess balances
- Surveys of how other firms of varying sizes handle their cash
- Listing of cash management banks in different parts of the country (Appendix 9) and a list of services they offer (Appendix 10)
- Average bank pricing of specific cash management services in four regions of the country—Northeast, Southeast, Central, and West
- Insights on bank-calling programs and methods of soliciting accounts
- Useful cash-management-related resources such as names of bank safety rating services, financial software programs, and financial books (Appendixes 8, 11, and 12, respectively)

This book will be different from other small business and financial books that you have read. It will explain the tricks of the trade from an insider's perspective. As a nationally recognized cash management expert, I've saved hundreds of companies and financial institutions tens of millions of dollars. I will provide you with an insider's viewpoint and save you money, no matter what size your firm.

Cash Cash Cash is loaded with money-making ideas. Look for them. Keep your pen handy. Mark up this book. It's your guide to improved cash flow.

What *Cash Cash Cash* Does Not Cover

This book is not all-encompassing, nor is it meant to be. Certain complex subjects need a separate book. Other authors have covered these areas. Therefore, the following topics have *not* been covered in this book:

- Investing
- Borrowing
- Cash forecasting
- Financial accounting

Available books for investing and borrowing are listed in Appendixes 11 and 12.

2

Cash Flow Is the Name of the Game

Without Cash You're Bankrupt

Money is round. It rolls away. — *Sholem Aleichem*

Keep on Top of Your Cash Flow

It's amazing how many business people lose sight of cash flow. That's the crucial building block for financial success. No matter how fantastic your company's products, sales force, quality control procedures, and management, your company will not survive unless you can generate sufficient cash to sustain the business. Cash is the fuel for your business, as it is for your car.

Learn to Manage Your Cash Flow

Unfortunately, too many business owners spend most of their time developing new customer markets, perfecting their products or services, and just running day-to-day operations. Cash flow usually does not rate a high priority until cash gets tight. Don't let your company join the ranks of failed businesses; learn how to manage your cash flow.

Source: Richard J. Maturi, "Staying Afloat," *Entrepreneur*, January 1989, p. 102.

Sophisticated accounting and bookkeeping entries will *not* save the day. Too many business owners concentrate on running the business but neglect the cash flow.

Know the Key Cash Management Objectives

What is cash management? Listed below are many of the activities that constitute the crux of cash management. Cash management is simply the effective handling of your cash to maximize its use—having the right amount in the right place and at the right time. This definition parallels what your business must do to stay in business—having the right product or service positioned at the right market segment, at the right time. Remember, a dollar saved by effective cash management is equivalent to a profit of a dollar on your product or service, because it increases the bottomline.

Cash management objectives are universal:

1. *Collect fast.* Collect money from your customers as fast and as often as practical and deposit your checks the same day as you received them. Throughout this book,

Exhibit 2-1 Cash and information flows must be managed. (Adapted by permission from Security Pacific National Bank.)

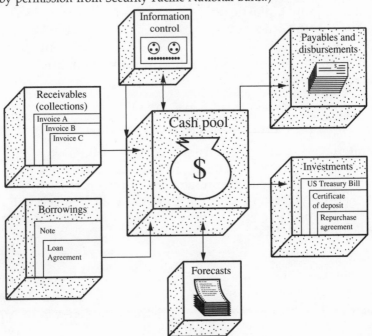

we'll be using terms such as receipts, remittances, or cash collections to refer to the money that customers remit to your company. All these terms are interchangeable.

2. *Disburse slowly.* Spend your money as slowly as possible, but within legal constraints and industry practice. We'll be referring to three different types of disbursement checking accounts: zero balance accounts (ZBAs), controlled disbursement, and remote disbursement. They operate differently. We'll explain which ones you should use.

3. *Concentrate funds.* Gather or mobilize your money from multiple banks (if you use more than one bank) to one bank for more productive use. Money sitting in five banks, for example, may be earning you no interest, and may even be costing you an opportunity loss. Terms such as cash concentration, funds mobilization, and funds concentration all refer to the practice of consolidating money to a central depository account known as a "concentration," or "master," account.

4. *Invest or borrow.* Invest or borrow money based on your short- and long-term cash needs of your business.

5. *Obtain daily information.* Obtain information from your banks and from internal sources on your daily cash in flows and outflows. Terms such as balance-reporting and information-reporting systems will be used interchangeably to refer to bank information systems offered to customers.

Financial Control

Typically, the little company quickly outgrows its financial control system or has trouble putting one into place at all. As a result, the simplest items, like keeping track of cash or tracking exactly how the business is doing, get lost. . . .Small business owners [may] find themselves out of financial control. They should start with a good control system right up front, so there is constant knowledge about what is going on.

Source: Robert Waterman (Author of *The Renewal Factor*), "Big Ideas for Your Small Business," *Changing Times*, November 1989, p. 57.

Know the Value of a Day's Interest

"Time is money," as Benjamin Franklin said. By instituting only a few of the sound cash management techniques in this book, you can make yourself money (much more than the price of this book). How much can you gain by collecting your customer remittances a few days earlier or by paying your vendor invoices a few days later? That depends upon a number of factors, including the dollar value of your firm's receipts or disbursements, the level of interest rates, and the number of days you can increase or decrease the float in your system. Float will be explained in detail in Chapter 4.

Let's look at a few different scenarios, as shown in Exhibit 2-2. For comparison, varying revenues and three interest rates are shown, as well as the interest earnings for one and four days.

Let's review an example in which a company has $20 million in annual revenues and can obtain its customers' checks four days earlier than usual throughout the year. The company can earn $22,222 a year if this money is invested at 10 percent interest rate. At 15 percent interest the earnings increase to $33,333 a year.

See the formula on the next page. Note that 360 days is used as the denominator. This is the industry practice for money market investments.

Exhibit 2-2.   Annual interest earnings attainable at varying revenues and interest rates.

Annual Revenues	Days Saved	Annual Interest Rate		
		8%	10%	15%
$100,000	1	22.22	27.77	41.66
	4	88.88	111.11	166.66
$500,000	1	111.11	138.88	208.33
	4	444.44	555.55	833.33
$1 million	1	222.22	277.77	416.66
	4	888.88	1,111.11	1,666.66
$20 million	1	4,444.44	5,555.55	8,333.33
	4	17,777.77	22,222.22	33,333.33
$100 million	1	22,222.22	27,777.77	41,666.66
	4	88,888.88	111,111.11	166,666.66

$$\text{Interest earnings} = \text{principal} \times \frac{\text{annual interest rate}}{360} \times \text{time}$$

$$= \$20 \text{ million} \times \frac{.15}{360} \times 4 = \$33,333$$

Your interest earnings increase the larger your annual revenues and the more days you save by collecting remittances early. The **percentage** of savings obtainable by a company with $100,000 in revenue is equivalent to the savings of a company with $100 million in revenue. A savings of $111.11, then, is worth as much to a company with $100,000 in annual revenues as $22,222 is to a company with $20 million in annual revenues.

Ride the CAMOL

To get a better perspective on the value of money, look at Exhibit 2-3, which shows the **Ca**sh **M**anagement **O**pportunity **L**adder (CAMOL). The CAMOL (pronounced "camel") con-

Exhibit 2-3. Cash Management Opportunity Ladder

Buyer	Elapsed Number of days		Seller	Elapsed Number of days
Order Goods	1		Send Catalog	1–10
Receive Goods	1–10		Receive Order	1–4
Receive Bill	1–34		Send Goods	1–15
Process Bill	1–28		Send Bill	1–30
Mail Payment	1		Receive Payment	1–4
Payment Clears Bank Account	3–6		Process Payment	0–1
			Deposit Payment	0–1
Total days	8–78		Money from Deposited Check Available	1–4
			Total days	6–69

tains two scenarios. One is for a buyer of goods or services, and the other is for a seller. Notice the wide variation in elapsed days for most of the steps. Managing the steps in the ladder by eliminating time delays can save you money as a buyer and seller.

Time Delay Has a Cost

Whether you're the buyer or seller of goods or services, there are delays in the process that inevitably cost you money. As the buyer you want to receive your order as quickly as possible, but you'd like to delay payment as long as possible. As the seller, you want to ship your goods as quickly as you can, and receive payment as soon as you can. Your firm, like all firms, is involved in both sides of this process.

As you see from the ladder, there are wide discrepancies in the time taken for the various steps. The longer delays in the process are expensive. For example, consider how two sellers handle their businesses:

Steps	Seller A	Seller B
Receives order	September 1	September 1
Sends goods to buyer	September 2	September 15
Sends bill to buyer	September 2	October 10
Receives payment	October 2	November 10
Processes payment	October 2	November 11
Deposits payment in bank	October 2	November 12
Receives availability on deposited check	October 4	November 14

Notice that seller A received money about 40 days earlier than seller B, even though they both received the buyer's order on the same day. Seller A's internal system for processing orders and cash is far superior to Seller B's lackadaisical approach. Seller A can earn interest on this money for 40 days while Seller B is still waiting for payment. For example, Seller A can invest $10,000 from a transaction for 40 days at 8% annual interest and earn $88.88.

$$\text{Interest earnings} = \text{principal} \times \frac{\text{annual interest rate}}{360}$$
$$\times \text{ days invested}$$

$$= \$10,000 \times \frac{.08}{360} \times 40 = \$88.88$$

The lesson to be learned from this simple example is that significant cash management opportunities exist in the mundane areas of shipping, billing, and cash handling for the seller of goods. The buyer of goods, on the other hand, has control over how and when to process and mail payment, as well as which bank to use to disburse the check. These steps, if handled properly, can also provide cash management opportunities. Therefore, savvy firms will "ride herd" on the CAMOL and manage every step on the ladder in their best interests. You should try to eliminate delays if you're the seller and lengthen them on the payment side if you're the buyer.

Cash Management Is Easy to Understand

The objective of this book is to provide you with the knowledge to assess, improve, and manage your firm's cash flow effectively. As a result, your bottom-line profits should improve. This knowledge could mean the difference between keeping your firm in business or filing for bankruptcy, especially if your business is only a few years old.

Learning how to improve your cash flow is critical to your company's future. Fortunately, you can easily understand and implement the cash management techniques that are applicable to your company, and many banks offer cash management products that can make your job of managing cash easy.

Unfortunately, most entrepreneurs and small business owners and some financial managers of small- to middle-market companies have been neither sufficiently educated about these cash management techniques and bank products nor provided with an easy-to-follow action plan on the effective use of them. This book will will do both.

A Wasted Commodity

Cash is not an asset but a liability, a wasted opportunity, unless it is earning money for its owner. Cash . . . is one of the most misunderstood, misidentified, and wasted commodities in the business world.

Source: Alfred De Salvo, "Cash Management Converts into Working Assets," *Harvard Business Review*, May-June 1972, p. 92.

Big Companies Aren't Necessarily Sophisticated in Cash Management

You may ask,"If cash management is so easy to understand and implement, then why isn't everyone doing it well?" I ask an equally enlightening question. "Don't all corporations over $250 million in sales effectively manage their cash?" The answer is NO.

After consulting with hundreds of companies, I've found that no significant correlation exists between a firm's size and its cash management sophistication. Surprisingly, many of the largest companies in the country aren't maximizing their cash flow, even though they have staff devoted solely to that function.

These large companies have trained individuals with titles such as "cash manager," "manager of banking," and "corporate cash manager." They report to assistant treasurers or directly to the corporate treasurer. In some companies, the controller manages the cash management function. These individuals have varying knowledge about cash management techniques that may be self-taught, learned from other individuals in the firm, or obtained from books, seminars, or bankers. Nevertheless, too many of these companies do not have sophisticated, well-run, or totally efficient and effective cash management systems. Why is that? There are many reasons, stemming from attitudes such as the following:

- *Let's do things the way we've always done them.* Most companies have conservative cultures in which the status quo is unquestioned and innovation is frowned upon.

- *Putting out the daily brush fires.* Financial managers may be overworked with daily minutiae and repetitive tasks and may not have time for future planning.
- *Don't rock the boat.* Companies do not want to disturb their exisiting banking relationships and therefore may not change to a bank with a more innovative service or a price advantage. The political environment in the company and the situation with bankers (e.g., board relationships) does not permit a relationship change without great personal risk.
- *The bank is selling, but we ain't buying.* Some bank cash management sales people do not use consultative selling to find the right product to meet the company's needs, but instead try to sell a product that the company does not need or want. Consequently, the firm's financial managers may not even know what services are offered by the firm's bank.

This list could go on ad infinitum, but I think you get the point. How effective do you think the 18.9 million small- to middle-market businesses are in managing their own cash with limited personnel and capital? *Cash Cash Cash* will provide you with the knowledge to effectively manage your cash.

Haven't Banks Been Providing Cash Management Products to Small and Middle-Sized Businesses for Years?

Most banks have only recently been awakened to the vast potential for providing loans and operating services to the small and middle-sized companies. Previously, the largest banks concentrated on providing services to companies with over $250 million in annual sales. In this market segment, the banks obtain larger profits. Economies of scale pay off in higher profit margins. That's as it should be. Banks are in business to make money, just like you and I are. As we will see in the chapter entitled "More Surveys Provide More Insight," small and middle-sized businesses are not very satisfied with commercial banks' response to their banking needs.

3

Manage Your
Working Capital
Components

Take an Active Role or You'll Be Sorry

In this business, you can't win 'em all.
—Johnny Roselli

Handling your working capital effectively can greatly improve your cash flow. This chapter focuses on three critical elements of working capital—accounts receivable, inventory, and accounts payable.

Invoice and Accounts Receivable Policies Should Be Tightened

Manage Your Invoice and Receivables Process

Two areas that too many small businesses neglect are invoicing and accounts receivable management. If well managed, both these areas can add to your bottom line, but if mismanaged, they can lead to real cash flow problems.

Tips on Turning Receivables into Cash

1. Get *detailed financial data* from a new customer.
   - Two credit references
   - Bank names, addresses, and account numbers
   - Copies of all checks for future reference

---

2. Make customer sign a *personal guarantee.*

3. Obtain *motor vehicle numbers* of all customers' cars. This can be useful in case judgment against customer is warranted.

4. Maintain *accurate accounting records and use a tickler system for follow-up.*

5. Place customer on *C.O.D. basis.*

6. *Work out payment schedule* for customer who needs time.

7. Determine if there are any *existing judgments or liens* against the customer.

Source: Eric J. Weiss, "Your Business and the Law," *Business Journal of New Jersey,* May 1986, p. 24 (emphasis added).

Pay Attention to Your Invoices

After selling your firm's product or service, you must generate an invoice before you can get paid. Everyone knows that, right? Doing it right, however, involves the following time-saving steps.

1. *Obtain customer orders by faster means than mail.* For example, have the customer fax the information to you, or set up an electronic tie-in to your personal computer (PC) through a modem. Consider using Electronic Data Interchange (EDI) to eliminate paper (see Chapter 7).

2. *Process orders quickly.* But, make sure the order is handled no later than the date specified by the customer.

3. *Prepare the invoice the same day.* Don't wait a few weeks, just because that's when you normally do it, especially for a large invoice amount.

4. *Mail the invoice out the same day it is prepared.* Don't wait a few days, especially at the beginning of a week, because if you mail it Thursday or Friday, you'll lose the weekend mail float.

5. *Smartly design your invoice.* Clearly lay out your amount due, due date, discount for early payment, and penalty interest for late payment. Indicate your mailing address

in bold letters, and request that the duplicate copy of the invoice be attached.

6. *If you use a lockbox* (a post-office box strategically located near your customers, to reduce mail time) to collect your remittances, *don't put your regular office address on the invoice*; otherwise your smart customers will mail the check to your office instead of your P.O. box, thereby gaining a day or two of extra mail float.

Develop Accounts Receivable Guidelines

1. *Check the financial health of new customers before offering them credit.* You may use one of the many rating services (e.g., Dun & Bradstreet). Also ask customers for five references from other businesses they are dealing with. Obtain cash, not a check, on your first order from a new customer. Have a detailed credit screening, approval, and risk process in place. Adhere to it.

2. *Make sure your invoice terms are not too generous.* Common terms are net 30 days (meaning that full payment is due within 30 days), but vary by industry.

3. *Give discounts for early payment.* This may be cheaper than borrowing money against receivables. If you offer a discount for early payment, then be careful not to offer too large a discount, unless you need the money because of a cash flow squeeze.

Will Your Customer Take a Discount?

Suppose you send a customer an invoice for $10,000 with terms of 1.5/10 net 30. This means that your customer will receive a 1.5 percent discount off the invoice amount if you are paid within 10 days. No discount is offered after 10 days, and full payment is due by the thirtieth day. Does your customer have a financial advantage to pay early, assuming his opportunity cost of funds is 11 percent?

Paying on the Tenth Day

To compare different payment scenarios, we use the present value formula. The basic concept is that having money today is worth more than having that same amount in the future.

$$\text{Present value} = \frac{\text{Cash received } n \text{ days from today}}{1 + \text{interest rate } (r)}$$

First, calculate the discount by paying in 10 days $= 10,000 - (10,000 \times .015) = \$9,850$. For 10 days, the PV is

$$\text{Present value} = \frac{9,850}{1 + [0.11(10/365)]} = \$9,587.33$$

The PV of Paying on the Thirtieth Day

No discount is taken, so

$$\text{Present value} = \frac{10,000}{1 + [0.11(30/365)]} = \$9,240.51$$

ANSWER: It is cheaper by \$346.82 (\$9,587.33−\$9,240.51) for the customer to pay the invoice in 30 days. The customer would want a higher discount rate than 1.5 percent to pay early. Actually, in this case the discount would have to be 7.31/10 just to equal the present value at 30 days without a discount.

4. *Charge penalty interest to customers who pay late, and charge back customers who take discounts after the discount period.* Too many companies are lax or bashful about charging their customers for late payments. Be firm. You can be selective, of course, if you know certain customers are having their own cash flow problems, but letting customers pay late is the same thing as lending them money!

5. *Don't procrastinate about following up on late payers.* Set up a standardized method for following up; for example:

   • Send out letter after five days overdue.

   • Call on the tenth day overdue.

- Call or write on fifteenth day overdue.
- Call or write again on twentieth day overdue.

On the thirtieth day, do one of the following:

- Send letter out from your attorney.
- Turn over to a collection agency.
- Use a collection attorney.

In your discussions, ask your customer when you will be getting paid. Take good notes. Don't send new merchandise if bills are still unpaid. Remember that bad debts hurt *your* bottom line. *Be vigiliant, and hang tough.*

6. Have an *aggressive* policy on *handling returned checks* and *obtaining a fee* from your customers who issue them.

Look for Six Danger Signals To Avoid Bad Debts

Companies can reduce their bad debt losses by looking for these danger signals:

1. Customer pledges accounts receivable to a bank that has claims on the customer's assets.
2. Other suppliers have suits or claims against your customer. These data can be obtained from credit-reporting firms.
3. Customer does not provide you with financial information. Why not? Is there a problem?
4. Customer delays making payment and has many excuses.
5. Customer's credit rating is lowered.
6. Customer frequently changes banks.

Source: Mark Robichaux, "Dealing With Deadbeats: Call Early and Often to Collect," *The Wall Street Journal*, July 18, 1989, p. B1.

Consider New Return Item Product to Cut Your Bad Check Losses

Bad check losses are a business expense that should be minimized by tight internal controls. Once you know that a customer's check has bounced, you must take immediate action.

Usually, the first step is to tell your bank to redeposit the check, unless the bank does it automatically. Typically, 30 to 60 percent of your checks will clear on the second try. Obviously, then, 40 to 70 percent are returned again.

A new service to speed up the bad check process is offered by Transworld Systems, Inc. (TSI), in conjunction with about 50 banks and two third-party vendors nationwide. The banks offering the service call it "Return Item Lockbox." (*Note*: banks offering this service are noted in the bank product matrix in Appendix 10.) Here's how the service works:

1. Your bank electronically sends your customer's name, address, and check face amount to TSI as soon as it is notified of a check return.

2. TSI mails up to five nicely worded collection letters to your customer asking for payment of the face amount plus a $15 processing fee to be sent to your bank.

3. Upon payment receipt, the bank notifies TSI to end the collection process.

4. The check amount is credited to your bank account, as is the $15 fee.

5. Your bank charges your account $7.50 per check at month-end.

On average, TSI claims that 62 percent of all customers send in payment, and 90 percent of those send in the $15 fee:

Key Point 1: Your checks are not redeposited before TSI takes over. So you may be giving up some unnecessary money since TSI's average hit rate is only 62 percent. However, if you're collecting on only 30 percent of your redeposited checks, this service may be attractive to you.

Key Point 2: If you don't use TSI, your firm should send letters to your customers requesting a fee for processing their bad checks. Be careful in setting the amount so that you don't charge your customer more than is legally permitted in your state.

For more information on this product, contact TSI at (212) 422-6622 or write to them at 56 Pine Street, New York, NY 10005.

Use Automated Cash Application Procedures to Save Money

You can update your accounts receivable records in a manual or automated manner. For example, if you use or plan to use a lockbox bank (explained in Chapter 5) to speed up the check collection process, consider having the bank send the accounts receivable information electronically to your company. The bank can be instructed to capture the invoice numbers and check dollar amounts as it processes your checks each day and place the information on an electronic medium such as a diskette or magnetic tape for daily transmission to your company. This can be done over the phone and tied in directly to your computer to update the accounts receivable records.

The bank can simultaneously mail you a photocopy or laser image of each check along with the envelope (if you need it to determine mailing date) and any other accompanying documents returned by the customer. Your personnel can either use this information as backup or use it to manually enter the data into your accounts receivable program.

Manage Your Inventory

Inventory Control Is Critical

Excessive inventory or its mismanagement can cripple your cash flow. Consider the case of a supermarket that has a warehouse packed to the ceiling with goods, and the refrigerators and freezers are also full. These idle goods can be thought of as "frozen" cash.

Small companies in particular may be forced by certain suppliers to buy more inventory than they need. For example, a car dealership may be required to order a specific number of cars from the manufacturer. All unsold cars represent an economic cost to the dealer. That is why businesses must carefully assess the true cost of carrying this inventory in terms of cash flow and the opportunity cost of funds tied up in inventory.

Ten Steps to Review in the Inventory Process

One approach to minimizing the cost of inventory is to review every facet of your inventory operation. You should have answers to the following questions:

1. Do you have a forecast by day, week, and month of what you expect to sell for each item stocked? If so, do you compare your forecast to the actual sales to determine the variances? Do you then adjust your next forecast accordingly?

2. Which items account for 80 percent of your sales? These should be managed as tightly as possible. Perhaps you can minimize ordering other items that are selling poorly or infrequently.

3. How fast can you get inventory once you order it—an hour, a day, a week, a month? The faster the better, since you don't have to stock it for a long time. Many manufacturing companies use "just-in-time" inventory, which enables them to receive the supplies the day they need them and not before.

4. How do you order inventory—by mail, by phone, or by electronic connection to your supplier via a computer? One of the largest car mat companies in the country receives orders by computer terminal from the automobile manufacturers for their rubber car mat needs. This system is fast and efficient, and it eliminates paper purchase orders.

5. How much inventory do you order? Do you order extra just to save a few cents an item? Determine what your *economic order quantity* should be by speaking with inventory experts and skilled accountants or by using available software packages.

6. Do you rely on just one or two suppliers? Perhaps they are not as competitive as others, or not as flexible on the minimum quantity you can order, or not as reasonable on their delivery schedule. Shop around for other vendors and mention to the original vendors that you

use multiple suppliers. You may see a major improvement in the way you are treated, because the existing suppliers do not want to lose your business.

7. How frequently is inventory analyzed to determine its life span and composition?

8. Do you know the cost of holding your inventory?

9. Do you have a policy for determining obsolete inventory, and how and when to get rid of it?

10. Do you have a complete inventory reporting system that provides the necessary information to manage the process?

Be Actively Involved in Reducing Inventory Costs

The key is to minimize inventory, which is the equivalent of cash sitting in a noninterest checking account—it's a cost to your business. Look for specialized PC inventory software for your particular industry. Make sure it tracks raw materials, work in progress, and finished goods by day. Work with suppliers who will deliver at the last minute, but make sure they're reliable. Minimize ordering in advance.

Accounts Payable Policies Need to Be Defined

Besides inventory control and accounts receivable policies, you need to craft your accounts payable policies and procedures wisely. You can be devious, playing games with your vendors, but you may risk your company's reputation, depending on how far you go.

Develop a Company Disbursement Policy

Every company has expenses and other obligations that must be paid. These include daily operating expenses, payroll, trade payables, and possibly dividends to shareholders. Some companies stretch their payables to extreme limits, thus jeopardizing their credit rating and company image. This isn't very wise. Other firms pay all their invoices within terms or even before they are due because they want to maintain excellent vendor, employee, and shareholder relations. These positions are the two ends of the spectrum; the majority of companies use a policy between these extremes.

Some companies, because they are in severe financial condition, begin delaying payments first to vendors, and then to employees and shareholders. This strategy may exacerbate the situation: Vendors will stop shipping supplies and employees will resign and possibly sue for payment. Then the company will have no options left.

Don't Ignore Ethics

In developing a disbursement policy for your company, you must take into account the ethics of how you treat your employees, vendors, and shareholders. Paying late, maximizing check-clearing float using remote disbursement, maximizing mail float using remote mailing, and taking discounts after the discount period are probably all unethical. Consider the financial benefits of these practices in relationship to the more important moral and ethical considerations. Then make your decision and be sure everyone in your company as well as each of your vendors, is clear on your policies. If your company becomes known as unethical, this could have major negative implications for your business future.

Ten Key Factors to Evaluate

In handling your disbursements, you should decide on your company's disbursement policy and then prepare a written policy and guidelines. You will need to answer the following questions:

1. Will you take discounts, if offered? How small a discount will be financially beneficial?
2. Will you take discounts *after* the discount period? (It is unethical!)

3. Will you always pay within terms or develop your own payment schedule (e.g., pay in 40 days instead of 30-day terms)?

4. Will you pay on time or late, and will you have specific payment terms with each vendor?

5. Will you try to maximize check clearing float on vendor payments by using a remote disbursement bank to gain float at the vendor's expense? It may be unethical.

6. Will you use remote mailing to delay payment to vendors by sending your checks to a distant geographic area to be mailed? It may be unethical.

7. Will you have a computerized accounts payable system, a manual system, or a hybrid of the two?

8. Will you personally sign every check issued, delegate the responsibility, or use a facsimile signature plate?

9. Will you pay employees weekly or biweekly, and will you pay by check or electronic payment?

10. Will you issue cash advances and company credit cards?

Let's address these issues in more detail.

Discounts

How Do You Determine Whether to Take a Discount?
Suppose you have an option of paying a $1,000 invoice in 30-day terms or paying on the twelfth day and taking a 2 percent discount (2/12 net 30). Assume that your opportunity cost is 8 percent. Here are two methods for determining which is cheaper?

a. The present value (PV) of the $1,000 payment in 30 days is

$$PV = \frac{\$1,000}{1 + [.08(30/365)]} = \$993.47$$

The present value of taking the discount and paying $980(= $1,000 - [.02 \times $1,000]) on the twelfth day is

$$PV = \frac{980}{1 + [.08(12/365)]} = \$977.43$$

It is cheaper by $16.04 ($993.47 − $977.43) for you to take the discount.

b. Another way of analyzing this is to use the future value (FV) formula, where i is the interest rate (or opportunity cost) and d is the number of days the funds can be invested. (Note that you use (30 − 12 =) 18 days for this calculation because you lose use of the money after payment.)

$$FV = \text{Discounted payment} \times [1 + i(d/365)]$$
$$= [\$1,000 \times (1 - 0.02)] \times [1 + .08(18/365)]$$
$$= \$980 \times 1.003952$$
$$= \$983.87$$

Thus, it cheaper by $16.13 ($1,000 - $983.87) to pay on the twelfth day and take the discount. The PV and FV formulas yield slightly different results due to rounding errors.

Another consideration besides the current interest rate is whether you have the money to pay within the discount period. You certainly don't want to borrow money at a higher interest rate than the value of the discount! Keep in mind that a 2 percent discount in 10 days is equivalent to 52 percent annualized over 260 business days per year.

Do You Take Discounts after the Discount Period? For example, do you pay in 25 days, taking the discount, when the discount period is 12 days? Some firms try this technique because it saves them money if the receiving company does not disallow it. Ethically, this practice is very questionable and certainly doesn't give the receiving company great faith in your honesty.

Payment Terms

Do You Always Pay within Terms? Make sure your company does not follow the policy of "C.O.D."—Cleaning Off

Desk—when paying invoices. That is, your staff should not be paying today the invoices they receive today, just so they have clean desks by the end of the day. I've found too many companies doing this. One interesting example was a well-known Japanese consumer electronics firm. The senior financial managers didn't think their company used the "C.O.D." approach. But after inquiring, they found out to their amazement that they were. As a result this practice was halted immediately.

Some firms always pay their invoices late no matter what. For example, a billion-dollar communications firm we'll call XYZ paid all its invoices in 60 days, even though most invoices specified terms of 30 days. When a supplier called to complain, XYZ said that its policy was 60 days, and that if the supplier was unhappy with the arrangement, XYZ would get another supplier. Few complained after that, and they continued doing business with XYZ. Large companies like this may be able to get away with this practice. But small and medium-sized firms should pay their invoices on time.

Other firms pay some invoices late and others on time, depending on the vendor and their own cash flow needs. Some firms pay a day or two late without receiving any negative feedback.

In your case, you have to decide on the best policy for your firm. You should take into account the image you want your company to have in the marketplace, your credit rating, the benefits of having high-quality, reliable suppliers who want payment on time, the payment practices in your industry (e.g., is there a norm?), and your cash flows to support the payment of the invoices. Being late once in a while is much different from having a premeditated plan always to pay late. Your vendors will quickly size you up for better or worse.

Do You Establish Specific Terms with Each Vendor?
Different vendors require different terms. For example, your largest vendor should be providing you with much better terms than your smallest vendor. Volume discounts and better terms are negotiable. Make sure a knowledgeable person deals with vendors; otherwise you will end up paying more than you should. Don't neglect to re-evaluate terms if economic

conditions change or if your volume keeps rising. Have an automatic review process of all major vendor terms every six months or every quarter.

Check-Clearing Float Extension

Remote Disbursement versus Local Disbursement.   Some years ago, the director of finance of one of the major tire companies asked me if I knew a bank in Hawaii he could use as a disbursement bank. He wanted to use a remote disbursement bank where the checks took a long time to be presented. His intent was clear: obtain maximum check-clearing float on checks sent to vendors, knowing that the vendor depositing the check would be receiving delayed availability.

At the opposite extreme was the cash manager of a large auto firm who said to me that his company would not consider changing disbursement banks if his valued vendors would receive worse availability on their deposited checks than they currently received. His company was using banks in a few Federal Reserve cities, where the checks quickly cleared against his account.

Remote Mailing and Zipcode Selection.   Two large manufacturing firms had some interesting approaches to vendor disbursements:

- One large steel company used a Troy check printer that automatically printed the entire check face of the check, as well as the MICR line (magnetic ink characters at the bottom of a check) of one of eight banks. The bank selection was based on the vendor's zip code address; the bank farthest from the vendor's mailing address was selected.
- Another manufacturing firm, based in the Northeast, couriered its vendor payments to Montana and mailed them from there to gain mail float.

These four examples represent the extremes. Three of these companies couldn't care less about the vendor, whereas the other company cared a great deal about its vendor relations.

You have to decide on the policy for your firm and whether you'll engage in these questionable practices.

Use an Automated Instead of a Manual Accounts Payable System

Many large companies use accounts payable software that handles the processing of all payables, as well as the automatic printing of checks on a predetermined date. Other large and middle-market companies handle their accounts payable function manually, believing they are saving money by not automating. Most small businesses can use a PC with an off-the-shelf accounting package that contains a payables module. The low price of PCs and software makes them affordable for most small businesses.

Appendix 12 contains a listing of accounting packages that contain an accounts payable module. Middle-market firms may require mainframe systems. There are numerous vendors of mainframe systems such as Management Science of America (Atlanta, GA) and McCormick & Dodge (Natick, MA) as well as others that offer comprehensive software.

If you're a small business, don't make the mistake of keeping your payables system manual because you don't want to spend $500 on a software package. Also, don't think that your system is fully automated just because you print your checks on a printer. A fully automated accounts payable system matches the receiving document (if there is one) with the purchase order and invoice. Some people ask me, "Why should I pay for a package that will be used to pay out money?" This question is short-sighted because the software's time-saving and automated record-keeping features will pay for themselves many times over.

Check Signing: How Is It Done?

Who signs your checks? Here are your choices:

1. You, the owner of the business, can sign *all* the checks.
2. Another trusted individual can sign some or all of them.

3. Checks over a certain amount (e.g., $1,000) can require two signatures.

4. A facsimile plate can be used to automatically print the signature when checks are being printed.

The method you select should have built-in safeguards to prevent internal fraud if you have employees other than yourself involved in the process. If you use facsimile plates, make sure they are locked up when not in use. Some business owners feel they must exercise complete control of their firm by signing every check, whether for $1 or $10,000. This policy is ridiculous. You can always be selective and sign checks over a limit such as $500.

Make sure that the individual responsible for the accounts payable function is *not* also responsible for reconciling your bank statement. Otherwise, you are looking for trouble. Keep these two functions separate. Make sure that your bank accounts are reconciled *monthly* and that any discrepancies or strange entries are brought to your immediate attention.

Automate Payroll Processing and Use Direct Deposit of Payroll

You should assess how often employees are paid and whether you should pay by check or use direct deposit of payroll (DDP). The ideal situation is to pay your employees monthly using DDP. Try not to pay employees weekly: pay at least every two weeks instead. The less frequently you pay, the more money you have in your bank account for other uses, and the less expensive the payroll process and banking costs.

DDP. If you have a *stable* work force, consider setting up a DDP program for everyone. This program uses no payroll checks. On payday the employee's net pay will automatically be in his or her bank account. This is accomplished by having each employee sign an authorization form agreeing to have his or her pay credited to specific bank account(s). You provide this information to your bank along with the net pay, and the bank prepares electronic credits called Automated Clearing

House (ACH) transactions for distribution to the appropriate banks through a countrywide ACH network. The employee can select any commercial bank, savings & loan, or thrift institution for receipt of pay if the institution is a member of the ACH network, as most banks are. Even if your employees are in different cities across the country, the DDP program can work very well.

DDP has numerous benefits to both the employer and the employee:

BENEFITS TO EMPLOYER

1. No checks issued

2. Less expensive than using checks

3. Lower banking costs

4. No lost or missing checks to replace

5. Shows interest in improving employee-employer relations

BENEFITS TO EMPLOYEE

1. Pay automatically credited to bank account

2. Pay can be divided and placed in two banks

3. No time wasted at bank to cash check

4. Pay deposited automatically, even during vacation

5. All funds available on payday; no bank holds on money

DDP employee participation is dependent on the marketing effort you put forth. In most states, employees must be given an option of receiving a check or DDP, and in other states the employer can decide on the method. So before making it mandatory, check your state labor laws.

Direct deposit can also be applied to reimbursing employees for expenses and trips. Instead of issuing a check, create an ACH credit to their bank account using a bank information reporting system's ACH initiation module.

Consider Three Payroll Processing Alternatives. In preparing your payroll, you have three options:

1. An in-house preparation using your own staff
2. A bank's payroll-processing unit
3. A third-party service vendor, such as Automatic Data Processing (ADP Employer Services, 1 ADP Blvd., Roseland, NJ 07068, (201)-994-5000) or Paychex Inc. (911 Panorama Trails, Rochester, NY 14625, (716)-385-6666)

In determining which approach is best for you, consider the following:

- Cost of performing the service internally versus performing it externally
- Deadlines for the outside providers
- In-house staff and expertise versus what's available outside
- Need for special software package in-house
- Skill and time needed to interpret tax laws and regulations, and to file proper forms on specified dates

Eliminate Cash Advances and Encourage Credit Card Usage

Issue Travel and Entertainment (T & E) Cards to Key Employees. To conserve cash, you should consider *not* providing employees with *cash advances* for travel and entertainment. They can drain your cash and result in unnecessary bookkeeping and trips to the bank to get cash. Instead, provide them with a corporate travel and entertainment card such as Citicorp Diners Club or American Express. Each month you can have the monthly statements sent directly to you and you can pay the bill; alternatively, you can have each employee pay the bill and reimburse each one. Remember that these bills require payment upon receipt since they are not credit cards. Also, you can peruse the statements to make sure that the expenses are in line with your corporate travel and lodging policy, which I'm sure all of you have developed and distributed to your employees.

Consider Personal Credit Cards. Another approach is to have your employee use a personal credit card and submit a monthly expense report for reimbursement. If an employee complains that his credit limit can't cover his business and personal charges, then offer to pay the expense of having him obtain a card solely for business. Some banks offer credit cards at no fee or a low fee, so be on the lookout for them. Another advantage of credit cards is the 25-day grace period before payment is due. Take advantage of this float by not paying credit card bills early.

Buy a PC Now If You Don't Have One

Even the smallest firm should have a personal computer with an accounting package that contains *at the minimum* general ledger, accounts receivable, and accounts payable modules. A listing of software vendors that offer accounting packages for small businesses is provided in Appendix 12.

Synthesis

This chapter covered three critical components of your working capital—accounts receivable, accounts payable, and inventory control. Paying attention to these areas and using the ideas presented in this chapter will improve your control and your cash flow.

4

Everything You Always Wanted To Know About Checks But Were Afraid to Ask

Check Availability Delays Can Kill You

Stanford didn't teach me how long it takes out-of-state checks to clear. We had constant cash-flow problems at first because of this. —Richard Huttner, quoted in *The Wall Street Journal*, Roger Ricklefs and Udayan Gupta, "Traumas of a New Entrepreneur," May 10, 1989, p. B1.

Check Holds Hold You Up!

As most of you know from dealing with banks as consumers, banks place a hold on the checks you deposit for a specific time period before you can use the money. This time delay is needed to determine whether the check is good. The bank from which a check is drawn may bounce a check for many reasons:

- The account on which the check is drawn has insufficient funds, which means there is not enough cash in the account to cover the check amount. This kind of check is called an NSF check.
- The account is closed.
- The check is missing a signature, or the signature is invalid or forged.
- A stop payment has been placed against the check.

A bounced check, referred to by bankers as a "return item," is a rare occurrence. Fewer than 1 percent of all processed checks bounce.

Banks place a hold on *all* checks because of the infinitesimal chance that a few of them will bounce. The banks do not want unpaid checks returned to them after they have made funds available to their depositors. The reason why all checks are held is simple: The bank does not know ahead of time which checks will bounce.

Banks Make Money on Check Float

Incidentally, banks make a significant profit on check float on checks held. For example, a bank may place a hold on an out-of-town check for seven business days, when in actuality the check clears back to the drawee bank in one day. The bank has earned six days of float earnings on that one check. On a $3,000 check, for example, that amounts to earnings of $4.00 ($3,000 $\times .08/360 \times 6 = \$4.00$). Imagine how much the bank earns on millions of dollars of checks, when the bank receives use of the money days before the depositor does.

Prior to 1987, banks held consumer-deposited checks from one to fifteen days, depending upon the source of the checks and the individual bank's hold policies. With the passage of Expedited Funds Availability Act in 1987, and in particular the execution of the Federal Reserve Bank's Regulation CC, the hold times have been reduced to a maximum of seven days in most cases. This legislation was brought about by Congressional and consumer-group protests about the delayed availability of deposited checks. Both groups argued that the holds on checks were unduly long and that check depositors were entitled to faster use of their money.

Businesses Are Treated Differently on Deposited Checks

Banks treat businesses and corporations much better than they treat individuals. Banks provide availability of funds on checks deposited by most businesses in zero, one or two days, depending upon the drawee bank location and the time of day the checks are deposited at their bank.

Before learning the tricks of the trade in check availability, you must understand both the components of a check and the process of clearing checks in the United States.

All About Checks—The More You Know the Better

What are those funny-looking numbers on the bottom of your business checks? Exhibit 4-1 shows a business-sized check. You'll notice that it is different from your personal check, which is typically six inches wide.

MICR Line Carries Critical Information

MICR (Magnetic Ink Character Recognition) was adopted for the MICR line in 1956 by commercial banks, the Federal Reserve, equipment manufacturers, and check printers to automate the manual process of sorting checks. The banking system began using the MICR line technology in 1961. The key portion of the check is the MICR line across the bottom. The MICR line is printed in magnetic ink by the check printer during the check-printing process. The other information on the check is usually printed in regular ink. Bank check sorters can read the MICR automatically at the rate of thousands of checks per minute.

Check serial number

The MICR line contains four distinct fields that must always be printed in the same location on each check. The first field contains the check serial number. In our example, the serial number is 0001. The MICR serial number matches the number printed on the face of the check. This number is used to reconcile checks at the end of the accounting period. Checks that have been paid or are still outstanding can be easily identified.

Exhibit 4–1 A corporate check. (This check was designed and printed by Model 656 Laser Check Printing System, manufactured by Digital Design, Inc.)

Digital Design, Inc.
8400 Baymeadows Way
Jacksonville FL 32256
800-733-0908/904-737-0908

Friendly National Bank
Downtown Branch
Jacksonville, FL 32256

Check No.: 0001

Date: 6-15-90

$\dfrac{2\text{-}90}{068}$

Pay Exactly: *Ten Thousand and 00/100 Dollars*

Amount: $ 10,000.00

Non-Negotiable

Pay
To The
Order Of:

Les Masonson
Cash Management Resources
20 McGarrah Road
Monroe, NY 10950

William D. Meadow

⑂000 1⑂ ⑂068383907⑂ 389 27⑂8938⑂

check   transit-   account
serial   routing   number
number   code

⑂000 1000000⑂

dollar
amount

40

Transit-routing code

The next field is the American Bankers Association transit-routing field. This number identifies the specific drawee bank. The first two digits represent the Federal Reserve District in which the bank is located.

Bank Identifier. The third digit in the transit-routing code indicates whether the bank is in a head office city (1) or another city. The fourth digit usually specifies the availability, and the next four digits represent the bank's unique identifier. The last digit (7 in the exhibit) is a verification digit that is used to identify encoding errors during processing.

Federal Reserve District Codes
and Selected Transit-routing Codes

Federal Reserve District Codes and Cities:

01 Boston	07 Chicago
02 New York	08 St. Louis
03 Philadelphia	09 Minneapolis
04 Cleveland	10 Kansas City
05 Richmond	11 Dallas
06 Atlanta	12 San Francisco

ABA transit-routing codes (without the verification digit) for selected banks and other institutions:

Citibank (NYC)	0210-0008
First Chicago	0710-0001
Valley National (AZ)	1221-0002
Chase (Syracuse)	0213-0937
U.S. Treasury	0000-0050
U.S. Postal Money Order	0000-0020
U.S. Central Credit Union—Wichita	3011-8962
Republic Savings Bank—Benton	2839-7203
American Express® Travelers Cheque	8000-0005

Account Number Field

This field designates the customer's account number.

Dollar Amount Field

The last field is the dollar amount field. The amount is encoded on the check (e.g., printed in MICR by machine) either by the first bank in which the check is deposited or by the depositor, and it is done with a special MICR encoding machine. If you scan your personal checks received from the bank in your monthly bank statement, you'll see that they are all MICR-encoded in the dollar amount field. Many retailers and utility companies "pre-encode" their customer checks with the dollar amount before depositing them in order to obtain lower per-check pricing.

Some of your checks may contain a white strip attached to the bottom edge of the check or be placed in an envelope with a clear glassine window. These checks were rejected by a bank's check reader/sorter and were repaired so that the MICR line could be read by the reader/sorter.

Fundamentals of Check Clearing

Now let's cover how checks clear—that is, how checks get from the deposit bank to the drawee bank. The easiest way to explain this subject is to use examples. The banks and availabilities mentioned in the following examples are not necessarily reflective of the actual availability that they offer. They are used for instructive purposes.

Let's take the simplest case first. In all cases, assume you are a business depositor as opposed to a consumer.

Case 1. On-us check

Suppose you have a checking account at Chase Manhattan Bank in New York City. Today you deposit a check from one of your customers that happens to be drawn on this bank. What availability would you expect to receive on this check, and how will Chase clear this check?

You should receive zero-day (immediate) availability on the check because it is drawn on the same bank where it is deposited (known as an on-us check). Basically, the check stays at Chase and is processed internally. Chase MICR-encodes the dollar amount, processes it, credits your account, and debits your customer's account. The customer receives the check with his or her bank statement.

Case 2. Local check

Suppose that today before 3 P.M. you deposit a check in your Chase account that is drawn on Manufacturers Hanover Trust Company in New York City. What availability would you expect to receive on this check, and how will Chase clear this check?

You should receive no worse than one-day (next-day) availability on the check, since it is drawn on a local bank in the same city. Chase MICR-encodes the check, sorts it into a bundle with other checks drawn on Manufacturers Hanover, and brings them to the New York Clearing House at 100 Broad Street. There they are given to Manufacturers Hanover.

Actually, all 11 commercial bank members of the New York Clearing House exchange checks with each other in the early morning hours each weekday. The banks settle up at the end of the day on the books of the Federal Reserve Bank of New York where each bank maintains an account.

Case 3. Transit check (out-of-town check) drawn on a Fed city

Suppose today you deposit a check in your Chase account that is drawn on the Bank of America in San Francisco. What availability would you expect to receive on this check, and how will Chase clear this check?

Believe it or not, you will probably get one-day availability, because the check is drawn on a bank in another Federal Reserve City. Of course, you'll have to deposit the check by Chase's internal deadline to receive next-day availability. Remember, both New York and San Francisco are two of the twelve Fed headquarter cities. (See the preceding list of Federal Reserve District Codes and Cities.) Typically, checks deposited in a major bank in a Fed city can be cleared to a bank in another Fed city in one day. That is why you receive one-day availability.

Four Ways to Clear Transit Checks.   After MICR-encoding and sorting the check, a bank has four options in clearing an out-of-town check. In this case, Chase can use one of the following methods:

1. *Local Fed office.* The check may be delivered to the Fed RCPC in Jericho, NY, to be processed to the Fed of San Francisco and presented to the Bank of America. The Fed has 48 offices in the United States, most of which process checks. These include the 12 head offices, 25 branches, and 11 Regional Check Processing Centers known as RCPCs. See Appendix 1 for the full listing. The Fed system clears about 34 percent of all checks.

2. *Direct Send to Drawee Bank.* Chase may send the check directly by courier to the Bank of America with other checks drawn on the bank. This is called a Direct Send. Couriers deliver the checks using private planes or commercial aircraft.

3. *Direct Send to Fed Bank.* The check may be sent directly by courier to the Fed of San Francisco to be presented to the Bank of America.

4. *Direct Send to a Correspondent Bank.* Chase may send the check directly to a correspondent bank (for example, to First National Bank of Chicago), which will forward the check to the Bank of America. A correspondent bank performs check processing and check clearing services for other banks. Their availability deadlines and their pricing

are competitive with direct sends to the drawee bank or local Fed office.

Use of a Direct Send Is an Economic Decision.   Chase's decision of which check-clearing method to select is based on economics. Factors to be evaluated are the time of day Chase receives the check; the availability offered by the drawee, Fed, or correspondent bank based on its own deadlines; and the cost of sending the check. The cost of using a direct send is higher than the cost of using the local Fed, but the availability obtained is usually one day faster. There is obviously a trade-off involved. The higher the dollar value of the checks is, the more likely the bank is to use a direct send, if all other factors remain constant.

Case 4. Transit check drawn on a non-Fed city

Suppose today you deposit a check in your Chase account that is drawn on a small commercial bank in a town in Montana. What availability would you expect to receive on this check and how will Chase clear this check?

The availability you will receive will probably be two days, because this check is not drawn on a Fed City or another major city. Chase will probably clear this check through the local Fed because a direct send will not provide any faster availability and will be much more expensive. Actually, most checks like this one are called "country items" because they are drawn on banks in smaller towns and cities. Some banks are able to clear country items in one day, although it is not very common.

Availability Is
What Counts

Why spend all this time on the check clearing process? Who cares? Remember, the faster you receive the availability, the faster you can use the funds in your checking account for other purposes. You can't use the funds on today's check deposits until they're available.

To recap what we've covered so far:

Type of Check Deposited	Typical Availability Granted by Deposit Bank
On-us item	0 day
Local item	1 day
Out-of-town item drawn on Fed city	1 day
Country item	1 or 2 days

This availability is not from a specific bank's schedule, but reflects what you should receive from your banks.

Become an Availability Sleuth

Do you know the exact availability you are receiving on each check deposited at your bank? If your answer is "no," don't be embarrassed. Many business owners and financial managers don't know the answer. How do you determine the availability your bank is currently providing on deposited checks? Take the following steps.

Obtain a Bank Availability Schedule

Simply ask each bank you use for check deposits for a copy of its availability schedule. The format and details of this schedule vary widely from bank to bank.

Track a Week's Check Deposits

For one week, write down the transit-routing code and dollar amount for each check deposited and the total dollar amount of checks deposited each day.

Compare Transit-Routing Codes to Bank's Availability Schedule

Look for the transit-routing code of each check and write down the bank's availability and its deadline. For example, if the schedule indicates that a 1210 transit-routing–coded check would receive one-day availability if deposited by 11 P.M., then you'll know if your deposit made the deadline.

Calculate Availability for Daily Deposit

To do this, set up a table like the following:

Availability Study

Check T-R Code	Availability Granted	Check $ Amount	Dollar Days*
0210	1	1,000	1,000
1210	1	9,000	9,000
0311	2	12,000	24,000
1113	2	3,000	6,000
		Totals 25,000	40,000

* Dollar days = availability granted × check amount

Assuming that this $25,000 deposit was made on Monday, the available funds on Tuesday should be $10,000 ($1,000 and $9,000 checks). On Wednesday $15,000 ($12,000 and $3,000 checks) should be available. The average availability of this deposit is 1.6 days, calculated as follows:

$$\text{Average availability} = \frac{\text{Dollar days}}{\text{Total dollar amount of checks deposited}}$$

$$= \frac{40,000}{25,000}$$

$$= 1.6 \text{ days}$$

Obtain a Daily Bank Balance Report

Each day obtain the balance in your account and the availability granted. You can obtain this information by phoning the bank each day or by using the bank's automated balance reporting system. Compare your figures with the bank's. If they agree, then you are gettting the availability stated in the schedule. If your numbers don't agree, then resolve the discrepancy with your bank.

Compare Your Average Availability with
Account Analysis Statement

As we'll see later in Chapter 10, you should obtain a monthly account analysis statement from most banks. If you divide the average float figure on this statement by the average amount of your daily deposits, you'll obtain the average availability. As long as the bank hasn't adjusted the average float figure for noncheck transactions or other adjustments, this calculation should be accurate.

What Does a Bank's Availability Schedule Look Like?

Commercial or Business Account
Availability Schedule

Look at Exhibit 4-2, which is an illustrative schedule. This schedule is provided to the bank's business customers (sometimes referred to as commercial accounts). It is the same one provided to the bank's consumer customers. As you can see by looking at the routing numbers, the availability on certain out-of-town checks is five business days! That stinks. Believe it or not, many banks hold certain checks for seven days.

Ask the bank if it has a corporate availability schedule. Ask why you aren't receiving corporate availability. Keep in mind the following three points on availability:

1. Businesses should receive the same availability as offered to the bank's large corporate customers.

2. You can negotiate with certain banks to receive a fixed availability on all your checks. This is known as a "corporate float factor". For example, you might tell the bank you want to receive an average availability of 1.25 days on all your checks, no matter where they are drawn. Some banks will agree to this, but other banks will tell you they can't change their policy for you. That type of response tells you about the bank's personal service motto. In any event, make sure to speak with the highest-ranking

Exhibit 4-2. Hypothetical availability schedule offered to unsuspecting business customers

Day Checks Available	Bank Transit-Routing Codes		
First business day after deposit	Cash & traveler's cheques Electronic payments U.S. Treasury checks		
Third business day after deposit	0210-0008 0219-0945 0602 0210-0012 0310-0004 0603 0210-0030 0430-0030 0219-0105 0520-0027		
Fourth business day after deposit	2260 2213 0214 2220 2219 2223 0214		
Fifth business day after deposit	Checks not listed above		

Note: This schedule does not portray any specific New York City bank. It is an incomplete schedule shown for illustrative purposes only.

officer in the branch you deal with to see if there is anything that can be done for you. The more money and accounts (business and personal) you maintain at the bank, the better your chances are for a positive response.

3. Make sure that your banks don't give you one-day delayed availability on cash and electronic payments. Here are two examples of common bank policies applied by a bank to its small business and consumer customers:

A. Cash deposits are always available on the business day after the day of deposit. The same rule applies to all cash and Travelers Cheque deposits, whether made at a teller or at an automated teller machine.

B. Electronic deposits such as directly deposited Social Security payments and wire transfers are available on the business day following deposit.

Demand same-day availability. Why is the bank delaying availability on cash? There is no excuse for it.

Corporate Availability Schedule
Is What You Deserve

Many banks offer small businesses the same availability schedule as they provide large corporate accounts. If your bank does, that's a feather in your cap! It's also a good sign that the bank is treating the small business customer fairly. As you can see in Exhibit 4-3, this schedule is much more comprehensive than the one-page business account schedule. This schedule from National Bank of Detroit is only one page of a 10-page schedule that also contains supplementary tables.

This is the type of schedule provided to large corporations. Each bank schedule has a different format, unique deadlines, and its own rules. This schedule is typically used for assigning availability to customers who maintain lockbox accounts at the bank.

Lockboxes

A lockbox is a special arrangement with a bank that allows the bank to pick up your mail at the post office around the clock and process your checks for rapid availability. Chapter 5 contains a detailed discussion of lockboxes.

Availability Schedule Components

You'll notice that the schedule has the following components:

1. *Availability deadlines.* Checks must be in the bank by this time, or else an additional day's availability will be added. For example, a check deposited from Philadelphia National Bank will be available in zero days if it is deposited by 9:30 A.M. Monday through Friday. Otherwise, availability is two days.

2. *ABA transit-routing codes.* The codes for specific banks or cities are listed with their associated deadlines. For example, the transit-routing code 0310–001 is Philadelphia National Bank.

Exhibit 4-3. Aggressive corporate availability schedule (Reprinted with permission of the National Bank of Detroit)

* NATIONAL BANK OF DETROIT CORPORATE AVAILABILITY SCHEDULE — FED. RES. DISTRICT	END POINT–ABA*	Midnight (Mon.-Th.)	2:15 a.m. (Mon.-Fri.)	5:30 a.m. (Mon.-Fri.)	8:00 a.m. (Mon.-Fri.)	9:30 a.m. (Mon.-Fri.)	2:00 p.m. (Mon.-Fri.)	6:00 p.m. (Mon.-Fri.)	6:00 p.m. (Mon.-Th.)	Branch (Mon.-Th.)	Branch (Fri.)	4:00 p.m. (Sat.)
2nd District Con't.	Jericho RCPC (0214, 0219, 2214, 2219)	1	1	1	1	1	1	1	1	2	1	0
	Utica RCPC (0213, 2213)	1	1	1	1	1	1	1	1	2	1	0
3rd District	Philadelphia City (0310, 0360, 2310, 2360)	0	1	1	1	1	1	1	1	1	1	0
	Philadelphia National Bank (0310–0001)	0	0	0	0	0	1	1	1	1	1	0
	Girard Bank (0310–0003)	0	0	0	0	0	1	1	1	1	1	0
	Fidelity Bank (0310–0050)	0	0	0	1	1	1	1	1	1	1	0
	Philadelphia RCPC (0311, 0312, 0313, 0319, 2311, 2312, 2313, 2319)	1	1	1	1	1	1	1	1	2	1	0
4th District	Cleveland City (0410, 2410)	0	1	1	1	1	1	1	1	1	1	0
	Central National Bank (0410–0004)	0	0	0	0	0	1	1	1	1	1	0
	National City Bank (0410–0012)	0	0	0	0	0	1	1	1	1	1	0
	Ameritrust Bank (0410–0068)	0	0	0	0	0	1	1	1	1	1	0
	Cleveland RCPC (0412, 2412)	1	1	1	1	1	1	1	1	2	1	0
	1st National Bank, Toledo (0412–0005)	0	0	0	1	1	1	1	1	1	1	0
	Huntington Bank (0412–0008)	0	0	0	1	1	1	1	1	1	1	0
	Cincinnati City (0420, 2420)	0	1	1	1	1	1	1	1	1	1	0
	Fifth Third Bank (0420–0031)	0	0	0	0	1	1	1	1	1	1	0
	Central Trust Co. (0420–0039)	0	0	0	0	1	1	1	1	1	1	0
	Provident Bank (0420–0042)	0	0	0	1	1	1	1	1	1	1	0
	Cincinnati RCPC (0421, 0422, 0423, 2421, 2422, 2423)	1	1	1	1	1	1	1	1	2	1	0
	Pittsburgh City (0430, 2430)	0	1	1	1	1	1	1	1	1	1	0
	Pittsburgh National Bank (0430–0009)	0	0	0	0	0	1	1	1	1	1	0

* Availability expressed in business days from date of credit.

Each bank generates its own availability schedule based upon its mix of check deposits, its direct-send cut-off times, its local Fed's check-deposit cut-off times, other internal operating constraints, the availabity of couriers and airflights, and competitive pressures from banks in the same city. For a detailed example of instructions for reading an availability schedule, see Appendix 2.

In summary, you *should make sure that you receive the corporate availability schedule*. This schedule provides the fastest availability times that the bank offers. If you have a small business and you find that the bank will not give your deposits corporate availability, then find out what you have to do to get it. Also, shop around locally to determine the availability offered by other banks. Negotiate with your bank once you have the ammunition! Remember to determine the financial impact of the delayed availability before spending time and hard work pursuing other alternatives.

What Do You Look for in Corporate Availability Schedules?

Learning to read corporate availability schedules is almost an art. In many cases, you have to read between the lines as well as all the footnotes to understand clearly the availability you are being assigned. The key factors to look for are the following:

1. *There is a cut-off (deadline).* To receive the availability, your checks must be in the bank's processing center by this deadline. The processing center could mean the bank's lockbox department or its check processing department. The deadline does not refer to check deposits at a branch office or main office teller window unless these are specifically stated. So ask your bank, if the information isn't clearly specified.

2. *Later-in-the-day deadlines are desirable.* These are more beneficial than earlier deadlines because you may have additional checks that will make only the later deadline, but can still gain faster availability.

3. *The deadlines are for checks with MICR-encoded dollar amounts.* These checks are referred to as "pre-encoded" or "pre-conditioned."

4. *Most banks' schedules are subject to change.* The bank may or may not notify you of a change beforehand. Some banks state that the schedule is subject to change without prior notification, so call your bank every quarter to check.

5. *Availability is usually stated in business days.* Saturday, Sunday, and certain holidays are not considered business days. For example, a check deposited on Friday that the bank assigns one-day availability will give you usable funds on Monday.

6. *Most banks pass on 100 percent of their availability to their corporate customers.* Others pass on a percentage of what they revceive, but the full availability is preferable.

7. *Some banks use "fractional availability."* This refers to providing the customer with a percentage of the availability over a two-day time-frame. For example, receiving availability with a fraction of 97 percent on a $10,000 check means that $9,700 is available tomorrow and $300 is available in two days. Fractional availability is used to capture the lost availability that a bank may encounter owing to factors such as equipment failure and transportation and weather delays.

8. *Rejected checks may receive one-day deferred availability.* This counts for any rejects that result from internal bank processing. Thus, high-quality dollar-amount encoding by the bank or by the company (if checks are pre-encoded) is critical for minimizing rejects.

9. *Some banks may assign delayed availability to thrift institution checks.* Check with your bank and carefully read the availability schedule. Thrift checks are denoted by transit-routing fields beginning with "2" in the first digit.

5

Collect Your Money Fast

Faster Than a Speeding Bullet

I've got all the money I'll ever need—if I die by 4 o'clock.
—Henny Youngman

Get your money fast. That's the point of this chapter. You can receive payment for your goods and services in six ways:

	Remittance Type	Typical Users
1.	Cash (coin/currency)	Retail businesses: newsstands, restaurants, convenience stores, department stores, and so on
2.	Wire	Brokerage firms; oil, commodities, and other such industries that require payment in "immediate funds"
3.	ACH (Automated Clearing House)	Insurance firms, mortgage companies, utilities, and other such companies that obtain the agreement of their consumer customers to debit their account electronically for repetitive small dollar payments
4.	Credit card	Retail businesses: see above
5.	Debit card	Retail businesses: gasoline stations, supermarkets, and so on
6.	Check	Most types of businesses except fast-food restaurants, newsstands, etc.

Remittance Types

Cash Is Fast

There are tens of billions of cash transactions in the United States each year, a number far surpassing the number of all other payment methods used. As far as total dollar volume, however, cash has less of an impact than other methods because of the small size of individual transactions. Some businesses accept only cash, such as most fast-food chains and newsstands and certain retail chains. A major risk facing business owners, besides theft and robbery, is the possibility of accepting counterfeit bills. Each year retailers lose millions of dollars because of counterfeits.

Counterfeit Money Detector

Vistatech Enterprises Ltd., a New York City–based firm, has developed the smallest device on the market for detecting counterfeit bills, which don't contain magnetic particles found in real money. Using the firm's $100 pen-size device, the retailer can rub the magnetic sensor over the bill. If it is real a green light goes on.

Source: Emily T. Smith, "This Gizmo Gets Tough with Legal Tender," *Business Week,* June 5, 1989, p. 98.

Wire Transfers Are "Cash"

Domestic wire transfers are handled over the FedWire, which is a countrywide funds transfer system owned and operated by the Federal Reserve system. The system moves money electronically between banks for its customers. FedWire transactions number 350,000 a day and are valued at over $1 trillion a day. The three most common cash management uses of Fedwire for small businesses and middle-market firms are for disbursements (38 percent usage), concentration (31 percent) and collection (29 percent), according to Trans Data Corporation (*Corporate Cash Management Survey Results,* 1989, p. 5, hereafter referred to as TDC-1).

FedWire is the method used least often for one company to pay another, because it is the most expensive. The average outgoing wire transfer costs about $10. Moreover, the sending company's bank account is debited the same day the wire is sent. Thus, the sending company does not benefit from any float delays.

Automated Clearing House (ACH) Gains Popularity

The ACH is a method for transacting electronic debit or credit transactions, depending on its application. The ACH instrument was first used in 1972 as a substitute for paper checks for small dollar transactions. In the context of this chapter, the ACH is used by selected industries to collect remittances from their customers who are consumers and not corporations. Companies in such industries as the following use preauthorized ACH debits to obtain payment from their *consumer* customers: cable TV, utility, insurance, mortgage companies, and banks. The consumer must provide a written authorization to the company giving permission to debit his or her account once a month for the debit transaction. Exhibit 5-1 illustrates the process.

The average cost of an ACH debit is about 11 cents. Besides the preauthorized debits, there are a few other payment methods that use the ACH to move the funds through the banking system to collect money. Automated Teller Machines (ATMs) are used by some consumers to pay credit card bills. The telephone bill-paying service offered by numerous financial institutions and the home banking services available to users of personal computers (PCs) can generate ACH credits or paper checks (credits) to retailers, utility companies, local merchants, and other vendors across the country.

Credit Cards Have Risks as Well as Benefits

Credit cards are used by over 50 million Americans to pay for many types of retail purchases. Credit cards are issued by banks, retailers, oil companies, telephone companies, and

Exhibit 5-1. Use ACH pre-authorized debits to get your consumer receipts.

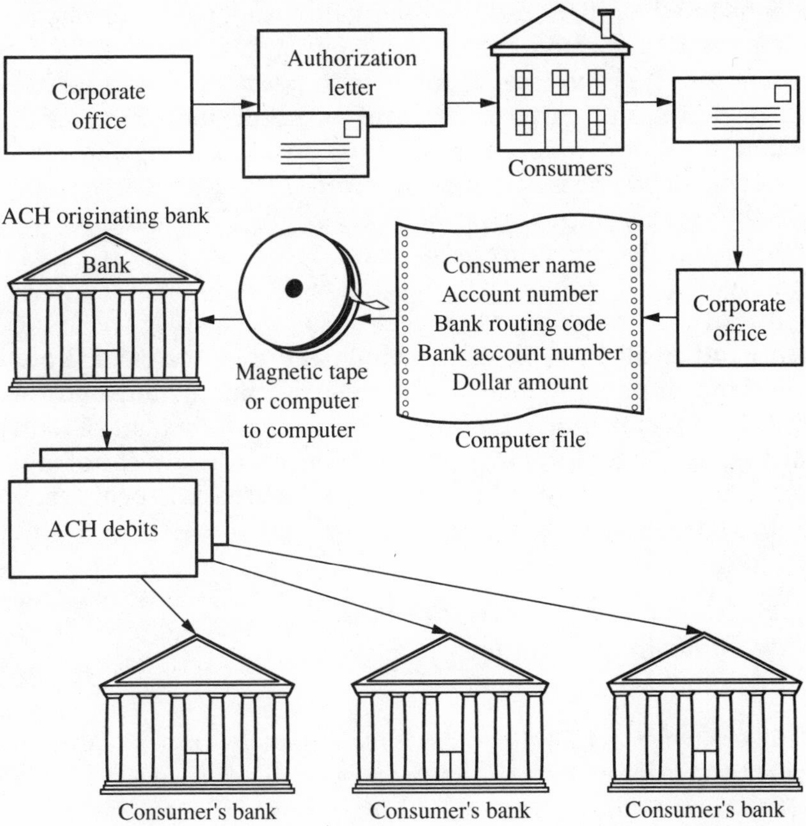

other firms such as airlines, auto rentals, and hotels. Also, charge cards are issued by American Express and Citicorp Diners Club for travel and entertainment. The volume of credit card transactions and the associated dollar volume increase yearly. In 1989, there were about 3 billion card transactions, valued at almost $220 billion. Typically, the customer has a period of 25 to 30 days from the billing date to pay for the purchases. After that date interest is charged.

Fraud Losses Grow

Credit card fraud is a growing problem for card issuers, who have consequently imposed some regulations for cardholders.

Retailers must be alert so that they are not charged for transactions in which they did not follow the proper procedures, as agreed with the credit/charge card company.

To minimize problems, retailers with heavy card volume use desktop or cash register credit card authorization terminals to obtain an authorization number prior to completing the sale. Other small businesses that can't afford this type of service still use the weekly paper bulletins to check for "hot" cards. They then check the signature and expiration date. Nevertheless, the credit card crooks are having a field day. They can get your carbon copies out of garbage cans in the back of shopping malls and create new plastic imprints, and they can call in your credit card number to mail order firms and charge thousands of dollars of merchandise before you get your statement. Credit card firms are continually searching for improved technology. In the future a "smart" card with an imbedded microchip may be the answer to eliminating fraud.

Home-based and Mail-order Businesses
Have Difficulty Obtaining
Credit Card Merchant Banks

Retailers with actual storefronts can usually find a bank to accept their credit card drafts for processing. However, that is not so for most home-based and mail-order businesses. Banks are leery of providing this service for these businesses because of the potential for fraud and the perceived high risk. Even long-established home-based firms with excellent credit histories and increasing sales have problems in this area.

Debit Cards Are Still Underused

Debit cards are not very popular, because the transaction is debited to the user's account on the same day or within a few days. This is unlike credit cards, where payment is not due for almost a month. There is no real incentive for a consumer to use a debit card, except that it is a substitute for carrying cash. Debit cards do not have widespread acceptance. They are offered by many gasoline companies, a few supermarket chains, and banks, among others. Their impact on the average small-or medium-sized business is negligible. Supermarkets are experimenting with their use in conjunction with their point-of-sale (POS) cash registers. So far, acceptance by consumers has been encouraging, but widespread use is many years away. Transaction volume remains low.

Checks Are the Most Prevalent Payment Instrument

By far the most frequent payment instrument used by businesses to pay other businesses and by consumers to pay companies is the ever-popular paper check. Because of its importance and its pervasive use as a payment instrument, the remainder of this chapter will focus on how to turn your checks into available funds quickly. Statistics on the composition of the population of check issuers are provided in Appendix 4.

The Myth of the Checkless Society

Currently an estimated 52 billion paper checks are processed in the United States each year. Check volume is growing at the rate of nearly 4 percent per year. Clearly, the use of checks is very popular and the volume of checks processed continues to grow, but it is growing at a slower rate than it did in the 1960s and 1970s. Predictions made in the late 1960s about a "cashless" and "checkless" society by 1990 were slightly wrong!

Checks Continue to be Popular

Why are checks so popular? The answer is simple. Banks process checks very efficiently and at very low cost. Also, checks are easy to use and individuals are very comfortable using them.

Your company has a financial incentive (e.g. float earnings) to use checks to pay other companies instead of using electronic payment instruments, but your company must convert checks to cash upon their receipt from your customers. As a disburser of funds, checks provide you with float until they are cleared back to the drawee bank account. You should understand the different types of float and the ways they affect you.

There Are Four Types of Check Float
You Should Know About

The following are the four types of float associated with checks:

1. *Mail float.* This is measured from the time a check is mailed by a customer until it is received at your office or your lockbox bank.

2. *Processing float.* This type is measured from the time a check is received until it is deposited in your bank account.

3. *Availability float.* This is measured from the time the check is deposited until you can use the funds as cash.

4. *Check-clearing float.* This float is measured from the time the check is deposited until it clears back to the drawee bank.

The typical time associated with each type of float is as follows:

Float type	*Typical float range*
Mail	One to five calendar days
Processing	One hour to one day
Availability	Zero to two business days
Check-clearing	One to three business days

Minimize Mail, Processing,
and Availability Float

As the *recipient* of checks from your customers, your strategy should be to *minimize* the collection float:

Collection Float = Mail + Processing + Availability Float

On the other hand, as the *disburser* of funds to your vendors, your objective may be to maximize your disbursement float within your corporate constraints.

Disbursement Float = Mail + Processing
+ Check Clearing Float

Your company may want to extend mail and check-clearing float. These disbursement issues and the float benefits will be explored in detail in Chapter 7.

Your objective should be to obtain your customers' checks as fast as possible after they are mailed and to deposit them in your bank account without delay so that they quickly become available funds.

The Typical Small Business Check-Processing Scenario Is Distressing

Small businesses usually request customers to send their checks to their office. After the mail is opened each day, the checks and invoices are processed, and the accounts receivable files are updated to reflect the payments. The checks are set in a batch with a deposit ticket for delivery to a local bank by 3 P.M. that day or perhaps for deposit in the bank's Automated Teller Machine (ATM) after hours. Some companies use the bank's night depository to make deposits after hours. A company may also choose to deposit checks the next day if there are many remittances or more important priorities.

Is there anything wrong with this small business approach from a cash management perspective? You bet! There are a lot of problems:

1. *All checks should be deposited by 2 or 3 P.M. depending on bank's deadline.* You should do this the day the checks arrive to obtain same-day ledger credit (funds posted to your account but not yet available) and to start the availability clock. Posting to the accounts receivable file may delay the deposit of checks. The checks should instead be photocopied, if there is a small number of them, or the invoices should be marked as paid. Pick up your mail before 9 A.M. in the post office. Also, have a staff member come in earlier, hire a temporary agency person, or have another person at your company help with the check-preparation process on heavy volume days.

Of course, before you hire outside help, you should do a cost-benefit analysis to determine if the one-day gain in availability warrants the cost of the temporary. For example, assume you need a temp for four hours every Monday to process checks that would normally be deposited Tuesday. If you assume the temp cost is $8 per hour or $32 per day, what is the minimum dollar value (DV) of checks that would result in a breakeven situation?

$$\$32 = (\text{DV of Checks}) \times \frac{.08}{360}$$

or

$$\text{DV of Checks} = \frac{32(360)}{.08} = \$144,000$$

The checks, then, would have to total $144,000 or more to warrant the cost of the temp, assuming you would receive one-day faster availability on these deposited checks.

2. *Checks deposited at the ATM after 3 P.M. lose one day of availability.* This is equivalent to depositing the checks the next business day. Some banks have a noon deadline.

3. *You have no real evidence that you actually deposited checks at an ATM.* You can obtain a receipt for the transaction, but that receipt does not mean that the bank actually received your checks. If the bank mishandles your checks or loses them, then you'll have to give it proof of your deposit. That means you must provide a photocopy of the checks or possibly even require the remitters to reissue checks if you did not make photocopies.

4. *You have no evidence that you deposited anything at a night depository.* The bank does not provide any receipts. Using a night depository should be avoided, if possible. If you have no safe in your office, or if there is no safe place for your checks, then consider the night drop.

5. *Small businesses do not operate on weekends.* Therefore, any checks arriving at the post office on Saturday or Sunday will not be received until Monday morning.

6. *The checks are not MICR dollar-amount encoded.* If the volume of checks you receive annually is large, it may pay to buy a desktop MICR-encoding machine (average cost: $3,000) to pre-encode the check's dollar amount before deposit. Banks charge 3 to 5 cents less per pre-encoded check. To break even on the machine over a five-year period, a company would need to receive 15,000 checks a year, if you assume an average savings of 4 cents a check.

How You Handle Your Checks Makes a Difference

As you can see from this example, the simple process of handling customer checks can have *negative* cash management consequences. If you don't think through the timing of your check preparation and deposit process, the updating of the accounts receivable files, and the timing necessary to make the bank's daily deposit cut-off, then there is a good chance that you will not obtain the most prompt availability on your check deposits. Also, you now understand the potential risk—however small—that you take in using ATMs and night depositories for check deposits.

Beware of Bank Deadlines

Keep in mind another important point. Even though some banks are open until 5 P.M. on certain days of the week, that doesn't mean you will receive same-day credit for your checks deposited by 5:00. Find out what the bank's deadline is for same-day deposit. You may be surprised to find that some banks use 2 P.M. as the cut-off time, even though they are open until 3 P.M. or even later. The availability clock will be delayed one additional day if you deposit the checks past the deadline. Check with your bank on its policy.

Make Special Arrangements with Your Bank

If you have clout with your bank because of a personal or business relationship, then you may be able to deposit checks after the bank's normal closing hours without losing availability.

You should ask the bank when it completes its own processing for the day and what its deadline is for sending the checks out for clearing. In some areas, bank branches may send their checks to a regional bank processing center or to the bank headquarters in a nearby city. These centers may continue the check-processing activities until midnight or later before dispatching the checks for clearing.

Try to arrange with the bank to drop off your checks after 6 P.M. at its regional center or downtown at the main office on days when you have a large volume of checks, and cannot make your deposit by its normal closing hours. The bank may want you to MICR-encode the dollar amount on each check. You can do this by buying a desktop encoding machine.

Evaluate Lockbox Banking Alternatives

Is there a better way for your company to collect checks than to accept them at your office? Yes, there is, and it is called "lockbox" banking. Fewer than 5 percent of small businesses, about 30 percent of middle-market companies, and over 60 percent of large corporations use this more sophisticated cash management method to collect their customer remittances instead of collecting checks in their offices. They use a "lockbox"—a post office box in which a bank can remove mail (checks) around the clock for deposit and check clearing. The typical flow of a lockbox is shown in Exhibit 5-2.

Most Small Firms Use One Lockbox Location

Small companies use one lockbox location. The actual number used depends on the location of their customers, the total dollar value of their remittances, and the banking costs. The larger a company's sales are, the more lockboxes it uses. However, even for $1 billion firms, more than four or five locations are unproductive.

Lockbox Benefits Are Numerous

Companies use lockboxes because of their many benefits:

Exhibit 5-2. Use lockboxes to speed your checks into the banking system. (Adapted by permission from Security Pacific National Bank.)

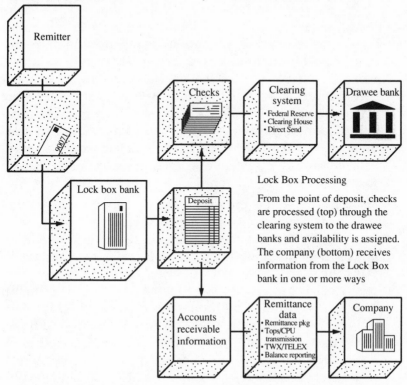

Lock Box Processing

From the point of deposit, checks are processed (top) through the clearing system to the drawee banks and availability is assigned. The company (bottom) receives information from the Lock Box bank in one or more ways

1. *They minimize mail float.* Customers are directed to send their checks to the closest lockbox to their mailing location.

2. *They minimize processing float.* The bank uses high-speed processing equipment, around-the-clock processing (including weekends) and a large staff to process the checks and clear them within hours of receipt.

3. *They minimize availability float.* The bank operates seven days a week and provides rapid availability assignment.

4. *They provide accounts receivable information quickly.* Information is available in the format (hard copy, magnetic tape, or diskette) desired by the customer.

5. *They eliminate the need for internal staff to process remittances.*

Two Types of Lockbox Plans Are Available

There are two types of lockbox plans offered by banks:

- *Wholesale lockbox*—corporate-to-corporate remittances. A wholesale lockbox is offered to companies that receive large dollar remittances (e.g., over $1,000) in moderate volume (e.g., 1,000 to 5,000 checks a month) from other corporations. Usually, the company does not return the original invoice with the check, which then requires manual handling. Thirty-one percent of companies with sales of between $50 million and $250 million use wholesale lockboxes, but only 7 percent of companies with sales between $5 million and $20 million use this service (TDC-1, p. 8).

- *Retail lockbox*—consumer-to-corporate remittance. A retail lockbox is offered to companies that receive high volumes (e.g., 50,000 or more checks per month) of consumer remittances that are low in value (e.g., $50 to $250 each). Typically, a returned document is provided by the company which the consumer sends back with the payment. This can be handled by the bank's automated equipment. Companies using retail lockboxes include insurance firms, utility companies, mortgage companies, retailers, cable TV firms, gasoline companies, and credit card organizations. Use of retail lockboxes by $50 million to $250 million companies is 16 percent, compared to 10 percent for companies with sales between $20 million and $49.9 million and 4 percent for companies with sales of less than $20 million (TDC-1, p. 9).

Wholesale Lockbox

We will first focus on wholesale lockboxes. A lockbox system is not necessary or advisable for every size business. Small businesses with less than $5 million a year in sales would probably not benefit from a lockbox approach because the bank charges would more than offset the gain in float. As a general rule of thumb, banks charge about $1 per check for wholesale lockbox usage, which includes all the bank's associated charges, not just the charge per check. In reality, you must obtain exact pricing from your banks.

Case 1: Company with $10 million in annual sales

Let's work through an example with a fictional company that has $10 million in annual sales to see if a lockbox is a worthwhile investment. ABX company is based in Philadelphia, Pennsylvania. The company manufactures floral baskets to be sold in department stores throughout the United States. Annual sales are $10 million and are growing at 20% per year. ABX bills its customers (department stores) monthly and receives their remittances in the Philadelphia office. ABX processes the checks received each day and deposits them in a local bank.

XYZ Bank has performed an analysis for ABX on the benefit of using a lockbox bank in Chicago to collect all its remittances. ABX receives 2,500 checks annually with an average dollar value of $4,000. The bank's analysis found that an average of one day in mail float and one day of availability float could be saved by using a Chicago lockbox, compared to the company's current method of handling remittances in Philadelphia. ABX also found that its banking costs would increase from $1,200 a year to $2,500 by using a lockbox bank. Should ABX proceed with a lockbox bank?

Determine the Value of Two Days of Float.   First, let's determine how much money ABX can save by obtaining use of its funds two days earlier. (Assume 8 percent is the annual interest rate.)

$$\text{Annual float benefit} = \text{annual remittance dollars} \times \frac{\text{interest rate}}{360}$$
$$\times \text{ number of days saved}$$

$$= \$10,000,000 \times \frac{.08}{360} \times 2$$

$$= \$4,444$$

$$\text{Annual net benefit} = \text{Annual float benefit}$$
$$- \text{additional lockbox costs}$$

$$= \$4,444 - (\$2,500 - 1,200)$$
$$= \$4,444 - 1,300$$
$$= \$3,144$$

In summary, ABX gains \$4,444 in additional float earnings, but has incurred an additional \$1,300 in bank costs. Thus, there is an actual gain of \$3,144 in using a lockbox. ABX may decide that this small savings does not warrant a change. I will discuss the factors that you should take into account in considering a lockbox after presenting the other cases.

Case 2: Company with \$25 million in annual sales

What if ABX sales were \$25 million a year? Would a lockbox be more cost-beneficial? Assume that annual lockbox banking costs rise to \$3,750 and that Philadelphia banking costs rise to \$1,600. Let's work it out.

$$\text{Annual float benefit} = \$25 \text{ million} \times \frac{.08}{360} \times 2$$

$$= \$11,111$$

$$\text{Annual net benefit} = \$11,111 - (\$3,750 - 1,600)$$
$$= \$11,111 - 2,150$$
$$= \$8,961$$

In this case there is an annual benefit of \$8,961 a year by using a Chicago lockbox. ABX may decide that this size benefit warrants the use of a lockbox.

Case 3: Company with \$50 million in annual sales

Annual lockbox banking costs are \$5,000, instead of \$2,000 at the existing Philadelphia bank.

$$\text{Annual float benefit} = \$50 \text{ million} \times \frac{.08}{360} \times 2$$

$$= \$22,222$$

$$\text{Annual net benefit} = \$22,222 - (\$5,000 - 2,000)$$

$$= \$22,222 - 3,000$$

$$= \$19,222$$

In this case, the annual benefit is \$19,222. ABX would probably be inclined to use lockbox.

Factors to Evaluate In Deciding on Wholesale Lockbox Feasibility

When deciding whether your firm should use a wholesale lockbox, consider the following:

1. *Annual sales collected by check.* The larger your sales are the more likely it is that a lockbox would be beneficial and would be used. Interestingly, 91 percent of middle-market firms that *use* lockboxes use either a wholesale or a retail lockbox. Of the these companies that use lockboxes, 70 percent use wholesale lockboxes. Larger companies are more likely to use lockbox services. For example, companies with sales ranging from \$50 million to \$250 million are five times more likely to use the service than companies with sales below \$20 million (TDC-1, p. 8).

2. *Location of your customers.* If most of your customers are located near your office, then perhaps a lockbox would not be beneficial since their checks would be in the mail only a day or two at most. However, if your customers are located across the country, then you must perform a cost-benefit analysis to determine the potential benefit in your case. Banks can offer you assistance with this analysis by using a specially designed lockbox model, which we'll explore shortly.

3. *Dollar amount of the checks.*   When analyzing your remittance data, you should focus on the customers that send
the largest dollar checks. Your lockbox should be located
as close to them as possible. The 80–20 rule may be
true in your case; that is, 20 percent of your customers
may provide 80 percent of your dollars. Review your customer remittances to determine which customers are your
largest and from which cities their checks are mailed.

For one month, keep a list of all your large checks. For
these accounts, write down each customer's name, mailing city, date of mailing and date received. Then obtain
mail times from a bank that subscribes to the Phoenix-
Hecht Postal Survey™ to determine alternative lockbox
cities. Appendix 5 lists the banks that receive this survey.
More about this later. Lockbox cities with the fastest
mail receipt times are Atlanta, Chicago, Dallas, Charlotte,
Pittsburgh and Los Angeles.

4. *Float reduction provided by lockbox banks.*   This encom-
passes mail, processing, and availability float. The more
days reduced, the larger the potential annual benefits.

5. *Incremental cost of lockbox banks.*   Compare this to existing
bank costs. The larger the incremental costs at the lockbox
bank, the less likely the lockbox solution will pay for itself
(and vice versa).

6. *Level of interest rates.*   The higher the interest rate is, the
higher the annual benefit will be.

Lockboxes Are Used Most by Larger Companies,
But Some Smaller Firms
Also Use Them Successfully

Small businesses are infrequent users of lockbox services
because of the lack of financial benefit, but middle-market and
especially larger companies are heavy users of bank lockbox
services. For example, a company with $150 million a year in
sales could gain $66,666 a year ($150 mm × .08/360 × 2) in
annual float benefits by using a lockbox, if two days can be
saved. A $1.5 billion company would save $666,666 a year for

a two-day improvement, and about $100,000 a year from only a 0.33 day improvement! Obviously, any incremental bank cost must be subtracted from these gains to arrive at the annual net benefit. Twenty-five percent of all middle-market companies use lockbox services, but only 4 percent of small businesses with sales of under $5 million use lockboxes (TDC-1, p. 7).

Lockbox usage in middle market companies varies by industry, according to Trans Data Corp.

Industry	Usage
Manufacturing firms	50%
Other industries	21
Business services	20
Wholesale trade	19
Construction	10
Retail trade	9

Once you determine that a lockbox is feasible, then you have additional decisions to make:

1. In which city or cities should you place your lockboxes? This can also be determined by an analysis of the mail time and availability data.

2. How many lockbox cities do you need? Most small firms need only one location. Usually, a Fed city is selected to obtain the best mail and availability float.

3. Which banks should you use for lockbox services once you've narrowed down the cities?

Banks Perform Lockbox Studies For A Fee

Firms that directly receive customer checks totalling over $25 million should consider having a bank perform a lockbox study. Also, companies that have larger dollar inflows and are currently using a single lockbox site should consider reviewing their lockbox system's effectiveness every three years. Many of the regional and money center banks use the Phoenix-Hecht Lockbox Micro Model™ to analyze the check data for small and middle-sized companies. This model runs on an IBM PC or compatible and provides the customer with optimal and alternative lockbox city locations. Bank pricing for this model analysis varies widely, but it typically ranges between $500 and $2,000. Some banks charge for entering the check data into the model as well. A few banks do the model analysis for free because they want to get the company's lockbox business. Check with your bank to determine its charges.

Data Requirements

The company needs to provide the bank with remittance data from a representative month so the model results are not skewed. Remittance data can be provided in any of three ways:

1. Customer dollars aggregated by three-digit zipcode or customer dollars entered by individual check
2. Use of computerized check data from a diskette
3. Customer check dollars assigned to specific sending locations based on population weight or assigned equally among zipcodes

Bank Runs the Model and Provides Recommendations

After the bank inputs the check data, it executes the model, which contains the latest Phoenix-Hecht Postal Survey™ mail and availability times for surveyed receiving cities, data on certain banks' specific availability times, and a list of certain lockbox networks. The bank can force specific cities into the solution for comparative purposes. The model produces many useful reports and breakdowns of the information. Exhibit 5-3 is a typical abbreviated optimization analysis prepared by a bank to compare the various solutions for one, two, or three lockbox locations. In this exhibit, the optimal city of Chicago provides an annual benefit of $64,480 from the company's existing New York City lockbox location. Adding a second lockbox in Philadelphia would provide an additional benefit of $11,132. Likewise, adding a third site in Los Angeles would

Exhibit 5-3. A Lockbox Micro Model Optimization provides useable solutions for one to three sites.

One Site / City	Total Float* (Days)	Existing System Float (Days)	Difference (Days)	Annual Float Gain at 6%
One Site				
Optimal: Chicago	3.35	4.73	1.38	$64,480
Selected Alternatives:				
Pittsburgh	3.45	4.73	1.28	59,940
Cincinnati	3.51	4.73	1.22	57,178
Atlanta	3.55	4.73	1.18	55,445
Philadelphia	3.72	4.73	1.01	47,463
Two Sites				
Optimal: Chicago, Philadelphia	3.12	4.73	1.61	75,612
Selected Alternatives:				
Chicago, Pittsburgh	3.16	4.73	1.57	73,318
Chicago, Oklahoma City	3.25	4.73	1.48	69,377
Three Sites				
Optimal: Chicago, Los Angeles, Philadelphia	2.99	4.73	1.74	81,430
Selected Alternatives:				
Chicago, San Francisco, Philadelphia	3.00	4.73	1.73	80,853
Chicago, Oklahoma City, Philadelphia	3.01	4.73	1.72	80,394

* Mail and availability

Note: The existing system is a lockbox in a New York City bank.

provide a $5,818 advantage over the two-city optimal. In this case the most practical solution is to move the lockbox from New York City to Chicago. The addition of more than one location is not that beneficial after taking into account the costs of a second lockbox bank.

How to Select a Specific Wholesale Lockbox Bank

Let's assume that you've had a bank perform a lockbox model study that indicated that your optimal lockbox system is a two-city solution of Chicago and Charlotte. Which banks do you select in those cities?

Follow these eight steps:

1. Obtain a copy of the each bank's *NCCMA/BAI Wholesale Lockbox Questionnaire* response. This document contains the critical information on each bank's lockbox service and its capability. The questionnaire is divided into eight sections and covers all aspects of a bank's lockbox service.

   1. Mail processing
   2. Lockbox processing
   3. Check processing and funds availability
   4. Data transmission
   5. Deposit and balance reporting
   6. Pricing and account analysis
   7. Lockbox network supplement
   8. Electronic payments supplement

2. Determine what aspects of the bank's service are most important to your company, and then assign the appropriate weights to each question. Also make sure to factor in any bank relationships you have with existing banks in these cities.

3. Use a spreadsheet program or a manually prepared matrix to compare banks. Rank the banks from highest to lowest scores.

4. Arrange to visit the banks with the top scores. Tour their lockbox operations and then compare each bank's operation based on specific criteria that you think are important.

5. Select a bank and sign a lockbox agreement.

6. Ask the bank to provide you with a Destination Directory that indicates which customer zipcodes should remit to which lockbox address.

7. Assign the appropriate post office box and city to each customer's invoice and accounts receivable record.

8. Enclose a notice with your next invoice indicating your new mailing address. Request that customers change their records to reflect this change. Follow up and contact customers who do not address their remittances to the correct address.

Wholesale Lockbox Networks Can Offer You Faster Check Collection

Prior to 1983, if a company needed more than one lockbox location, it had to use banks in different cities. With the development of "lockbox networks," companies can use one bank and gain the benefit of multiple city collection points. This provides reduced mail, processing and availability floats, in general. There are four types of networks in existence.

Mail Intercept

A bank collects mail from local post-office boxes in multiple cities in addition to collecting mail in its headquarters city post office. The bank instructs the post office in these cities to package the mail and send it by Express Mail the next day to their headquarters for processing. An example of a bank offering this type of service is Continental Bank in Chicago, which was the pioneer in developing this concept. This bank currently has post-office boxes in eighteen cities (including Chicago) and has the mail forwarded to Chicago for processing.

Bank Consortium

This is a group of unrelated banks that offers multiple collecting points. The customer has to use only one of the banks in the consortium to gain the benefits of all collecting locations. One example of this type of network is ImageNet, which consists of banks using the same processing equipment. Banks in ImageNet include Bank of Boston, Citizen's & Southern National Bank (Atlanta), Boatmen's Bank (St. Louis), Security Pacific National Bank (Los Angeles and San Francisco), NCNB Texas National Bank (Dallas and Houston), Harris Bank & Trust Co. (Chicago), and Philadelphia National Bank.

Processing Centers

This type of network is either wholly owned by one bank, by a bank holding company or bank affiliates. The bank opens post-office boxes in selected cities, sets up processing facilities (if they don't already exist), hires staff, and encodes checks before depositing them on-us or in local correspondent banks for clearing. The most prominent providers of this service include

- **Pittsburgh National Bank** (Pittsburgh, Philadelphia, Dallas, Louisville, and Cincinnati)–this network is called Acce-laNet
- **Chemical Bank** (Chicago, Dallas, Atlanta, Newark, and New York City)
- **Citibank** (Wilmington, Delaware; Chicago, and Los Angeles)
- **Citizens & Southern National Bank** (Atlanta, Dallas, Tampa, and Columbia, South Carolina)
- **First National Bank of Chicago** (Chicago, Newark, Dallas, Charlotte, and Los Angeles)
- **First Wachovia** (Charlotte, Dallas, and Atlanta)
- **Mellon Bank** (Philadelphia, Pittsburgh, Boston (retail and custom lockbox only), Chicago, Dallas, Atlanta, and Los Angeles)
- **NCNB National Bank** (Charlotte, Columbia, SC; Atlanta, and Tampa)
- **Sovran Bank** (Chattanooga, Memphis, Nashville, Norfolk, Richmond, and Washington D.C.)
- **First Interstate** (15 sites in seven western states)

Evaluate All Factors

When considering a wholesale lockbox system, you should also consider the capabilities, pricing, and quality of these networks. Perform the same type of analysis as you would on individual banks. Make sure that you understand who bears the responsibility of errors. Since you are only dealing with one bank, errors committed by other banks in a network have to be corrected and compensation given to you.

Use Retail Lockbox for Consumer Remittances

As we mentioned earlier in this chapter, retail lockbox is characterized by a high volume of low-dollar consumer-to-corporation payments. There are two additional distinguishing features of a retail lockbox. The first is that the company sends the consumer an invoice that is printed with Optical Character Recognition (OCR) characters (Exhibit 5-4). The OCR line contains the customer's account number and payment amount. OCR is not similar to MICR and is not printed in magnetic ink.

The second feature is the inclusion of a return envelope. The objective is to encourage the consumer to return the invoice in the return envelope, which has a preprinted address or a window through which the address shows on the invoice.

Retail lockbox is used by about 10% of middle-market companies. Some firms handle the function internally because they believe they have better quality control and lower cost than banks can offer. That is why many utility and insurance firms perform their own remittance processing inhouse.

Economical Decision Not to Use OCR Invoices

A company using a wholesale lockbox does not usually use OCR invoices or return envelopes. The reason is economical. Most business customers would not return the original invoice or the envelope, because their accounts payable system automatically prints a check with a stub or invoice detail.

Exhibit 5-4. OCR document and return envelope speed your remittances to cash.

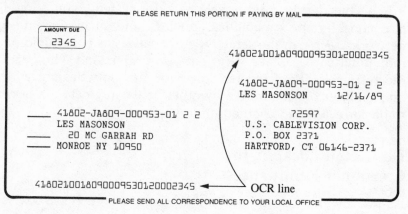

Determine Internal Costs

Selecting a retail lockbox provider is easier than selecting a wholesale lockbox provider. The first step is to determine the cost of performing the processing internally, if you want to consider that option. This involves costing certain factors:

- Space allocation (rent per square foot)
- Internal labor

- MICR-encoding equipment purchase or lease
- MICR equipment maintenance
- Supplies (MICR ribbons, stationery)
- Cost of availability given up by not working on weekends and holidays

Obtain Bids from Outside Sources

The next step is to obtain bids from retail lockbox banks and third-party retail lockbox providers such as NRC Express Payment Network (30 processing centers countrywide), National Processing Company, Sears Payment System, Inc., and EDS Retail Remittances, Inc., among others. These third-party providers offer competitive pricing and multiple receiving locations. However, they do not necessarily provide service in the immediate area that a company has its customer base.

The addresses and phone numbers of these vendors and others are provided in Appendix 6.

Local or Countrywide Need?

There are two types of retail lockbox needs—countrywide and regional. Some companies have a national consumer base and may need multiple collection points across the country, such as American Express (credit card payments), Sears, Roebuck & Co. (Sears and Discover Card payments), and Exxon Corp. (gasoline payments). Other companies have customers in a local area or geographic region such as Pacific Gas & Electric, Consolidated Edison Company of New York, and Kingston Cablevision.

Critical Evaluation Factors

In selecting a retail lockbox provider, whether it is a bank or third-party vendor, the most important factor for most companies is *price* per remittance (check). The all-in price (price including all the bank charges plus per-item pricing cost, information reporting, exception processing, outgoing wire transfer, and so on) can range from $0.08 to $0.29 per check, depending on the monthly check volume, processing requirements, customized handling requirements, and exception processing (e.g., checks without invoices).

Although availability and mail time are important factors, they are in many cases secondary to price. Let's take an example. Able Cable TV Company receives 50,000 consumer remittances a month with an average value of $25. It has received two proposals from banks to perform the processing:

Bank A: This bank can save the company 0.5 day mail float and 0.5 availability float. Its price per item is $0.20 all-in.

Bank B: This bank can't save any float, but its price per item is $0.19 all-in.

Assuming both banks offer equivalent quality, which one offers the cheapest service?

Bank A

$$\text{Annual float savings} = (50,000 \times \$25) \times 12 \times 1 \times \frac{.08}{360}$$

$$= \$3,333$$

Annual cost of processing: $(50,000 \times 12) \times .20 = \$120,000$

Total Cost $= \$120,000 - 3,333 = \$116,667$

Bank B

Annual cost of processing: $(50,000 \times 12) \times .19 = \$114,000$

Thus, Bank B's cost is cheaper by $2,667. However, in neither case should a lockbox bank be used, because the float benefit is much less than the bank's cost!

Obviously, the larger the remittance size and the greater the float benefits, the greater the financial impact. Some third-party providers such as NRC have nationwide collection points that could have a significant float advantage for companies that collect remittances from a nationwide customer base.

Retail Lockbox Networks Are Advantageous

Only a few banks and third-party providers offer more than one retail lockbox collection point. Multiple collection points offered by the same provider is a known as lockbox network. Banks with more than one retail lockbox location include the following:

- **Citibank** (Philadelphia, Chicago, and Los Angeles)
- **Mellon Bank** (Philadelphia, Pittsburgh, Boston, Chicago, Dallas, Atlanta and Los Angeles)
- **PNC Financial Corp.** (Philadelphia, Pittsburgh, Louisville, Cincinnati, and Los Angeles)

There are benefits to the company of using multiple collection points:

- Reduced mail, availability, and processing float compared to a single location
- Improved control and problem resolution from use of only one bank instead of multiple banks
- More competitive price based on volume discount because all checks are processed by one bank
- One tape or computer-to-computer transmission of data (accounts receivable information)

Get a Written Lockbox Agreement

If you decide to use a bank or third-party provider for your retail or wholesale lockbox service, be sure to get a written contract so that each party knows exactly what to expect from the other. Be sure to include minimum operating performance criteria, pricing guarantees, specific instructions on how each item is to be handled including exceptions, and a plan for handling compensation in case of errors.

Synthesis

This chapter focuses on the fastest ways to get your money from your customers. Wire transfer and ACH are the fastest methods, but lockbox is the most often used. In collecting remittances, remember to minimize mail, processing, and availability float.

6

Concentrate on Funds Concentration

Put All Your Eggs In One Basket

Electrons are the ultimate carrier pigeons. —David L. Boyle, Vice President, Citicorp/ Citibank, February 25, 1987

If your company uses only one bank for deposits, then your funds are already concentrated. You can skip to the next chapter, unless you want to understand how larger firms than yours handle their cash concentration needs.

Three Objectives of Concentration

Concentrating, or mobilizing, your funds is important when you have two or more depository banks (also referred to as field banks). The principal objective is to move all your available funds into one main account called a "concentration" or a "master" account. In that way, the money can be effectively used for compensating the bank for services provided, for investing, or for paying down an outstanding loan. Additional concentration objectives are to use the least expensive concentration methods and to leave minimal balances in depository bank accounts.

83

Three Concentration Methods

The three concentration methods are the following:

- Check (Depository Transfer Check—DTC)
- Automated Clearing House (ACH)
- Wire transfer

These three instruments should be familiar to you. They are the same methods used to collect money from your customers. As you will see in the chapter on disbursements, these methods are also used to disburse funds.

Checks, ACHs, and wire transfers are the only three instruments that you have to understand when collecting, disbursing, or concentrating funds. The only differences are the ways in which they are used in those three circumstances.

Comparison of Concentration Methods

Here's how the three instruments compare for funds concentration:

Instrument	Concentration Bank Availability Assignment	Typical Cost
DTC	1–2 days	$ 0.75 originating bank 0.15 receiving bank
ACH	one day	$ 0.11 originating bank 0.11 receiving bank
Wire	immediate	$10.00 originating bank 6.00 receiving bank

Wire Transfers Have Limited Use

Wire transfers should be used for concentrating funds in three cases:

1. You need *immediate* funds today in the concentration account for investment, borrowing, or compensation.
2. The dollar value of the available funds to be concentrated is large enough to offset the $16 round-trip wire cost.

Both the initiating and receiving bank will charge for the wire.

3. You have inadvertently built up excess balances in the depository account that are a nonearning asset.

Wires are almost 18 times as expensive as DTCs and 73 times as expensive as ACHs, so they are used less frequently than ACHs. Thirty-one percent of middle-market firms that use wire transfers (75 percent) use them for concentration purposes (TDC-1, p. 5).

How to Calculate the Break-even Cost of a Wire

Before using a wire instead of an ACH, for example, figure out if the dollar value (DV) to be transferred warrants the use of the wire. The break-even formula on the round-trip wires is

$$DV \text{ of wire} = \text{cost of wire} \times 1/(\text{interest rate}/360)$$

$$= 16 \times \frac{1}{.08/360}$$

$$= \$72,007$$

Another way of looking at this equation is to ask yourself the following question. What amount of money do I have to invest today at an 8 percent annual interest rate to earn $16 in interest by tomorrow?

$$\text{Today's Investment} \times \text{Daily Interest Rate} = \text{Tomorrow's Interest}$$

$$TI \times (.08/360) = 16$$

$$TI = \frac{16}{.08/360}$$

$$= \$72,007$$

The wire value should be at least $72,007 to cost justify its initiation. Thus, wire transfers are cost-beneficial for large dollar amounts. Moving money from lockbox accounts by wire is usually a wise move, if the funds can be effectively used at the concentration bank.

The ACH is the Most Popular
Concentration Instrument

The ACH is the most popular method used to concentrate funds from field banks because:

- It is easy to prepare.
- It is the lowest cost method.
- It is electronic instead of paper.
- It is guaranteed next-day availability in the concentration bank account.

Depository Transfer Checks Were Popular
Until 1983

The ACH, as a concentration tool, became available only in 1983. Prior to that year, DTCs were used by most companies as the concentration method of choice. Now a DTC must be used in the place of an ACH when the deposit bank is not a participant in the ACH network. A DTC looks very much like a check, except for the following differences:

- The words "Depository Transfer Check" are printed across the top center of the check.
- No signature is required.
- DTCs are typically printed at night by the concentration bank using high-speed MICR printers, based on daily deposit information received from company sources via an automated deposit-reporting service.

Although DTCs are still used by about 25 percent of all companies, ACHs have surpassed DTCs in popularity for the reasons mentioned in the preceding section.

Ten Keys To Use
Concentrated Funds Effectively

Analyze the following factors when you are determining your concentration system strategy:

1. Round-trip cost of concentration instrument at both depository and concentration banks
2. Mix of deposit—cash, checks, credit cards
3. Balance or compensation requirement of depository banks
4. Availability assigned by depository banks on checks and credit card drafts
5. Availability provided by concentration bank when DTCs are used
6. Frequency with which the funds at each deposit bank should be concentrated
7. The dollar amount of the transfer, taking into account check and credit card draft availability
8. Choice of which concentration instrument(s) should be used
9. Use of employees or armored car service for daily deposit
10. Current cost of bank services related to the concentration process

How Do You Actually Accomplish Funds Concentration?

To illustrate how concentration can be accomplished, we'll use three cases, each one progressively more complex:

- *Case 1:* Concentrating funds from three lockbox banks
- *Case 2:* Concentrating funds from a 25-store restaurant chain that accepts only cash
- *Case 3:* Concentrating funds from a 50-store clothing chain that accepts cash, checks, and credit cards

Case 1: Concentrating Funds from Three Lockbox Banks

Let's assume that you have a lockbox system with banks in Chicago, Los Angeles, and Philadelphia. Each day you receive about $100,000 in remittances in each bank. Your concentration bank is located in New York City. There are three ways to concentrate funds. We'll review each one and point out the best approach.

Using Wire Transfers

How do you go about concentrating the funds by wire? The dollar amount of the transfers is large, so wire transfers could be a cost-effective technique. To concentrate money using a wire transfer, take the following steps:

1. Using your concentration bank's information reporting system, obtain yesterday's lockbox deposit totals and today's opening available balances.

2. Initiate "reverse wires" from the lockbox banks to the concentration bank for a specific dollar amount using the wire transfer initiation module. A reverse wire requests that the receiving bank send available funds of a specified amount to the requesting bank.

An alternative approach is to set up "standing instructions" at each lockbox bank requesting the bank to wire transfer all available funds or all funds above a certain available balance level to the concentration bank. The benefit of standing instructions is that you don't have to take any action to execute the wire, since the bank handles the transaction automatically. This second approach does not offer as much flexibility or control as the first approach.

ACH Concentration

Assume that in this same example, we decide to concentrate by ACH instead of wire in order to reduce the transfer costs. Take the following steps:

1. Using your concentration bank's information reporting system, obtain yesterday's lockbox deposit totals and today's opening available balances.

2. Initiate ACH debits (electronic transfers) to the lockbox bank accounts and ACH credits to the concentration bank account for a specific dollar amount using the system's ACH transfer initiation module.

An alternative approach is to set up "standing instructions" at each lockbox bank requesting it to send ACH credits of all available funds or all funds above a certain available balance level to the concentration bank. This second approach does not offer as much flexibility or control as the first approach.

ACH Disadvantages

The main disadvantage of using an ACH instead of a wire transfer is that the ACH credit will not become available funds in the concentration bank until the next day. Thus, balances will build up in the lockbox account overnight, every day, and especially on weekends. However, if you accurately estimate your receipts for the next day, then you can use the ACH to concentrate the funds at a lower cost than by using wire.

This one-day delay can result in building up balances in lockbox banks that greatly exceed the compensation necessary for services. Therefore, you must closely monitor the daily available balance position in each lockbox bank and initiate large dollar wire transfers once a week (on Fridays, for example). Alternatively, you could draw down a larger amount (e.g., 150 percent of the the previous day's daily deposit) in the daily ACH transfer. You can use historical information or an educated guess. However, you must be careful not to overdraw the account on a ledger or available balance basis.

Analyze Cost vs. Benefits

In summary, you must analyze the cost versus the benefits of using wires or ACHs. The factors to be considered are the following:

- Round-trip cost of each instrument
- Balance build-up in lockbox banks

- Potential earnings on wired funds
- Compensation requirements at lockbox banks

DTC Concentration

If we wanted to substitute DTCs for ACHs in the previous example, the process would change only slightly.

The process of using your concentration bank's information reporting system to obtain yesterday's lockbox deposit totals and today's opening available balances is the same. Instead of creating ACHs, however, you will use the bank's DTC transfer initiation module, if it is offered.

If this module is not offered, you will have to create three manual DTCs using the three DTC check books—one for each lockbox bank account. You may then deposit the DTCs at the concentration bank for check clearing. Availability will be assigned by the bank. Most likely all three DTCs will be given next-day availability because they are drawn on Fed cities. The potential problem of idle balance build-up can occur with DTCs as well.

Should the company use ACH or DTC to concentrate funds? The simplest approach is the automated ACH method, if a bank offers the ACH initiation feature. Remember, the ACH is cheaper, is guaranteed next-day availability, and eliminates paper.

Case 2: Concentrating Funds from Twenty-five Depository Banks

Now let's consider a more complicated concentration situation. Let's assume that a fast food restaurant chain has locations in 25 cities across the country. A local depository bank account has been set up for each restaurant. Daily restaurant deposits range between $1,000 and $5,000, depending on the day of the week and the restaurant location. The restaurants accept only cash, not checks or credit cards. Each day, the store manager deposits the day's receipts at the local bank. The company headquarters is in St. Louis, where its concentration bank is located.

How should this company concentrate its cash? Are wire transfers applicable in this case? Should DTCs or ACHs be used? We will evaluate each alternative.

Wire Transfer Approach

You are correct if you answered that wires would be too expensive for the transfer amounts involved. The daily wire charges alone, five days a week for 52 weeks, would cost $104,000 per year!

$$\text{Annual Cost} = (\$10 + 6) \text{ wire charges} \times 25 \text{ stores}$$
$$\times 52 \text{ weeks} \times 5 \text{ days a week}$$
$$= \$104,000$$

This cost does not include the charge for obtaining the information on the restaurant deposits each day and the cost of the internal time needed to input the wire information into a bank's information reporting system (wire transfer module).

Of course, you could concentrate by wire less often, perhaps once or twice a week, but this would leave idle balances in the field banks. These balances may be well in excess of those needed to pay the bank for its services. You would have to analyze all the variables to determine whether wires are feasible.

ACH Approach

Can ACH be used to concentrate the funds effectively and at low cost? Definitely, but how?

The first step is to get the daily deposit information from each restaurant. This can be obtained in a number of ways:

- If the store cash registers (POS terminals) are tied into the company's computer system, then the information on each store can be polled at a specific cut-off time each day.
- The store managers can call the headquarters office at the close of each business day and report in the deposit amount.

- The store managers can call a third-party deposit reporting service such as National Data Corporation or a bank's deposit reporting service to report in the daily deposit.

In the first two instances, the company would have to initiate 25 ACH transactions using the St. Louis bank's information reporting system (ACH initiation module). To minimize the amount of information to key-enter, the company should set up "repetitive" ACH transfers. The company would give the bank a list of the 25 local banks, their transit-routing codes, and their bank account number. The bank would store this information in its system.

Each day, the company would only have to input the dollar amount of the ACH transfer on the appropriate line number of the ACH initiation screen. The screen would be preformatted by the bank with lines numbered 1 to 25. The bank already knows the banks that correspond to each line. If the bank does not have the line number capability, then each bank's information will have to be entered manually.

The bank will then automatically create 25 ACH debits that night, one drawn on each of the local banks, and will arrange one ACH credit (for the total amount of the debits) that will be available funds the next day in the concentration account.

Use a Third-Party Reporting Service or a Bank's Deposit Reporting Service

To automate the ACH concentration process completely without the company headquarters getting involved in the process, a third-party or a bank's deposit reporting service can be used. At the end of each day, the restaurant manager calls a toll-free number provided by the service and reports the daily deposit. After the deadline, the service prepares a magnetic tape of the deposit data and transmits it by phone to the St. Louis concentration bank. (If the St. Louis bank offers a deposit reporting service, then no tape has to be created.) That bank then automatically prepares the 25 ACH debits and sends the ACHs through the ACH network that night.

A third-party reporting service will charge for each phone call, for initially setting up the service, and for preparing and sending the tape. A typical phone call charge is $0.60. The service will provide a report of all phone calls, the time of the calls, and the dollar amount reported. This can be sent to the company by facsimile or first class mail. This document can be used as the audit trail and as a record showing which restaurant managers did not report.

ACH Concentration System Cost Example. How much would ACH concentration cost, taking into account transaction charges only? Without a third-party service it would be

$$\text{Annual Cost} = 25 \text{ ACHs/day} \times 52 \text{ weeks} \times 5 \text{ days}$$
$$= 25 \,(.11 + .11) \times 52 \times 5$$
$$= \$1,430$$

With a third-party service

$$\text{Annual Cost} = \$1,430 + (25 \text{ calls} \times .60/\text{call} \times 52 \times 5)$$
$$= \$1,430 + 3,900$$
$$= \$5,330$$

The transaction costs for ACH are much lower than the cost even for **weekly** wire transfers:

$$\text{Annual Wire Costs} = (\$10 + 6) \text{ wire charge} \times 25 \times 52$$
$$= \$20,800$$

Using Deposit Anticipation

Is there a way to lower the costs of concentrating the funds in this example but still use the ACH mechanism? Yes, there is. You can use *deposit anticipation* to estimate deposit amounts for upcoming days and include the estimate in the day's deposit notification. Deposit anticipation is a technique that can be used to concentrate funds less often than daily. For deposit anticipation to work successfully, the daily deposits should be predictable with a high degree of accuracy, and the composition of the deposit should be mostly cash. However, this technique can be used with checks, as long as the percentage of one- to two-day availability is stable.

Deposit anticipation can be successfully used in cases in which deposits are all cash, and when historical data exists for each store daily for at least a few months. Let's work out an example at one restaurant.

Week 1

Monday:

Daily deposit:	$2,000
Estimate for Tuesday's deposit:	$1,700
Monday's phone call:	$2,000 + $1,700 = $3,700

Tuesday:

No phone call made	
Actual daily deposit:	$1,900

Wednesday:

Daily deposit:	$1,400
Adjustment for Tuesday:	200 (1,900 −1,700)
Estimate for Thursday's deposit:	$2,100
Wednesday's phone call:	$1,400 +200 +2,100
	=$3,700

Thursday:

No phone call made	
Actual daily deposit:	$1,800

Friday:

Daily deposit:	$2,300
Adjustment for Thursday:	−300 (1,800 − 2,100)
Estimate for Saturday's deposit:	$3,100
Estimate for Sunday's deposit:	$2,800
Estimate for Monday's deposit:	$1,900
Friday's phone call:	$2,300 −300 +3,100
	+2,800 +1,900 =$9,800

Saturday:

No phone call made	
Actual deposit:	$3,300

Sunday:

> No phone call made
> Actual deposit: $2,900

Week 2

Monday:

Actual deposit:	$1,600
Adjustment for Monday:	−300 (1,600 − 1,900)
Adjustment for Saturday:	200 (3,300 − 3,100)
Adjustment for Sunday:	100 (2,900 − 2,800)
Estimate for Tuesday's deposit:	$1,700
Monday's phone call:	$1,600 − 300 + 200 + 100 + 1,700 = $3,300

Continue the same pattern on Wednesday and Friday each week.

Using deposit anticipation allows the store to make ACH transactions only three days a week instead of five days, resulting in an annual deposit reporting cost savings of $1,560 [$3,900 − $2,340, or (25 stores × 52 weeks × 5 days × 0.60) − (25 stores × 52 weeks × 3 days × 0.60)], and an annual ACH savings of $572 [$1,430 − $858, or (25 ACHs × 0.22 × 52 × 5) − (25 × 0.22 × 52 × 3)]. The total annual savings is $2,132 per store.

Deposit anticipation can be used when the next day's receipts can be forecast with a high degree of accuracy (e.g., 90 percent) and when the receipt patterns are fairly stable from week to week. Anticipation works well because the ACH transaction created one day always clears the deposit bank on the next business day. For example, Monday's ACH is debited to the deposit bank on Tuesday.

DTCs could be used in place of ACHs, but that would result in a higher cost without any benefit. DTCs must be substituted for ACHs if the deposit bank is not a member of the ACH system. Nonmember banks cannot accept ACH credits or debits. Thus, if in our example three depository banks are not ACH members, then DTCs will have to be used instead. In the United States, the vast majority of commercial banks and savings and loans are ACH members.

One other caveat you should be aware of is that the DTC may be assigned two-day availability by the concentration bank. This will result in the build-up of balances in the deposit bank. In this case, you may want to use a wire transfer every two weeks to retrieve any residual balances in the depository banks.

Case 3: Concentrating Funds from Fifty Clothing Stores

Let's assume your company owns 50 clothing stores across the western United States. The stores deposit between $2,000 and $8,000 a day in a local bank. The deposit is 20 percent cash, 35 percent checks, and 45 percent credit cards (Visa®, MasterCard®, and AT&T Universal Card). Your store managers deposit the day's receipts, including the credit card drafts, in a local bank by 3 P.M. Any sales after that time are deposited the next day. Assume that each bank provides two-day availability on the credit card drafts. Sales on a day-to-day and week-to-week basis can be predicted with only a 60 percent degree of accuracy. How would you concentrate the funds to your New York City concentration bank?

Because of the relatively low dollar amounts, you probably wouldn't use wire transfers, especially with 50 stores involved. Wire transfer costs alone would be $208,000 a year.

ACH, in combination with a deposit-reporting service, would be the most logical approach. Manual DTCs would be cumbersome and time-consuming, and automated DTCs prepared by the concentration bank would not offer any advantages over automated ACH. Of course, any ACH nonmember local banks would require that DTCs be used. This would not be a problem because the bank could be given a list of banks that use ACH or DTC.

Depositing Cash, Checks, and Credit Card Drafts

One issue we must address is that 35 percent of the money deposited is in the form of checks and 45 percent of the money is in credit card drafts. Availability provided by the deposit bank will be one and two days for the checks (depending on where they are drawn), and two days for the credit card drafts. (Some banks provide immediate or one day availability on credit card deposits.)

Creating an ACH today for the total amount of the deposit could potentially *overdraw the account* when the ACH debit hits the account tomorrow, because some of the checks deposited today are not yet available funds tomorrow. None of the credit card dollars are available funds either. This situation is referred to as a *negative available balance position* or an uncollected funds position. The book balance is positive, but the available balance is negative.

How do you resolve this problem of varying availabilities on checks and the two-day availability on credit card drafts? You can create the ACH for a dollar amount less than today's deposit; for example, 50 percent of the total deposit. Once a week, on Friday, you can call the banks to obtain the available balance and move the excess funds out by wire.

An alternative approach is to leave an average deposit from one or two days in each account all the time. This balance cushion will hopefully avoid any negative balance conditions as well as handle any return items (bounced checks).

No matter which option you choose, you should monitor the accounts weekly and adjust the balances or ACH amount to meet current conditions.

Deposit anticipation would probably not work very well in this case because of the composition of the deposit and the difficulty of predicting tomorrow's balance with a high degree of certainty.

How often should the funds be concentrated from each store? Based on the difficulty of using deposit anticipation, the recommended approach is to prepare daily ACHs using one of the two approaches we have mentioned. DTCs can be substituted when the field banks are non-ACH member institutions.

Based on our evaluation of three concentration cases, the recommended concentration approach is:

1. Use wire transfers to move large dollar amounts from lockbox banks

2. Use automated ACHs for most applications instead of DTCs

3. Use DTCs when depository banks are non-ACH members

Zero Balance Collection Accounts Can Segregate Your Receipts

Firms with divisions or branches may want to keep separate accounting records of receipts for each branch. To accomplish this goal, the firm can set up zero balance collection accounts in the concentration or lockbox bank. Each division's receipts would be deposited in the appropriate account each day. Each night the bank would automatically transfer the funds from each account into the concentration account. Thus, no funds would remain in the zero balance accounts overnight.

Retail Store Deposit Tracking

Retail establishments such as restaurant chains, supermarkets, gasoline stations, and convenience stores require a way to segregate their store locations' bank deposits for accounting purposes. Firms in one geographic area can accomplish this goal by using one or two banks with branches near all store locations. Many banks offer a deposit reconciliation service where each store uses a specially encoded deposit ticket. All the deposits for each day are credited to one bank account, but the deposit information from each store is kept separate. The firm saves money because only one bank is needed, instead of separate accounts at each store location.

Synthesis

We've reviewed the three objectives and three methods to concentrate funds. By taking into account the availability and cost of each instrument, you can devise a concentration strategy that will meet your exact needs.

7

Disburse Slowly

Slower than a Snail

The money is always there but the pockets change.
—Gertrude Stein

Small Businesses Unwisely Use a Regular Checking Account for Disbursements

Small businesses don't really think about how they disburse their money. More than 90 percent of these businesses use regular checking accounts at their local banks to disburse and deposit their checks. The number of checks deposited and disbursed is manageable, so using one bank appeals to most business owners. However, there is one significant disadvantage of using one account for both purposes. **Excess balances** are kept in the account by most small businesses because of the uncertainty of when your disbursement checks will clear the account. Small business owners don't want to risk having inadequate balances, which can result in the bank bouncing their checks because of "insufficient funds," so they are fighting a constant battle to guess how much to keep in the account. Numerous surveys such as those presented in Chapter 12 have shown that as a group, small businesses keep much higher balances than necessary to pay for bank services.

Firms Should Use More Sophisticated Disbursement Accounts

Companies should not use one checking account for both deposits and disbursements unless their annual revenues are below $100,000 a year. Using one account is short-sighted for the following reasons:

1. It is not known with certainty when every check issued will be paid against the account.
2. Sufficient daily balances to offset all checks clearing are not known with certainty.
3. Any patterns in check clearing for specific types of payments such as payroll, trade payables, and operating expenses will be difficult to track because they are all mixed in one account.
4. The balance position will have to be monitored at least weekly, if not daily, to ensure that sufficient balances are maintained in the account so that a negative ledger balance or an uncollected balance position does not occur.
5. You may be keeping an excess balance in the account and giving up an opportunity to pay an outstanding loan or make an investment.

Use Zero Balance Accounts— They're Simple to Use

Firms should use separate checking accounts for different types of disbursements—payroll, petty cash, and trade payables—for accounting purposes, ease of reconcilement, and for control. And if your company has different divisions or subsidiary companies, you should set up separate accounts for each one, to maintain separate accounting integrity. These should not be regular checking accounts, but rather *zero balance accounts* (ZBAs).

No funds are kept in ZBAs. Using these, you write checks as you normally do. However, when the checks clear your bank against the ZBA account, the bank's computer system automatically offsets these checks (debits) with a credit from another account that you must maintain at that *same* bank, called a "master" ZBA account. Another name commonly used for this account is a "concentration" account.

Enough money must be maintained in the master account to cover all ZBA disbursements. Otherwise, the bank can "bounce" your checks unless you've previously arranged for a credit line to automatically kick in to cover any funding short-falls.

The diagram below (Exhibit 7-1) depicts a common ZBA arrangement. Here the master account funds seven ZBAs—

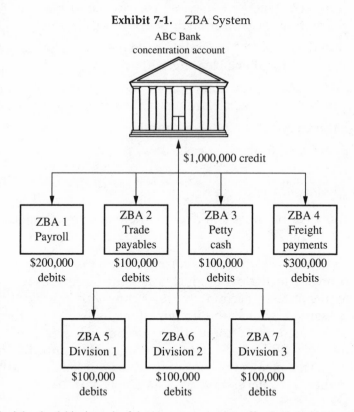

Exhibit 7-1. ZBA System

ABC Bank
concentration account

$1,000,000 credit

ZBA 1 Payroll	ZBA 2 Trade payables	ZBA 3 Petty cash	ZBA 4 Freight payments
$200,000 debits	$100,000 debits	$100,000 debits	$300,000 debits

ZBA 5 Division 1	ZBA 6 Division 2	ZBA 7 Division 3
$100,000 debits	$100,000 debits	$100,000 debits

Each night, the debits in each of the seven accounts are offset by individual credits from the concentration account at the same bank. Therefore, the opening balance in each ZBA is zero.

payroll, trade payables, petty cash, freight payments, and three divisions.

ZBA Advantages

Your company gains eight benefits from using a ZBA approach:

1. No funds are maintained in ZBAs.
2. Funds are maintained in one master account.
3. ZBAs eliminate the possibility of having excess balances in multiple accounts.
4. Different types of payments can be segregated for accounting, organizational, or control purposes.
5. Different types of payments can be easily reconciled and analyzed for check-clearing patterns.
6. ZBAs can be used for payments in which the dollar amount of checks clearing is fairly stable (e.g., payroll).
7. Easier reconcilement of accounts.
8. Better able to forecast cash flow.

ZBA Disadvantages

In addition to nominal extra costs, there are also three drawbacks to using ZBAs:

1. *Total daily balance need is unknown until the next day.* One problem is that you must maintain sufficient balances in the master account to cover any ZBA checks being presented against the account that night. The difficulty is that you don't know the minimum balances you need to cover ZBA checks clearing on one day until the next day. This means that on some days your balances will be higher than necessary, and on some days they may fall short.
2. *Excess balance potential.* With ZBAs, your bank notifies you the following morning with the total dollar value of checks presented against each account the previous day.

Thus, you have a one-day information lag, so you must guess and keep more balances than you might desire. Over the course of the month, this may result in keeping "excess" balances.

3. *Overdraft potential.* On the other hand, keeping minimal balances could result in frequent overdrafts, requiring bank financing at premium interest rates (e.g., prime + 3 percentage points).

In conclusion, ZBAs have many advantages. However, because users do not know the dollar value of the checks clearing against the account until the next morning, they also have a major drawback.

ZBA Usage Is Higher as Company Size Increases

Small businesses are minimal users of ZBAs. Middle-market and large firms are more frequent users of this cash management product. Ninety-three percent of the largest banks offer ZBAs, according to Trans Data Corporation (TDC-1, p. 24). Also, branches of large banks offer this service in the same state. Community or small commercial banks may not offer it, so check with your banks.

ZBA Users

Sixty percent of the firms with annual sales of $50 million to $250 million use ZBAs, which is high in comparison to 40 percent of the firms with sales of $20 million to $49.9 million and 20 percent of the firms with sales of $5 million to $19.9 million (TDC-1, p. 24).

Controlled Disbursement Accounts Come to the Rescue

About 150 banks across the country offer controlled disbursement services (TDC-1, p. 17). To overcome the drawback of not knowing the total dollar amount of disbursement checks until the next morning, banks have developed a more powerful ZBA called a controlled disbursement account. Banks offering this account can provide **same-day early morning check-clearing totals** to their customers. The disbursement bank can notify a company by 11 A.M. EST (8:30 A.M. in some cases) of the total dollar value of checks that will be charged to its account that night. The customer either wires in the funds from another bank to cover the disbursements or transfers funds from another account at that bank, if additional accounts are maintained there.

Thirty percent of companies with sales of $50 million to $250 million use controlled disbursement compared to only percent of the companies with sales of $5 million to $20 million. Overall 17 percent of middle-market companies use the service (TDC-1, p. 17). Another study indicates that almost 81 percent of all large companies (sales greater than $500 million annually) use controlled disbursement (*Powerful Position—for the Present*, Greenwich Associates, 1989, p. 34).

How Does the Controlled Disbursement Process Work?

How can a bank provide *same-day* check-clearing information, and how does it obtain this information so early?

Controlled Disbursement Banks Are Not Located in Fed Cities

Banks offering controlled disbursement services are generally not located in the 12 Federal Reserve cities, in which the Fed can present checks throughout the day. Continuous presentment would make it impossible to obtain a final check-clearing total early in the day and would negate the benefit of controlled disbursement.

RCPC Locations Are Used for Controlled Disbursement

Controlled disbursement banks are instead located in Regional Check Processing Centers (RCPCs). The reason for this is that the Fed in RCPCs presents checks to the banks only in the early morning hours, either in one or two early morning check presentments. No further checks will be presented to the banks by the local Fed until the following morning.

Fed Data Transmission of Check Clearing Totals

The controlled disbursement bank can receive check dollar amount totals by customer account number either by establishing a computer link (electronic transmission of MICR line data) with the Fed or by sorting the checks obtained from the Fed at its own facility. The bank can then notify the customer by telephone, facsimile, telex, or through its information reporting system. Telephone is the most often used method for providing notification information. However, automated notification methods such as PCs are becoming increasingly popular (Trans Data Corporation, *Bank Competitor Analysis: Information Reporting and Initiation Services Survey Results*, 1989, p. 3, hereafter referred to as TDC-2).

Same-day Account Funding by Wire Transfer Is Most Common Approach

The customer must then fund the account, usually by wire, the same day. Otherwise, the bank has the option of bouncing the checks or extending a loan to the customer overnight. The bank usually does not want to bear any risk that a company will go bankrupt overnight and be unable to meet its obligations.

Controlled Disbursement in California

Interestingly, most banks in California do not offer controlled disbursement in their own state, because there are no RCPCs there. These banks usually provide the service to their customers through a correspondent or affiliate bank in another state. For example, Wells Fargo Bank offers the service through United Bank of Grand Junction (Colorado) and through Pittsburgh National Bank (Jeannette, Pennsylvania). Security Pacific National Bank uses an affiliate bank in California to offer controlled disbursement in state.

In summary, controlled disbursement accounts have many positive features. They should definitely be used for vendor payments if a firm has annual disbursements over $50 million a year. In smaller firms, a cost-benefit analysis should be performed to determine whether it is a practical alternative since bank pricing for controlled disbursement is higher than for ZBAs or regular checking accounts. Regular ZBAs are used by many companies for payroll, petty cash, and miscellaneous payments. Payroll check clearings can be forecast with a high degree of accuracy, and petty cash and miscellaneous payments are small transactions, so there is no need for or benefit from using controlled disbursement services, which are much more expensive than regular ZBAs.

Remote Disbursement Accounts Are Still Being Used Today

Before the development of controlled disbursement in 1980, certain banks offered a disbursement service called "remote disbursement." Remote disbursement was born in 1967 in two banks, one in upstate New York and one in North Carolina. Other banks, especially in the Western states, also began offering the service.

Remote disbursement offers a company the opportunity to obtain extended check-clearing times on disbursement checks because the bank is located in a geographically isolated area. This extra clearing float translates into additional earnings, if the company can use the money elsewhere more productively.

Most remote banks offer same-day notification of check clearings and extended clearing time on the checks. Almost 25 percent of all large companies were using the service in the

---

Decreasing Float Time

In the 1970s check-clearing float for remote banks was three to four days. In 1989 it decreased to about 2.25 days for the top remote banks and to 1.75 to 2.00 days for other remote banks.

1970s and early 1980s. Currently only 16 percent of these large companies use the service, according to Greenwich Associates (*Powerful Position—for the Present*, p. 34). The primary users are in the retail and food industries.

Fed Is Against Remote Disbursement

The use of remote disbursement peaked in 1978. On January 11, 1979, the Federal Reserve issued a policy statement indicating that banks should refrain from offering any service that would delay the presentment of checks, including remote disbursement. Although this pronouncement was not a regulation or a law, many banks began de-emphasizing the service. Also, over the past dozen years, check-clearing float from remote banks has diminished because of Fed Reserve initiatives.

Is There a Difference between Remote and Controlled Disbursement?

Yes. The difference boils down to the intent of the company issuing the checks. A company using a remote account is mainly interested in extending its check-clearing float as long as possible, so that the funds can be invested until the account has to be funded. Of course, the vendor who deposits the remote check will most likely receive availability in two days instead of one day. Thus, the vendor will absorb the loss of the extra day or will complain to the issuing company, which may or may not do anything about it.

Float Is of Secondary Importance

Clearing float on controlled disbursement banks averaged 1.25 days in 1989. A company using a controlled account is mainly interested in receiving early morning check notification so that it can determine its daily cash position early in the day. Clearing-float gain is of *secondary* importance.

Many firms invest in the money market for overnight investments and can obtain the best rates and widest choice of instruments in the morning. That is why companies want to receive their clearing information as early as possible. If your company does not need early morning information or does not invest, then notification time may not be an issue.

Should you use a remote account or a controlled account for vendor payables? That is a solely business decision based on the annual net benefit, vendor relationships, image, your company's philosophy and policy, and the ethics. Don't forget the ethics issue.

Annual Reconcilement and Related Services

Companies using a ZBA, controlled, or remote disbursement account can take advantage of the automated account reconcilement (A/R) services offered by their bank. Twenty-five percent of middle-market firms use account reconcilement bank services. Also, 12 percent of smaller middle-market companies

---

Manual Reconciling Wastes Labor Hours

A few years ago I was visiting a division of an automotive company near Detroit. In a conversation with the controller about his cash management system, I asked how he reconciled his 10,000 vendor checks a month. He showed me a stack of paper about three inches high and said that each month his clerical staff typed the check serial numbers and issue dates on the sheets as checks were disbursed. At the end of the month, he received the cancelled checks from the bank, and his staff manually entered the paid date and reconciled the account by hand.

I then asked him if he knew that his bank could perform the reconcilement for him. Astonishingly, he said "no". I then explained to him that the bank could do the job faster, more accurately, and at lower cost. I think he was in shock when I left the meeting.

Obviously, neither his corporate headquarters treasury department nor the company's banks ever told him about this standard bank service. For years he had been doing it manually, wasting labor hours.

use A/R; 21 percent of the medium sized companies use it; and 40 percent of the largest middle-market companies use it (TDC-1, p. 23).

A/R services typically include the following:

- *Partial reconcilement.* The bank provides the company with a list (in paper or computer format) of all checks paid. Checks are listed by serial number during the reconcilement period. The company then reconciles the data inhouse, using a software program. One month is the usual reconcilement period, but some firms reconcile weekly or daily. Any beginning and ending date can be used, not just month-end.

- *Full reconcilement.* Here the company provides the bank with a list of check serial numbers and the checks' issue dates for the period, in paper or computer format. The bank's software performs a reconcilement based on the checks that have been paid. The bank can also provide reports of checks still outstanding, checks stopped, and checks paid without issuing information.

An Uninformed Controller

While consulting with a large outdoor-advertising (billboards) company, I saw hundreds of boxes of paid checks lining the shelves on the four walls of a conference room. These checks, I found out, were from 20 years ago to the present. The average check was $25 and was for the monthly rental of space for billboard promotion. I asked the controller why he kept these checks for 20 years. He said that in case there was ever an inquiry, he could refer to the check to respond.

Obviously, this controller did not know that banks offer microfilm or check safekeeping. Moreover, he is not required to keep cancelled checks for more than seven years, according to bank regulations. The fact that he retained the checks for a longer period of time could work against him in a legal dispute because he would have to produce the checks in question if they were still in his possession.

How long do you store your checks? Why? Make sure to check with your lawyer or accountant before making any rash changes.

- *Microfilm/microfiche.* The bank can provide microfilm copies of statements and checks in a predetermined order (e.g., paid date and serial number).

- *Check safekeeping.* Instead of returning your paid checks, the bank will store them for a specified time (e.g., 3 months) before destroying them. A photocopy can be provided by the bank at any time, if the company needs one. Another alternative is for companies to obtain a microfilm of their checks in serial number order and to keep the film in a safe location.

  Four percent of the smallest middle-market firms use check safekeeping, as well as 8 percent of the medium-sized companies and 10 percent of the largest middle-market firms (TDC-1, p. 23). You should strongly consider check safekeeping. There is no need to store boxes of checks on your premises or to pay to have them stored in a records storage facility.

- *Float report.* Some banks can provide you with a report that gives summary statistics on the average time between issuance and payment of your checks. An overall weighted statistic for all your paid checks indicates the average float time. This number can be tracked for each reconcilement period to detect any changes in check-clearing times.

- *Check sorting.* All banks can sort your checks in either serial number or dollar amount order before returning them. The checks can be filmed, sent back to you for storage, or kept by the bank before being destroyed.

- *On-line stop payments.* You can place stop payments (which cancel the check you issued before it is paid by your bank) on your PC on-line without having to call or write to the bank. Confirmation will be printed on your screen and you can create a hard copy on your printer for your files.

- *Single account/subaccounts.* Most controlled disbursement banks offer companies that need more than one disbursement account a money-saving option.

  Suppose your company needs four separate accounts— one for each of four divisions. Instead of using four accounts, the bank can set up one checking account number with a subaccount system. By designating specific digits in the serial number field of the check, the bank can reconcile and provide separate information to you as if you had four unique accounts. Banks' charge for each account is fairly high (e.g., $75 to $200 a month), so the use of this subaccount system provides significant savings. Some banks charge for subaccounts (e.g., $25 a month) but others do not. You always save over separate accounts.

Account Reconcilement Option

Do it yourself when

- you have fewer than 500 checks per month
- you have time or staff to do it
- you want to minimize expenses
- you have a PC-based Account Reconcilement package
- you can afford an Accounts Payable package with an account reconcilement capability
- your bank's price is exorbitant

Use a bank when

- you have high check volume (more than 500 checks per month)
- you need specialized reports
- no Account Reconcilement software meets your needs
- you do not have hardware/software to run program
- the bank's price is cheaper or equal to your cost
- you have no staff or time available

Drafts

Besides using checks for disbursements, some companies use drafts. The most common type of draft is called a *payable-through draft* (PTD). This instrument looks like a check, feels like a check, and smells like a check, but it is a draft. It has a MICR line, and it clears through the banking system as a check does. These are the distinguishing features of a draft:

- The words "payable-through" are printed on the face of the draft, typically in the lower left-hand corner.
- The draft is *drawn on the issuing company*, not on the bank.
- The draft is payable through a bank that acts as the intermediary for payment.
- The issuing company is responsible for verifying the signature, determining that the transaction is valid, and checking the endorsement.
- The bank must present the physical drafts or an electronic transmission of the draft data to the company for its review and approval within 24 hours before actually debiting the account.
- The company has the final right of acceptance and can return any drafts that it deems improper. The draft is returned through the Federal Reserve system.

The Origin of the PTD

PTDs were created in 1932. At that time, the U.S. Government wanted to charge banks a small tax on each check they processed. To avoid this tax, banks began using this new instrument, the PTD, which was not considered a check and hence was not taxed. In 1988, more and more banks offered an electronic delivery of the MICR line on the PTD to speed up the processing.

Use of Drafts for Field Office Payments

Drafts are used by companies to pay claims, by field offices to pay for local expenses, and by sales organizations to reimburse traveling sales staff. For example, the sales people each have a book of blank drafts. They can reimburse themselves at any time by preparing a draft payable to themselves and cashing it at their bank. The draft usually has a dollar limit printed on its face (e.g., $500). The company can review the draft and determine its validity before accepting it, because the bank physically or electronically delivers all the drafts that clear the bank every day.

Rapidraft® and Traveletter® Offer Money-Saving Disbursement Approach

Two unique payment systems are offered by Gelco Payments Systems, Inc., a firm based in Edina, Minnesota. They are called Rapidraft® and Traveletter®. Here's the story.

Rapidraft®

This product is used by firms that want to maintain centralized control over payables, even though they maintain geographically diverse branch offices, plants, sales offices, or distribution centers. Instead of opening up many local bank accounts and maintaining balances that are difficult to monitor and control, they choose a better way—using Rapidraft® (see Exhibit 7-2). Gelco custom designs a multipart PTD or a standard PTD with a company's custom-designed statement attached. The PTDs are distributed to the appropriate offices for normal payables use, and the recipient of the PTD deposits it as if it were a check. One copy of the PTD is sent to the main office for approval and the other copy is kept at the branch office location.

Advantages of Rapidraft®

1. Local autonomy maintained in issuing payments
2. No need to maintain a local bank account
3. No idle or wasted balances in local banks
4. Can use one bank as disbursement bank
5. Complete audit trail
6. Easy to generate and prepare management reports

Exhibit 7-2. Gelco Rapidraft® (Reprinted with permission from Gelco Payments Systems, Inc.)

FINLAY FINE JEWELRY CORPORATION
PETTY CASH RECONCILIATION

0001027

TOTAL PETTY CASH FUND: $ _____   GROUP NAME
LESS CASH ON HAND: $ _____   & NUMBER _____
LESS TOTAL RECEIPTS (MUST BE ATTACHED) $ _____   DATE _____
DIFFERENCE: $ _____

ACCOUNT NAMES	AMOUNT	ACCT. #	ACCOUNT NAMES (CONTINUED)	AMOUNT	ACCT. #
AUTO EXPENSES			SECURITY:		
GARAGE & PARKING		705-05	ALARM SERVICE CHARGES		738-01
MILEAGE		705-09	SECURITY EQUIPMENT REPAIRS		738-02
OTHER		705-08	SECURITY TESTS		738-03
DATA PROCESSING SUPPLIES		718-05	GUARDS		738-04
DATA PROCESSING EQUIP. REPAIR & MAINT.		718-11	LOCK REPAIRS & REPLACEMENTS		738-05
FREIGHT & POSTAGE			OTHER		738-07
FREIGHT CHARGES		230-03	STATIONARY AND OFFICE SUPPLIES:		
POSTAGE & SHIPPING		230-04	OFFICE SUPPLIES		761-03
OVERNIGHT DELIVERY		230-05	FORMS		761-04
JEWELRY REPAIR			XEROX		761-05
CHARGEABLE TO CUSTOMERS		202-04	OTHER		761-08
NON CHARGEABLE TO CUSTOMERS		202-05	SMALL OFFICE EQUIPMENT		761-10
MISCELLANEOUS EXPENSES			SUBSCRIPTIONS:		772-01
MISCELLANEOUS		777-01	OTHER ACCOUNTS (Not listed above)	AMOUNT	ACCT. #
PLANTS, FLOWERS, ETC.		777-02			
TAXI		777-09			
REPAIRS & MAINTENANCE					
MISCELLANEOUS (UNDER $500)		760-03			
CLEANING SERVICE		760-04			
MACHINE RENTAL		759-02	TOTAL RECEIPTS		
TELEPHONE		765-01	DIFFERENCE (From reconciliation above)		714-02
FOOD FOR MEETINGS		773-02	TOTAL CHECK		

"RAPIDRAFT" REG US PAT OFF   LITHO IN U.S.A.   "RAPIDRAFT" REG US PAT OFF   02797000 00

ACCT #								TOTAL
AMOUNT								

This instrument is void unless authorized by a RAPIDRAFT Authorization issued to the Drawer By GELCO PAYMENT SYSTEMS, INC., P.O. Box 35884, Edina, MN 55435-0884

R/D AUTH NO   DATE

GROUP NUMBER
2 1 — 9 6

FINLAY FINE JEWELRY CORPORATION   0001027

PAY TO THE
ORDER OF _____

THE
AMOUNT OF _____
NOT GOOD FOR MORE THAN **$500.00**

$ _____

NOT NEGOTIABLE

SIGNATUE OF RAPIDRAFT AUTHORIZATION HOLDER

PAYABLE THROUGH
NORWEST BANK LITCHFIELD, N.A.   75-188/919
LITCHFIELD, MINNESOTA

This Rapidraft Order was drawn strictly in accordance with the authority of said Rapidraft Authorization issued by GELCO PAYMENT SYSTEMS, INC. If any statement herein be untrue, we, the aforesigned, agree to pay to the drawer company upon demand the amount of this Rapidraft order and all expenses and damages arising from such misstatement

⑈0100010277⑈ ⑆09190188⑈

7. No need to maintain a central accounts payable department

8. Local vendor relations are maintained

9. Reduces overall administrative and banking costs

Rapidraft® Applications Are Numerous

The types of payments that can be made using Rapidraft® are numerous. They include the following:

utilities	freight
supplies	temporary agency
repairs	personnel
emergency cash	convention expenses
	sales incentives

Companies in the consumer goods industry also use this product to pay for co-op advertising, promotions, and early-buy allowances, among others.

Gelco's Service Bureau can handle the entire payment tracking and management process by managing the banking relationship, processing the information on the draft's face, cross-referencing and validating the data, producing accurate and timely management reports, and providing information to the company. This information can take a variety of formats, including magnetic tape, diskette, or hard copy. For companies that prefer to handle this entire process themselves, Gelco offers a software package dubbed "GelcoVectr".

Traveletter® Is Another Winner

This Gelco product focuses on travel and expense report management. The Traveletter® merges expense reporting, approval, and employee reimbursement into one transaction. This is accomplished with the Combo Expense Report Form, which is customized to each company's needs. Travelers receive payment as soon as they complete this form, without having to wait weeks for reimbursement. (For more information on these two products, contact Gelco Payments Systems, Inc., One Corporate Center, 7301 Ohms Lane, Edina, MN 55435. Phone: (612) 832-3561 or (800) 334-3526.)

Charge Card Purchases Can Reduce Immediate Cash Outlays

According to a *Wall Street Journal* article (April 7, 1989) entitled "Small Firms Increasingly Say 'Charge It,'" more and more small companies are issuing corporate charge cards to selected employees. The leading corporate card issuers are Citicorp Diners Club and American Express, but Visa®, MasterCard®, and AT&T Universal Card credit cards are also competing in this lucrative market. There have been numerous stories over the past few years of owners of fledgling companies who have saved their companies by using all of their charge cards to the hilt. Interestingly, a 1988 American Express survey found that over one-third of business owners were not aware of the existence of corporate charge cards.

Smaller businesses, according to the article, don't often complain about the high interest rate charges on their revolving credit card accounts. Moreover, many of them use their card's credit feature as a line of credit to manage their cash flow. Also, smaller firms seek higher credit limits than they receive on personal cards. One of the main advantages of using a corporate card, besides the prestige factor, is the receipt of a quarterly report from the card company delineating all expenses by employee and expense category (e.g., lodging, restaurants, travel).

Follow These Charge Card Guidelines
to Save Money

If your firm uses corporate cards, be sure to take the following precautions:

- Provide your employees with written guidelines on how and when the cards can be used.
- Provide specific limits on hotel room prices, meals, and transportation allowances.
- Spell out your policy on the use of first class air travel, if you permit it at all, and on your procedures for booking flights.
- Review the quarterly reports for each person to detect any abuses or questionable charges or practices.
- Reimburse employees for their expenses using a direct deposit to their preselected bank accounts (via the ACH) or consider using the Traveletter® approach.
- Don't use charge cards or credit cards as substitutes for the traditional borrowing methods, because the high interest rates on these cards (e.g., 18 percent) make them expensive in this case.

Disbursement Model Studies Can Identify Clearing Float Benefits

If you are interested in increasing your check-clearing float, then you can determine the financial benefits by having a bank perform a disbursement model analysis using a model such as offered by Phoenix-Hecht Disbursement Micro Model™. Fewer banks have this model than the lockbox model, so contact your bank to determine if it has this service. If your bank doesn't offer it, then you can contact Phoenix-Hecht at (919) 541-9339 to obtain a list of banks that provide it. Bank pricing for this model is similar to the pricing of the lockbox model.

Data Requirements

The company needs to provide the bank with disbursement check data from paid checks for a representative month so the model results are not skewed. This data can be provided in the following ways:

1. Total vendor dollars aggregated by three-digit sending zipcodes

2. Individual check data in hard copy or from a diskette

Bank Runs Model and Provides
Recommendations

After entering the check data, the bank executes the model using the latest available Phoenix-Hecht Clearing Study™. The study contains check-clearing times between selected deposit and drawee bank cities. The model reports provide insight into the current and optimal disbursement system. Exhibit 7-3 contains the optimization analysis of one to three locations. In this case, a company could increase its check-clearing float by 0.71 days, which is equivalent to $98,299 a year in annual float gain, assuming a 6 percent interest rate, by using a disbursement bank in Van Buren, Missouri, instead of its existing bank in Chicago. An additional $21,172 can be earned by adding a second disbursement bank in Ft. Wayne, Indiana. A third site would add $8,898 compared to two sites.

How to Select a Specific Disbursement Bank

When selecting a disbursement bank, follow these ten steps:

1. Have a bank use the Phoenix-Hecht model to determine optimal and alternative disbursement cities if you are looking to maximize check-clearing float. Keep in mind that the disbursement model can provide only disbursement *cities*, not specific disbursement bank solutions.

2. Determine which cities appeal to you based on their relative check-clearing times, early notification times, or both, depending on your corporate disbursement philosophy.

3. Obtain a listing of potential banks in these cities from the bank performing the study.

4. Send each bank a letter requesting information on its disbursement services. Be sure to include your specific

Exhibit 7-3. The disbursement model optimization report pinpoints float benefits.

Site	Cities	Days Gained	Annual Float Gain at 6% Compared To Existing System
Optimal one site:	Van Buren, MO	0.71	$98,299
Alternatives:	Waynesville, MO	0.70	98,159
	Crane, MO	0.64	89,118
	Hartford, CT	0.22	31,336
Optimal two site:	Ft. Wayne, IN; Van Buren, MO	0.86	119,471
Alternatives:	Ft. Wayne, Waynesville	0.83	116,015
	Hartford, Van Buren	0.78	109,000
Optimal three site:	Abilene, Fort Wayne, Van Buren	0.92	128,369
Alternatives:	Fort Wayne, Van Buren, Waynesville	0.90	125,005
	Fort Wayne, Van Buren, Hartford	0.87	120,650

Note: The existing system is a bank in Chicago.

needs (e.g., account reconcilement, check safekeeping, or microfilm, check volume, and number of accounts).

5. Request that the bank send you its *BAI Controlled Disbursement Questionnaire* response. This document contains critical information on each bank's service. The questionnaire has 85 questions divided into eight sections:

1. Background
2. Presentation
3. Processing
4. Notification
5. Funding methods
6. Disbursement services

7. Implementation

8. Pricing

Most banks will have prepared answers to this questionnaire and will be able to respond quickly to your request.

6. Determine which aspects of the bank's service are most important to your company. Then assign the appropriate weights to each of the eight categories and to the questions.

7. Use a spreadsheet program or manually prepare a matrix to compare banks. Rank the banks from highest to lowest.

8. Arrange for on-site visits with top scoring banks.

9. Select a bank and sign a written agreement.

10. Have checks printed and begin issuing checks on this account. Close out your old account after a month or two so that outstanding checks will have time to clear.

Ten Tips on What to Look for In Selecting a Top Controlled Disbursement Bank

1. Provides early notification (before 10:30 A.M. EST)

2. Provides automated means (information reporting service) of obtaining clearing totals

3. Accepts funding by wire the same day

4. Does not require you to maintain other bank accounts

5. Does not accept direct sends from other banks

6. Offers high-quality ancillary services (e.g., account reconcilement, on-line stop payments, check storage, and subaccounts)

7. Has rapid response time (24 hours or less) on normal inquiries

8. Guarantees price for at least one year

9. Offers competitive pricing (e.g., per-check charge of $0.12 to $0.15).

10. Accepts compensation in fees or balances, with no premium charged for fees.

Paying by Wire Is Not So Smart

So far, we've focused on paying obligations by check. As you remember from previous chapters, however, you can also pay by wire and by ACH, although most firms do not.

Wire Transfer

Paying vendors by wire is not nearly as common a method as paying them by check. When you pay by wire, your company loses use of the funds the day the wire is sent, and your bank charges you $8 to $10 for sending the wire. Your customer is also paying an incoming wire charge. There is no float benefit using wires, as there is with checks. According to TDC, of the 75 percent of the middle-market companies that use wire transfers, 38 percent use wires for disbursements (TDC-1, p. 5).

In certain industries, such as the petroleum, commodities, and securities industries, wires are common because of the large size of the transactions.

Key point. You shouldn't pay vendors by wire unless you are receiving some benefit, such as a price concession or a discount. Without these benefits, you're losing money. There are two types of wire transfers, repetitive and nonrepetitive.

Repetitive wires

A repetitive wire is one that is sent to the same account at the same bank on a frequent basis, such as daily or weekly. The only variable is the dollar amount. Repetitive wires are also known as predefined wires, line transfers, structured wires, and preformatted wires.

Repetitive wires are typically used for concentrating funds from lockbox banks and for paying for specific periodic types of transactions such as taxes or funding a payroll account in another bank.

Manual or automated

The transaction can be handled by manual or automated means. In the former case you call your bank contact and provide the dollar amount of the transfer. The bank will have previously been sent a letter by you specifying the banks, transit-routing codes, and account numbers that will be used for repetitive transfers, and it will have prepared a "linesheet" that contains this information. When you call, the banker simply places the dollar amount next to the appropriate line. This document is used as the authorization to send out the wires by the bank's wire transfer department.

Repetitive wires can also be easily executed using a bank's wire transfer initiation module of its balance reporting system. The screen contains blank numbered lines. You can input the dollar amounts and the wire will be handled automatically by the bank.

Nonrepetitive wires

This type of wire is infrequently sent to the same beneficiary, so the receiving bank, the account number of the receiving party, and the dollar value are variable information. These nonrepetitive wires also are known by other names, such as unstructured wires, free-form wires, and third-party transfers.

Nonrepetitive wires can also be handled either manually, by calling the bank with the information, or automatically, by using a bank's information reporting service. In both these cases, however, all the information must be provided. (In the previous case of repetitive wires, only the dollar amount is needed).

Key point. Use a bank's information reporting system to create automated wire transfers with a PC in your office. These transfers are up to 50 percent cheaper than manual transfers and can be executed quickly and accurately. Make sure your bank offers PC-initiated wires.

Internal Wire Transfer Fraud: Should You Be Concerned?

Definitely! You must have the proper controls in place, especially for free-form transfers, or else you run the risk of being unpleasantly surprised one day. Embezzlement of company funds and fraud are growing phenomena. The availability of PCs and the ease with which employees can use the bank's information reporting system to initiate wires increases the temptation for unscrupulous employees.

Here's How to Do It Right

You should focus your concern on free-form tranfers and the ways that they are accomplished at your company. Here's how they should be done:

- Free-forms should be input over the bank's information reporting system, not called in to the bank.
- Free-forms should not be sent by facsimile to the bank— anyone can photocopy a signature and obtain a password from a previously faxed transfer that is in your files.
- Two individuals should be assigned to do all free-form transfers—one should enter the data, and the other should verify and release the transfer.
- Each person should be assigned a unique password that will not be left lying around, written down anywhere, or shared with anyone, even in case of absence or vacation.
- In case of emergency or employee vacation, a back-up person should be trained to handle the transaction with his or her own password.
- Request that the bank call back another person at the company to verify the accuracy and authenticity of the wire.
- Passwords should be changed quarterly and whenever an employee leaves that job function or leaves the company.

Here's How to Do It Wrong

- One person does all your wires. (Caveat: one-person firm!)
- Two persons are involved—one inputting the data and one verifying the data—but they know each other's passwords.
- A few people in your company know the codes, which are left out in the open.
- Codes and passwords are rarely changed, even when a person leaves your company or is transferred to another department.
- When an employee calls in the transfer on the phone to the bank, everyone around can hear the password and codes.

Other Electronic Funds Transfer (EFT) Systems You Should Know About

In addition to wires, there are two other electronic systems that handle large dollar payments. FedWire handles domestic funds transfers, and CHIPS and SWIFT process international oriented transactions. ACH is the electronic payment system that handles mostly small dollar payments.

CHIPS (Clearing House Interbank Payment System)

CHIPS is operated by the New York Clearing House Association and is owned by its New York City member banks. CHIPS electronically ties together 140 domestic depository institutions and branch offices of foreign banks in New York City. On an average day, CHIPS processes about 200,000 transactions valued at $750 billion.

CHIPS handles many types of transactions: letters of credit, collections, reimbursements, foreign exchange, and the sale of short-term Eurodollar funds.

SWIFT (Society for Worldwide Interbank Financial Telecommunication)

SWIFT connects 2,360 financial institutions in 56 countries and processes about one million messages a day. SWIFT is not a funds transfer system like FedWire, but an *international* automated message-switching and transmission service for member banks. The information that SWIFT transmits about funds transfers for bank customers will be executed on a future day specified in the text of the message on the books of the receiving bank. SWIFT is owned by a Belgian cooperative of 1,460 financial institutions worldwide.

SWIFT messages allow institutions to circulate instructions on international payments, statements, and other transactions associated with international finance. About 80 percent of the CHIPS transfers are initiated by SWIFT messages.

Unless small businesses or middle-market companies send international-oriented transactions to their banks for transfer, they will probably not need to use either of these systems.

(ACH) Automated Clearing House

In the United States, paying by ACH is growing in popularity, but only for specific applications. It is most popular for companies that pay employees by direct deposit of payroll (DDP) and for the U. S. Government, which pays social security recipients their monthly payments by direct deposit. ACH disbursements are also useful for annuities, pensions, interest payments, and federal tax payments. Very few firms pay their shareholders using the ACH.

Private and public companies may offer the DDP service to their employees. Only 10 percent of all U. S. employees are on DDP. About 52 percent of social security recipients are on direct deposit. (Laura Cianci, "Direct Deposit Cuts Costs, Time," *USA Today*, December 13, 1989, p. 8B.) According to Trans Data Corporation (TDC-1, p. 11), 27 percent of the middle-market firms use DDP, as well as 18 percent of the smallest firms, 26 percent of the medium-sized firms, and 38 percent of the largest firms. Usage of DDP from 1985 to 1989 has been stable.

DDP Usage by Industry	
All firms	27 percent
Business services	52
Other industries	31
Manufacturing	30
Construction	23
Wholesale trade	21
Retail trade	20

Source: TDC-1, p. 11

Before you can send an ACH credit to a person's bank account, your company must obtain written approval from that person. That individual must supply his or her bank account number and bank transit-routing code and sign a release form to receive these credits.

Corporate Trade Payments

A more recent ACH disbursement application allows one company to pay another company using the ACH. This type of corporate-to-corporate payment is commonly referred to as a "corporate trade payment" (CTP). See Exhibit 7-4 for an illustration of this. These business-to-business payments can be formatted in various ways. Be aware that if you receive electronic payments from the U.S. Government that certain agencies use the CCD+ format.

Although it was first pilot-tested in 1983 and then approved for widespread use, CTP still has relatively low volume. Companies have limited interest in it, and there are standardization issues to overcome. Moreover, float is still an issue that

Exhibit 7-4. Corporate trade payment flow is straight forward.

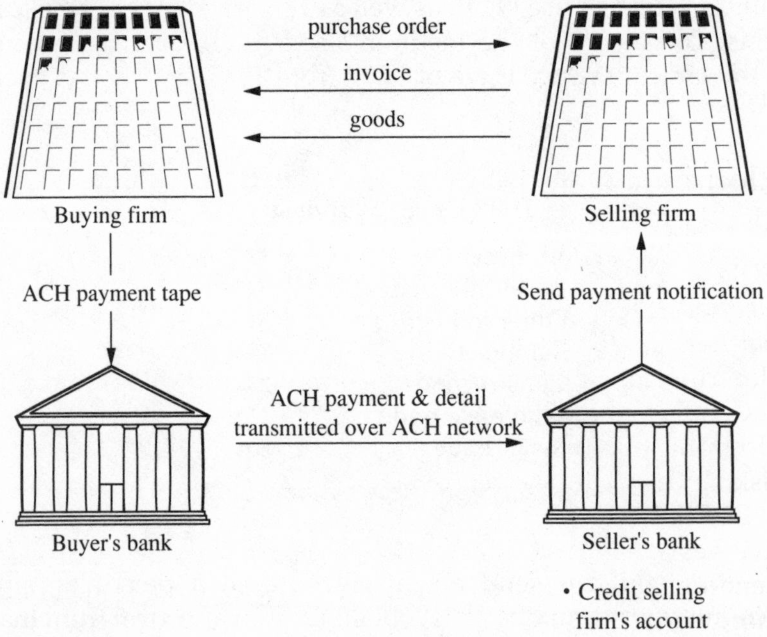

Buying firm

purchase order

invoice

goods

Selling firm

ACH payment tape

Send payment notification

ACH payment & detail transmitted over ACH network

Buyer's bank

Seller's bank

• Credit selling firm's account

keeps many companies from evaluating CTP in an in-depth manner. Use of CTPs is growing slowly. Only about 4 percent of middle-market firms used CTPs in 1986 and 1987, compared to 10 percent in 1988 and 1989. (TDC-1, p. 13)

Reasons Why CTPs Aren't Popular

According to TDC-1 (p. 13), there are several reasons why middle-market firms do not use CTPs:

No interest in service	70 percent
Don't know enough about it	16
No float/prefer checks	7
Other	5
Expense in converting systems	2

Also, according to TDC, CTP usage among middle-market firms is low—an average of four items a month. This minimal volume may be traced to the problem of locating other firms (vendors/suppliers) that can or want to accept CTPs. Moreover, the various CTP formats in use may be a stumbling block. Surprisingly, 4 percent of the firms that use CTPs indicate that it is their primary payment method, and 2 percent plan to make it their primary method.

Electronic Data Interchange (EDI) Use Is Minimal

EDI is the hottest area in cash management. It is the electronic exchange of business documents between trading partners (e.g., buyers and sellers). Business documents include invoices, bills of lading, price quotes, and shipping orders.

Companies have realized the cost and time benefits of using electronic transmissions instead of using paper documents and risking delays in the U. S. Mail.

EDI has been around for over 20 years, but only in the past five years has its value been perceived by many companies, vendors, and banks. Companies with sales over $1 billion are more likely than small companies to use EDI because of

economies of scale. Only 11 percent of middle-market companies use EDI (TDC-1, p. 16).

EDI Is Not Used Much

TDC-1 (p. 16) reports several reasons why middle-market companies are not heavy users of EDI (among nonusers of EDI):

Reason	Percentage
No interest in service	68%
Don't know enough about EDI	20
Expense of conversion	5
Difficulty with vendor cooperation	4

Over the next five years, more and more companies are
expected to begin using EDI. Even small businesses will be
able to participate by using reasonably priced software. There
are many software packages that you can buy that provide EDI
capability. Previously, EDI participation was available to large
companies and their customers and vendors. Now it can be
used by any firm that has a desire to accomplish these goals:

- to eliminate paper documents
- to reduce clerical cost
- to improve management of inventory
- to develop a more effective billing system
- to provide fast, accurate customer service

Synthesis

This chapter focused on the different approaches to use in disbursing your funds. Control, your firm's disbursement policy
and philosophy, and your desire to extend clearing float are
all critical elements that you should evaluate.

8

It's 10 A.M.; Do You Know Where Your Cash Is?

You Should Know by Now

"Information about money is almost as valuable as the money itself." —Walter B. Wriston, former Chairman of Citicorp/Citibank

---

You need timely information about your bank balances, deposits, incoming wire transfers and ACHs, disbursement check clearings, and maturing investments to manage your cash effectively and to determine your daily cash position. These figures must be accurate, timely, and easily accessible.

Information Reporting Systems Are Critical to Track Your Cash

Banks Use Various Approaches to Providing Information

In 1975 Chemical Bank developed one of the first balance reporting systems to provide information to its corporate customers. Since then banks have taken a variety of actions:

- Some developed their own information systems internally, which was an expensive option.
- Some bought software packages from vendors.
- Some used time-sharing services to provide the service.

- Some franchised another bank's system (e.g., the BankLink system is offered to banks by BankLink, Inc., an independent subsidiary of Chemical Banking Corporation).

When these information systems were first introduced, they were commonly known as "balance reporting systems," because their main feature was their ability to provide balance details. In the past two decades, however, the service has been expanded to provide much more data and has evolved into a bank information reporting service. Most banks have devised unique names for their systems rather than simply calling them information systems. Examples are InfoCash, Citi-Cash Manager, TRANSEND, MARS, FirstCash, Direct Connection, ChemLink, and CONFIRM. These names are either registered, trademarked, or copyrighted.

Most Firms Use One Bank's System

Small businesses and middle-market companies tend to use only one bank's system—typically their major relationship or credit line bank, or perhaps the bank where they deposit sizable sums of dollars (such as a lockbox bank). Large firms use multibank information reporting systems because of the need for extensive details.

Almost 50 percent of the middle-market companies surveyed receive daily balance information from their banks. Only 26 percent of the smaller middle-market firms used the service, compared to 66 percent of the larger middle-market firms (TDC-1, p. 19). Thirty-four percent of all firms use a bank's telephone information reporting, 22 percent use an electronic window (to access directly into the bank's computer), 15 percent use audio response, and 31 percent use other automated reporting services (TDC-2, p. 3).

Small Business Cash Management Information Reporting Systems

A handful of banks and vendors have developed information reporting systems specifically designed for small businesses and middle-market firms. Other banks sell their standard system with fewer features to the smaller companies. Organizations that offer specific small or middle-market information and software systems are mentioned in the following sections.

BankLink, Inc.

BankLink introduced the *MicroLink* product in 1986 for the middle market. MicroLink is marketed to firms with annual revenues ranging between $2 million and $100 million. It is a modular service with screen prompts to guide the user through the various functions, and it offers four functions:

- *Cash Manager*. This provides a daily cash flow report. It can be used with a spreadsheet and can send and receive funds electronically.
- *Check Manager*. This is an electronic checkbook. It can record, print, and obtain a status report on check disbursements (current and historical), and it provides a float analysis report.
- *Automated Payments and Collections*. These can initiate ACHs for any purpose.
- *Accounting Connection*. This service automatically reconciles your disbursed checks with your accounts payable information.

Business Banker, introduced in 1989, is a computerized banking service for the expanding small business with annual sales below $10 million. Accessed through a PC, Business Banker provides account balances, check clearing, and available deposits; executes transfers between accounts; and allows stop payment initiation on issued checks. Banks offering the Business Banker package charge about $50 a month. The first bank to license the product was Florida National.

Manufacturers Hanover Trust

Another bank provider, Manufacturers Hanover has offered *Interplex Business Manager* for middle-sized companies since

1986. This product automates and integrates specific cash management and bookkeeping procedures. It can communicate with five other banks, forecast cash, print checks, and integrate payables and receivables.

Harbinger Computer Services

Harbinger Computer Services, besides offering its EDI product, developed *InTouch Cash Manager*™ in 1985 for banks to sell to their middle-market and small business clients. Companies with annual sales ranging between $500,000 and $25 million are its target market although much larger firms use the service.

InTouch Features.   This PC-based business banking system offers the following features:

- Complete balance and transaction history for business and personal accounts at bank
- Check clearing
- ACH and funds transfers
- Electronic bank statements, as requested
- Automatic bank reconciliation (daily, weekly, monthly)
- Complete recordkeeping and report writing
- Check writing
- Downloads to spreadsheet and database programs
- Access to third-party information and news retrieval services
- Electronic mail and electronic calendar

InTouch Banks.   The following banks offer this product to their customers:

Marine Midland Bank
Buffalo, New York

Deposit Guaranty National Bank
Jackson, Mississippi

National City Bank
Cleveland, Ohio

Wells Fargo Bank
San Francisco

First National Bank
  of Atlanta
Atlanta, Georgia

Old National Bank
  in Evansville
Evansville, Indiana

Midwest Financial Group
Peoria, Illinois

InTouch Pricing. Typical bank charges for InTouch range from $35 to $75 a month, depending on usage. Most of these banks offer a free 30- to 60-day trial period for the product. Research compiled by Harbinger indicates that over a one-year period, average available balances of 100 companies using the service rose almost 22 percent and money market account balances increased by 34 percent.

Automatic Data Processing (ADP), Inc.

ADP offers *BalExpress*[SM] for small and middle-market companies. This simple, low-cost service starts at $25 a month. It is sold by ADP to banks to market to their customers. To use the service, a company enters a user number and password on a PC or terminal. The system authenticates the password and prints the balance report. The customer is then automatically disconnected from the system. Up to three accounts with as many as six fields of data can be accessed in this manner at the bank.

Another product offered by ADP through banks to small and middle-sized companies and selected retail customers is its *Bal-Express Touch-Tone* service. This allows the bank's customers to obtain the prior day's balance information by making a touch-tone phone call. The collected balance, ledger balance, total debits, and total credits are all obtainable. Businesses that want same-day information can use ADP's *Intra-day Touch-Tone* service, which provides such information as the day's balances, controlled disbursement, ACH debits and credits, and incoming wires. Each bank determines exactly what information will be available to its customers.

Third-Party Service Providers

About 55 percent of the banks offering information reporting offer the service through an outside vendor. Another 25 percent

---

use a combination of a vendor and internal resources. Three top vendors used by banks for information reporting are Bank-Link, with 31 percent usage; ADP with 28 percent and (NDC) National Data Corporation, with 20 percent (TDC-2, p. 29).

What Information Can You Obtain from an Information Reporting System?

Although most banks offer an information reporting system, the sophistication and the cost of the product varies greatly from bank to bank. Although money center banks (e.g., New York City, Chicago, and San Francisco) and regional banks offer the most highly developed systems, many smaller banks offer a barebones product. A top-notch system for large companies would not be needed by small and middle-market companies. Here are the features of a comprehensive information reporting system:

- *Toll-free phone number.* Free phone call to access system
- *Internal bank system.* Often less expensive than banks that use third-party systems
- *Twenty-four-hour access.* Excellent customer service feature
- *Balance reports.* Previous day's closing ledger; available current-day ledger; available one- and two-day float; and intraday balances

Balance Information Statistics

Of the middle-market firms receiving balance information, 80 percent receive previous-day data, 56 percent receive current-day data, and only 36 percent receive both current and previous day information (TDC-2, p. 28).

- *Account detail.* Previous day's total debits and total credits; dollar values and number of credits and debits; previous day's transactions; and intraday details
- *Lockbox detail.* Total number of items and dollars; immediate, one-day, and two-day availability; previous day's report; and intraday report

- *Wire transfer module.* Preformatted screen for initiating wires; repetitive and nonrepetitive wires; current- and future-date warehousing; offline repetitives for high-volume users; intraday incoming wires
- *ACH module.* Initiation of ACH debits or credits on pre-formatted screen; preparation of concentration debits; transactions for current and future dates; notification of incoming ACHs, including CTPs
- *Security reports.* Reports that indicate who used the system, when, and for what purpose
- *History reports.* Total debits and credits, 5 to 60 days of balance history including ledger and available balance
- *Controlled disbursement report.* Clearing totals for first and second presentments, if the information reporting system is housed in the same bank as the account.
- *Multibank balance reports.* Capability for other banks to provide their balances to this bank's system or to a third-party vendor to consolidate it for transmission to the bank or to the customer
- *Target balance report.* Calculation of target balance (the balance you're managing to each day so that you end up at the appropriate balance level by the end of the month) for each account for the period to date

Sample reports are shown in Exhibits 8-1 and 8-2.

Use of Information Reporting Systems

Middle-market firms use bank information reporting systems for little else than balance information, but the other information that some of these firms obtained from the bank was the following:

Detailed debit and credit activity	14 percent
Wire transfer initiation	8 percent
Same-day lockbox data	6 percent
Same-day controlled disbursement	6 percent
Same-day stop payment initiation	3 percent

(TDC-1, p. 20)

Exhibit 8-1.   Balance reports provide critical data. (Reprinted with permission of Security Pacific National Bank)

ABC COMPANY
SECURITY PACIFIC BANK
SPACIFICS
BALANCE HISTORY REPORT
BALANCES REPORTED AS OF 01JANXX–07JANXX
PRINTED ON 25JANXX 13:40 PST

DATE	LEDGER BALANCE	COLLECTED BAL	TOTAL DEBITS	TOTAL CREDITS
SPNB – SECURITY PACIFIC BANK				
CURRENCY USD DOLLAR				
ACCT 1123456 – DEMO CONCENTRATION ACCT				
01JAN	1,739,810.81 CF	1,316,673.60 CF		
02JAN	1,739,810.81 CF	1,316,673.60 CF		
03JAN	1,775,133.11 B	1,236,937.10 B	738,266.83 B	773,589.13 B
04JAN	2,042,809.10 B	1,589,490.06 B	355,360.20 B	623,036.19 B
05JAN	3,351,002.46 B	1,970,863.85 B	424,086.63 B	1,732,279.99 B
06JAN	1,684,779.89 B	1,295,664.75 B	412,180.20 B	650,651.93 B
07JAN	1,684,779.89 CF	1,295,664.75 CF		
TOTALS			1,929,893.86	3,779,557.24
AVERAGE	2,002,589.43	1,431,709.67	482,473.46	944,889.31

Average for date range

Source Codes
identify amounts as
bank-reported (B) or
carried forward (CF)

Bank and Account selection
Available from domestic and international banks in multiple currencies

How Do You Access a Bank's Information Reporting System?

You can access a bank's system at any time, but most companies access it early in the morning. To access the system, you can use your PC or a dumb terminal and a modem, or simply call either the bank's voice response system or a customer service person at your bank. The bank can also send you a fax transmission or a TWX/Telex or call you by phone.

Firms receive balance information using the following methods:

- 37 percent use a terminal or PC
- 37 percent call the bank by phone
- 19 percent have the bank call the company
- 10 percent use the bank's audio response system

In summary, 56 percent of the firms used automated means to obtain the information, and 44 percent use manual methods (TDC-1, p. 19).

Banks prefer automated means and typically price them lower than the manual service. Some companies use an automatic dialer connected to their PC, which dials the bank's system and obtains the information. It may store the information in the computer for immediate access when the employees arrive in the morning or may print the information on a printer.

Exhibit 8-2. Transaction reports give you the details. (Reprinted with permission of Security Pacific National Bank)

ABC COMPANY
SECURITY PACIFIC BANK
SPACIFICS
DETAIL TRANSACTION REPORT
REPORTED AS OF 24JANXX
PRINTED ON 25JANXX 13:38 PST

SPNB – SECURITY PACIFIC BANK

CURRENCY USD DOLLAR

ACCT 1123456 – DEMO CONCENTRATION ACCT

– CREDITS –

AMOUNT	DESCRIPTION	
71,636.05	LOCKBOX DEPOSIT 1234	
	DISTRIBUTED FUNDS: 0-DAY/	41,000.00
	1-DAY/	30,636.05
24,384.00	DEPOSIT 61233	
	FUNDS: ONE DAY AVAILABILITY	
112,936.90	DEPOSIT 61234	
	FUNDS: TWO DAY AVAILABILITY	
464,613.43	MONEY TRANSFER 712030024170	
	FUNDS: IMMEDIATE AVAILABILITY	
100,018.75	ZBA CREDIT FROM ZBA1 440987654	
	DISTRIBUTED FUNDS: 1 – DAY/	60,018.75
	2 + DAY/	40,000.00
773,589.13	5 CREDITS PRINTED	

– DEBITS –

AMOUNT	DESCRIPTION	
4,414.89	CHECK PAID 56791	
353,492.70	CHECK PAID 56793	
	FUNDS: VALUE DATE 891121	
372,883.68	MONEY TRANSFER 713020042070	
7,475.56	ARS DEBIT 912345	
738,266.83	4 DEBITS PRINTED	

Itemizes float on each transaction.

In 1989, 82 percent of all firms surveyed had access to a PC for treasury functions, compared to only 57 percent in 1986. Among firms that currently have access to a PC, 82 percent also have access to a modem (a device that enables a PC to send and receive information over phone lines) for treasury functions. Thus, banks have a significant potential to increase their marketing of automated capabilities to this marketplace (TDC-1, p. 21).

Security Is Critical—You'd Better Believe It

Be sure that you set up tight security so that only designated persons can access your cash management information or transfer money. Otherwise, you may be extremely sorry. Security is your responsibility, so do a thorough job and don't delegate it. Better safe than bankrupt!

An Inside Job Can Kill You

An internal fraud or embezzlement can occur at any company at any time, so be alert and do detailed periodic audits. Consider the well-publicized fraud that occurred in the mid-1980s at a well-known middle-market company based in Florida. Ironically, the company spent a lot of time interviewing and hiring a Chief Financial Officer, but didn't realize until it was $600,000 too late that his resume and references were a complete fake. The CFO set up bank accounts under a phony name and wired the money out before disappearing. This CFO had complete control over the cash management system and took advantage of the opportunity. The company did not learn until later that this was the 26th time that he had pulled this disappearing act at a company.

Set Up a Tight Security Program at Your Company

To minimize potential cash management fraud at your company, you should limit access to the bank's information reports to yourself, if you are the owner. If this is not practical because of the size of your business, then give authority to others to obtain information and make funds transfers. Before passing on this responsibility, however, you should take certain precautions. Listed below are the types of precautions you should take in handling funds transfers. Consult an expert, if necessary.

- *Do a background check.* Investigate any persons that will be handling cash management data, sending out wire transfers, or making cash management decisions. You don't want a person who is a compulsive gambler or who has other questionable character traits to use your company's money to satisfy his or her habits.
- *Assign different passwords to every authorized person.* This includes all people who are given access to the bank's system.
- *Assign a unique ID code to every person.*
- *Change passwords at least quarterly.* Also change them whenever an authorized person leaves your company or changes job functions.
- *Limit transfer amounts, number of transfers, and size of individual transactions.*
- *Instruct each person NEVER to reveal his or her code or password.* Tell employees not to write their codes down where others may see them.
- *Print a daily report on the system usage.* Look for illegal or unauthorized system use, especially wire transfer initiations, and immediately investigate any potential acts of unauthorized entry.
- *Set up at least one approver on all nonrepetitive wires.* Consider having the bank call back a senior person to verify the transaction's authenticity.
- *Keep a daily log of all transactions for future use.*
- *Require that employees avoid "copied" software.* Also instruct them not to use computer bulletin boards to obtain free software, because either type of software might contain computer viruses that could destroy computer files and possibly cause financial loss.

Three Ways to Handle
Nonrepetitive Wires—
Carefully, Carefully, Carefully

You have three choices in handling nonrepetitive wires:

1. Call in the transfer to a bank representative with a password and ID code. Request a bank call-back to a different person.
2. Use your bank's wire transfer module with the proper security, as already mentioned.
3. Send a fax transmission to the bank for execution with the appropriate authorized signature and password.

Ranking these methods from the standpoint of security, I would recommend 2, then 1, then 3. Controlling the process using a computer with dual passwords and a call-back is far superior to verbal or written (faxed) instructions.

The risk is higher for choices 1 and 3 because of the possibility that a clever inside person might gain access to the codes in the former case or might forge or photocopy a signature in the latter case. However, using a call-back procedure to an authorized person (who is not an accomplice) greatly reduces the risk in both cases.

Banks Are Not Immune to
Internal Crime

Wire transfer fraud is not only a problem that can happen at companies. Banks are prone to internal fraud attempts as well. In 1983, this became particularly apparent in the well-publicized case of fraud perpetrated by a man I'll call John Jones at a large West Coast bank. Mr. Jones gained access to this bank's wire transfer department. He had worked as a consultant to the bank a few months prior to the fraud, and the staff in the department knew him.

Once he was in the department, Mr. Jones had surreptitiously uncovered the wire transfer code words by observing the operating personnel who entered the wires on their terminals. He then wired out $10 million to a New York City bank to wire to his newly established account in a Swiss bank. After arriving in Switzerland, Mr. Jones bought uncut diamonds with the money. He was eventually arrested when he went back home to California, and the diamonds were recovered. While in custody of authorities, he was planning a similar caper at another bank! Last I heard, he was a consultant to the banking industry on wire transfer fraud.

Deposit Reporting

Retail firms need to report their daily deposits to a central location for cash concentration purposes. To report this information, they can use POS terminals (if they are interconnected to a central computer) or a telephone touch-tone deposit reporting service from a third party vendor or from their concentration bank, if this service is offered. If it is not available at your bank, one of the companies listed in the following section can be used, either through the bank or directly.

Noncash Management Information Reporting

Retailers and other firms may have information-gathering needs besides cash. Information needs may include such areas as sales, inventory, and production statistics. If this information cannot be consolidated by existing internal communications means, firms can obtain it by reporting the details to a third-party vendor. This vendor will then provide customized reports to the company.

The following firms offer information gathering services:

Provider	*Services*
Automatic Data Processing Network Services Division 210 North Clark Suite 1600 Chicago, IL 60602-5099 *Contact*: Lynne E. Fish Manager Marketing Sales Support (312) 346-1044	Deposit reporting, MIS reporting for sales, production, personnel, and inventory data from remote locations

Provider	Services
First Data Resources 10825 Farnum Drive Omaha, NE 68154 *Contact*: Lori Parriott Marketing Manager (402) 399-7738	Deposit reporting, credit card authorization, information reporting
National Data Corporation National Data Plaza Atlanta, GA 30329-2010 *Contact*: William L. Place Director of Marketing (404) 728-2138 (800) 344-1449	Deposit reporting, bank credit card authoriza- tions, healthcare data services, information reporting on sales and inventory collected from remote locations

Treasury Workstations
Have Entered the Scene

The latest development in information systems and technology is the treasury workstation. Workstations were developed in the early 1980s by a few vendors and banks.

A treasury workstation is a specialized group of integrated software modules designed for a PC. Using a modem to obtain bank information, a company can automate many of the manual cash management activities, generate the daily cash position, post bank data to the accounting system, and perform many of the daily number-crunching tasks by using a workstation. Other modules can perform even more tasks:

- Keep track of bank information (account numbers, addresses, phone numbers, account personnel, account signatories)
- Capture bank information electronically
- Initiate electronic funds transfers (ACHs and wires)
- Analyze account analysis statements
- Track investment portfolios
- Track outstanding debts

- Post data to the general ledger automatically
- Write reports in varying customized formats

Many small companies and banks entered the market place with their own workstations, but there were too many sellers for too few buyers. This resulted in a severe retrenchment. Today there are only a handful of major sellers including three or four vendors and a few banks. A licensing agreement with ADS Associates allows some banks to market a workstation to their clients. ADS is 49 percent owned by Bankers Trust Company.

The reason for the workstation debacle a few years ago can be traced to the following factors:

- Small firms were not well capitalized and had limited resources.
- Questions about availability and quality of training, customer service and maintenance, and enhancements were difficult to answer with certainty.
- The pricing of $10,000 to $100,000 for software was prohibitively expensive for many firms to justify, even though each module was priced separately.
- PCs were not then as plentiful or powerful as today's models.
- The biggest market for the workstation was the large company, but each company wanted customized software that was too expensive for vendors to develop.
- Some large companies built their own workstation because of their unique needs.

Today the workstation market is stable. In the last few years, there have been no new entrants. The remaining vendors and banks have a tested product that has found its place among many firms. However, few middle-market companies have found a need or financial justification for the product. Only as these companies reach sales of $500 million and beyond does their need for a workstation become more pressing. As the numbers of transactions and banking relationships increase, the impetus for automation and cost savings becomes stronger.

Many companies either internally develop their own workstations using spreadsheets, database management, and word
processing software or hire an outside programmer.

If you are interested in more information about workstation
vendors, see the list in Appendix 7.

Synthesis

This chapter covered information—one of the most important
cash management components. Make sure your bank can provide you with the information you need on a timely basis. Be
super critical of your wire transfer security. A word to the wise
is sufficient.

9

Is Your Cash Management System Providing Maximum Bottom-Line Profits?

Map Out Your System

"Never take anything for granted." —Benjamin Disraeli

"We think in generalities, we live in detail."
—Alfred North Whitehead

So far you've covered a great deal of material. You should now be knowledgeable about the cash management techniques that are at your disposal to help you maximize your company's cash flow. How can you easily and quickly get a handle on whether your existing cash management methods can be improved?

Use the Cash Management Action Plan (CASH MAP)

To accomplish this task, I've developed a unique worksheet called the *CASH MAP*—**Cash** Management Action Plan—that you can use. Refer to Exhibit 9-1. You can photocopy this sample or develop your own, depending on the complexity of your cash management system. All the critical information

Exhibit 9-1. CASH MAP

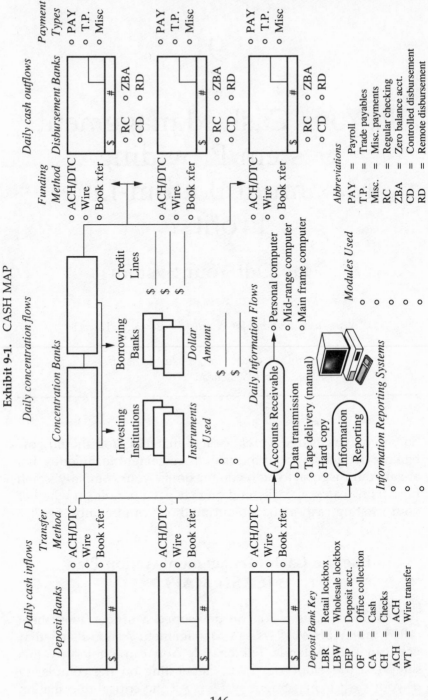

Daily cash inflows

Daily concentration flows

Daily cash outflows

Deposit Banks — Transfer Method
- ACH/DTC
- Wire
- Book xfer

Concentration Banks

Funding Method
- ACH/DTC
- Wire
- Book xfer

Disbursement Banks — Payment Types
- PAY
- T.P.
- Misc

- RC   o ZBA
- CD   o RD

Credit Lines

Borrowing Banks — Dollar Amount

Investing Institutions — Instruments Used

Daily Information Flows

Accounts Receivable
- Data transmission
- Tape delivery (manual)
- Hard copy

Information Reporting

Personal computer
- Mid-range computer
- Main frame computer

Modules Used

Information Reporting Systems

Deposit Bank Key

LBR = Retail lockbox
LBW = Wholesale lockbox
DEP = Deposit acct.
OF = Office collection
CA = Cash
CH = Checks
ACH = ACH
WT = Wire transfer

Abbreviations

PAY = Payroll
T.P. = Trade payables
Misc. = Misc. payments
RC = Regular checking
ZBA = Zero balance acct.
CD = Controlled disbursement
RD = Remote disbursement

146

about your existing system can be placed on this one-page form. A completed form is shown in Exhibit 9-2.

Let's go through your cash management system and fill out this form together. Make sure you have your account analysis statements, the volumes of all your transactions, and the associated dollar amounts handy so that you can proceed quickly through the process.

Cash Inflows

Indicate the names of depository and lockbox banks and locations where you make deposits under "Daily Cash Inflows." Also indicate the total dollar ("$") amount deposited in a typical month and the number ("#") of checks deposited. Use the symbols "LBR" and "LBW" for lockbox retail and lockbox wholesale. Use "OF" to specify if the checks are collected at a lockbox bank or are collected at an office address and then deposited in a regular deposit account. Indicate the types of receipts being deposited, such as cash (CA), checks (CH), ACH credits (ACH), or incoming wire transfers (WT).

Cash Concentration Method

Next show how you concentrate the funds—via ACH, DTC, wire transfer, or book transfer—for each banking relationship. Darken the appropriate circle under "Transfer Method".

Concentration Banks

Here, under "Concentration Banks," list your concentration banks and their locations.

Investment and Borrowing Institutions

Show the names of the institutions where you invest funds, if you invest. Typically, these would be commercial banks, investment banking houses, and other financial service providers such as money market mutual funds. Indicate average investment amount and list the types of investment instru-

Exhibit 9-2. CASH MAP

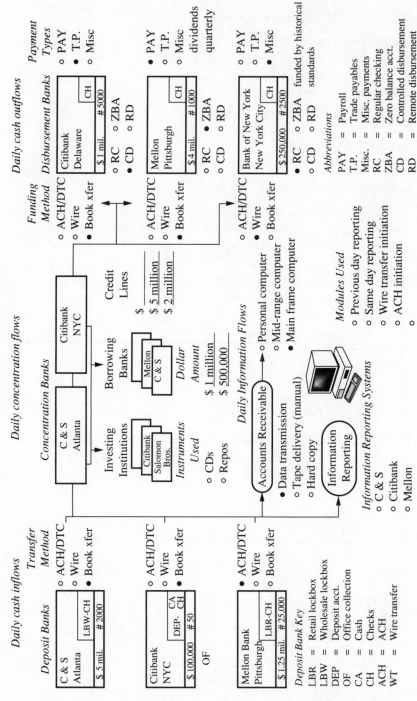

Daily concentration flows

Concentration Banks

C & S Atlanta — Citibank NYC

Investing Institutions
Instruments Used
- Citibank
- Salomon Bros.
- CDs
- Repos

Borrowing Banks
Dollar Amount
- Mellon — $ 1 million
- C & S — $ 500,000

Credit Lines
- $ 5 million
- $ 2 million

Daily cash inflows

Deposit Banks	Transfer Method
C & S Atlanta — LBW-CH — #2000 — $ 5 mil.	○ ACH/DTC ○ Wire ● Book xfer
Citibank NYC — DEP- CA CH — #50 — $100,000 OF	○ ACH/DTC ○ Wire ● Book xfer
Mellon Bank Pittsburgh — LBR-CH — #25,000 — $1.25 mil.	● ACH/DTC ○ Wire ○ Book xfer

Deposit Bank Key
LBR = Retail lockbox
LBW = Wholesale lockbox
DEP = Deposit acct.
OF = Office collection
CA = Cash
CH = Checks
ACH = ACH
WT = Wire transfer

Daily cash outflows

Funding Method / *Disbursement Banks* / *Payment Types*

Disbursement Banks	Funding Method	Payment Types
Citibank Delaware — CH — $1 mil. — #5000 — ○ RC ○ ZBA ● CD ● RD	○ ACH/DTC ○ Wire ● Book xfer	○ PAY ● T.P. ○ Misc
Mellon Pittsburgh — CH — $4 mil. — #1000 — ○ RC ● ZBA ○ CD ○ RD	○ ACH/DTC ○ Wire ● Book xfer	● PAY ○ T.P. ● Misc dividends quarterly
Bank of New York New York City — CH — $ 250,000 — #2500 — ○ RC ○ ZBA ○ CD ● RD — funded by historical standards	● ACH/DTC ○ Wire ○ Book xfer	○ PAY ○ T.P. ● Misc

Abbreviations
PAY = Payroll
T.P. = Trade payables
Misc. = Misc. payments
RC = Regular checking
ZBA = Zero balance acct.
CD = Controlled disbursement
RD = Remote disbursement

Daily Information Flows

Accounts Receivable
- Data transmission
- Tape delivery (manual)
- Hard copy

Information Reporting

○ Personal computer
○ Mid-range computer
● Main frame computer

Modules Used
○ Previous day reporting
○ Same day reporting
○ Wire transfer initiation
○ ACH initiation
○

Information Reporting Systems
○ C & S
○ Citibank
○ Mellon

148

ments you use (e.g., certificates of deposit, U. S. Treasury securities, repurchase agreements, bankers' acceptances, and money market or stock mutual funds). Similarly, indicate the banks where you borrow money and the dollar amount of your credit lines.

Cash Outflows

Now list your disbursement banks and their locations and indicate the type of account you have there (e.g., regular checking, controlled disbursement or ZBA, trade payables). Next, indicate the type of disbursements (e.g., payroll, trade payables, and miscellaneous). Also indicate the dollar volume and number of transactions each month. Show whether your disbursements are in check, wire, or ACH form by using the appropriate symbol.

Disbursement Account Funding Method

Show how you fund each disbursement account—book transfer at the same bank, ACH, or wire transfer from another bank—by darkening in the appropriate circle.

Information Reporting Systems

Indicate the bank information reporting systems and the modules that you use (e.g., wire transfer initiation).

If you use a lockbox bank, indicate how you get the information to your accounts receivable system (by data transmission, tape delivery, or hard copy).

Other Useful Information

Attach another page to the CASH MAP that contains additional useful information that could not be placed on the MAP. This can include such data as the following:

- Name, address, and telephone number of each bank relationship and key bank contacts, such as account officers and customer service representatives

- The method of compensating each bank—fee or balance or a combination of the two
- Compensating balance level or fees paid to each bank in the last calendar year by month
- Current year's target balance level by bank
- Your current year's cash management goals
- List of areas of interest (e.g., EDI, ACH direct deposit of payroll, cash forecasting)

This last area would be useful to have in case bankers or cash management sales representatives called on your company and wanted to know in what areas they could help.

Take This Diagnostic Review
Seriously—It Will Save You Money

Once you've completed the CASH MAP, compare it to the cash management techniques presented in previous chapters to see if there are any techniques that you can use to improve your cash flow. To help you with this process, answer the following questions.

Cash Inflows

1. Do your customers mail their checks to your office? If yes, why don't they send them to a lockbox bank instead to minimize the mail, processing, and availability floats? Can you justify the cost of a lockbox bank?

2. If you are currently using a lockbox system, when was it put in place? Has your customer base increased or has your sales increased substantially over the past three years? If these changes have occurred, then a a reevaluation may uncover some inefficiencies. Speak to your banker about performing a lockbox study.

3. Have you considered a lockbox network instead of using more than one bank? The float improvement and bank

cost savings can be substantial. Also, you need to work with only one bank.

4. Is your accounts receivable system automated using an up-to-date software package (internally developed or purchased off-the-shelf)? If not, you may be using an antiquated system that is expensive to run. Speak to software vendors and computer salespeople and obtain a demonstration of the package. Check vendor references.

5. How do you update your accounts receivable file? Do you use key-entry on a preformatted computer screen or a slower and more expensive paper-based entry system?

6. If you use a lockbox bank, does the bank send a data transmission to your company to automatically update your accounts receivable file? If not, why not?

7. Do customers send you wire transfers or ACH credits to pay for your goods or services? If not, can you negotiate this type of payment in your contract with future customers? As an incentive for customers to pay you electronically, perhaps you can give these customers a larger discount, if you already offer discounts.

Cash Concentration

1. What method do you use to concentrate your funds? If you use wires, are they cost-beneficial? Have you tried to minimize the use of wires for concentration unless it is absolutely necessary? If not, you are paying a high price for funds concentration.

2. Have you considered using the less expensive ACH? If not, why not?

3. If you use DTCs, have you considered replacing them with ACHs? If not, why not?

4. Do you have more than one concentration bank? Why? You probably need only one.

5. How often do you concentrate funds from each bank? You may need to concentrate weekly or monthly from

banks with low balances (e.g., $10,000 or less) and daily from banks with higher balance levels.

Cash Outflows

1. Do you use a regular checking account for depositing your checks and making your disbursements? This may be fine for very small businesses (e.g., companies with annual sales below $100,000), but it is not very effective for larger firms.
2. Do you use ZBAs? If not, why not?
3. Have you considered controlled or remote disbursement? If not, why not?
4. Consider these questions if you're using controlled disbursement:
   • Are you receiving good service, competitive pricing, early morning notification, and adequate account reconcilement services?
   • Can you get on-line stop payments in your account reconcilement service?
   • Have you considered setting up subaccounts to lower your account maintenance costs?
   • When was the last time you evaluated your bank and compared it to the competition? Three years should be the maximum time between evaluations.
5. What type of payroll account do you have? It should at least be a ZBA and be funded as the employee checks clear against the account.
6. Do you offer Direct Deposit of Payroll? If not, why not? If you do, what percent of your employees use it? If fewer than 50% use it, why is it not more popular? Have you thought of making it mandatory? Before taking that step, check out the labor laws in your state.
7. To minimize your payroll costs, do you use temporaries, part-timers and free lancers? Pay for help when you need it.

Information Flows

1. How many bank information systems do you use? If you use more than one, why?

2. How much do you pay for the service? Some banks charge a high price because they use a third-party vendor to provide the service. Get bids from other banks, if it's feasible.

3. Are you using a "Rolls Royce" information system with a high pricetag when you need only a "Yugo" barebones system to obtain daily balance data? Break down the pricing into modules and pay for only what you need. Your bank may be providing same-day information when prior-day information will do.

4. Do you have a Treasury Workstation? If you do, how is it working? If it does not work well, then consider another system. If you don't have a system, do you need one? Is it cost-beneficial? Get information from the service providers and decide. Workstations are most often bought by large companies and some larger middle-market companies. Small businesses would find them unnecessary and too costly.

Compare Your System to an Effective One

Now that you've gathered all the information about your cash management practices in one place and you've thought about the answers to the preceding questions, you are well on your way to finetuning your system to yield greater returns.

What components does an effective cash management system contain? Key point: The size of your cash flows and the size of your business determine which techniques are applicable to your case. Companies with effective cash management systems:

1. Use retail or wholesale lockbox systems or networks

2. Obtain data transmissions of accounts receivable data from lockbox banks

3. Collect consumer remittances by ACH instead of by check, especially if payments are repetitive (such as utility or mortgage payments)

4. Obtain rapid availability on their deposited checks, averaging between 0.75 to 1.25 days, and never hold checks overnight

5. Use ACH or wire transfers to concentrate funds

6. Use one concentration bank

7. Use one controlled disbursement bank and subaccounts, if necessary

8. Use separate accounts for payroll, trade payables, petty cash, and other specialized payments (e.g., freight or payable-through drafts).

9. Have banks perform full or partial account reconcilement

10. Use banks' check safekeeping services

11. Pay their employees using Direct Deposit of Payroll

12. Pay their employees once or twice a month, not weekly

13. Pay their invoices as late as possible—certainly not early unless the discount is financially favorable

14. Compensate their banks with fees only, or a combination of fees and balances

15. Use banks' information reporting systems and key modules such as wire transfer and ACH initiation

16. Obtain daily balance information on their large dollar accounts

17. Manage to a target level or to a minimum balance position, if they are paying by a combination of fees and balances

18. Use personal computers to keep track of their cash management activity, to obtain bank information, and to

prepare financial analyses and forecasts using database, spreadsheet, and graphics programs

19. Use short-term cash forecasts and prepare monthly or quarterly budgets
20. Invoice their customers promptly and charge for late payments
21. Monitor accounts receivable and take immediate action against late payers
22. Order the minimum amount of inventory

Compare these components with your cash management system. The more of these you have in place, the more effective your system will be in maximizing cash flow to the bottom line.

Remember that the *type and size of your business* and the *size of your cash flows* will have a major impact on whether the components mentioned above are feasible in your specific case. A cost-benefit analysis can be used to determine their financial impact. Be sure to factor in the reduction in labor hours, the elimination of paper, and other productivity savings obtainable by implementing specific cash management techniques.

Now is the time to assess your existing practices. It's easy to do using the CASH MAP. Don't wait another day, because you'll never find the time. Do it now! You'll be happy you did.

Synthesis

Now is the time to assess your existing practices. It's easy to do using the CASH MAP. I've provided you with a form and a checklist. Use them to develop your own format to meet your specific needs. Do it now! Don't wait another day, because you'll never find the time. You'll be glad you did.

10

Negotiation—The Way to Buy Bank Services

All Banks Are Not Created Equal

"Everybody's negotiable." —Muhammad Ali

"Small businesses don't have the time or expertise to manage their money as well as the large companies. So they leave more money in the bank than large companies." —Neil C. Churchill, Director, Caruth Institute of Owner-Managed Business, Southern Methodist University, quoted in Sanford L. Jacobs, "Banks Profit More on Loans to Small Firms, Study Shows," *The Wall Street Journal*, October 15, 1984, p. 35.

Understand the Past to Understand the Present

1950s and 1960s

Banking was once simple. The need was for credit/financing, a checking account, and wire transfers. A small or middle-market company maintained one or two banking relationships for both its credit needs and services. A company did not have a financial incentive to change banks unless the bank did not meet its credit demands or its needs for specific cash management services. Thus, most companies maintained long-term relationships with only a few banks. Also, there wasn't a significant difference in the basic bank services, so companies didn't do much comparison shopping. Large banks were not marketing very aggressively to this market.

1970s and 1980s

Economic conditions in this period were much more unstable. The prime rate and short-term interest rates began rising and hit double digits in 1974, 1979, 1980, 1981, and 1982. The prime rate hit 21.5 percent in December 1980. Treasury bill yields reached 16 percent in 1981. In the last two years, the prime rate hit a high of 11.5 percent and closed 1989 at 10.5 percent. These changes, along with regulatory actions in the late 1980s by the Federal Reserve Board and Congress, resulted in a change in the way in which companies viewed their banking relationships and the way in which banks viewed their potential clients.

Cash Management Pricing Increased by 100 Percent to 300 Percent in Past Decade

Banks "unbundled" their pricing for cash management services. Each bank service (e.g., for check deposits, lockboxes, and automated clearing house) stands on its own from a profit and loss perspective. Since 1980, banks have increased pricing on individual services from 100 percent to 300 percent. Savvy financial managers continue to analyze their existing bank services with a sharp pencil. Obtaining annual bids on service charges from bank competitors is becoming a common practice.

Banks Finally Cater to Small Businesses

The small business market was not a major target for most large and regional banks until recently. These banks preferred working with larger companies (e.g., those with annual sales exceeding $250 million) because the profit potential was greater owing to the larger volume of transactions and the demand for more types of services. This decision makes sense from the bank's bottom-line view.

More and more banks are now realizing the untapped potential in serving small businesses and are continuing to expand their marketing to middle-market firms. Banks continually search for markets to increase their income from noncredit services. Larger companies are overbanked and are more price-conscious than middle-market and smaller companies. Mergers and acquisitions are gradually reducing the number of large companies. This causes companies to prune banks.

Review Your Bank Relationships Periodically

Robert Frost's definition of a bank is "a place where they lend you an umbrella in fair weather and ask for it back again when it begins to rain." (*The Great Business Quotations*, compiled by Rolf B. White.)

Today companies are scrutinizing their banking relationships more frequently and are not showing as much tolerance for unsolved needs, problems, or noncompetitive pricing as in years past. Foreign banks and other sources of funds have reduced the need for commercial banks for credit needs.

Pricing and Quality Are Most Important

To middle-market companies, pricing and service quality are two of the more important factors in selecting a bank for cash management services. Companies will not think twice about changing banks if prices are substantially lower at another bank and the service quality is equal to or better than the quality of their existing bank. Small businesses still focus on the personal relationship with the account officer, the officer's knowledge of the company, and the bank's ability to provide credit when needed as the most critical elements. For small businesses pricing for banking services is a secondary consideration, but pricing on loans is critical.

Inexperience in Dealing with Banks Can Be Costly

Perhaps you do not have much experience in shopping for bank services and managing your banking relationships. You may not know:

- How to manage the relationship
- The approach to use in shopping for bank services
- How to negotiate for services
- What pricing is competitive
- What to expect from the account officer
- How to properly compensate the bank
- Whether fees or balance compensation is preferable.

Banking Problems

A 1989 survey of middle-market companies by BDO Seidman, *Pulse of the Middle Market*, provides insight on what problems firms have with their banks. Firms were asked, "What makes your banking relationship difficult?" Here are the responses:

Percent Responding	*Response*
29 percent	Unfavorable interest rates
27	Changing loan officers
18	Bank doesn't understand your business
11	Rules keep changing
8	Slow turnaround
7	Lack of stability

What to Look for When Picking a Bank

You Must Ask the Right Questions

Buying banking services is a lot like buying a car. The car has a sticker price, options, various payment plans, hidden costs and extras, an optional maintenance agreement, available customer service, and maintenance needs. In comparison, banks have a standard price list, optional services, payment options including fees and balances, costs you may not have been aware of after reviewing your account analysis statement, and customer service representatives or account officers to handle your account.

You know how difficult shopping for a car can be without a consumers' guidebook. Imagine shopping for bank services without any guidebooks or with limited knowledge. Luckily, this chapter can help you.

Selecting a bank is a logical process if you know what to do. As with a car, you work from your needs to your specific requirements. If you're inexperienced, then it can be frustrating, confusing, and time-consuming. You have to know the right questions to ask, sense when a bank may be fudging an answer, and understand what their answer means. Banking relationships are complex arrangements. They involve the personalities, politics, and financial conditions of both parties as well as external economic and competitive factors.

Selecting a Bank for Operational Services Can Be Mastered

Let's focus on the criteria to use in selecting a bank for handling your operational and transactional business. You must determine exactly what services you want the bank to provide. Are you looking for a credit line, cash management services, international capability, a combination of services, or the expertise of one or more bank specialists?

Step 1. Know What Services You Need

List the exact services you need, if you know what you need. For example, you may need a bank in California to process wholesale lockbox remittances from customers remitting large dollar checks mailed from states in the western United States. You may want the bank to process these remittances in a certain way and to send a data transmission of the accounts receivable detail to your company by 8 P.M. each night. You may want a controlled disbursement bank. You may want an ACH funds concentration system.

If you don't know exactly what services you need, then you should finish reading this book or reread the key chapters that review cash management techniques and bank cash management services. You can also speak to knowledgeable bankers, cash management salespeople, or bank or external cash management consultants who will take the time to explain the basic services to you.

Step 2. Contact Banks

After compiling your list of services, contact specific banks to determine if they offer the desired services. Consider banks in nearby and distant cities if bank location is not a critical issue in obtaining a credit line, for example, or in selecting a controlled disbursement bank. You may be unaware of the banks that offer the services you want and the banks that are particularly adept at those services. Use the surveys and directories shown in Exhibit 10-1 to gain insight into banks that offer the services you need. Refer to Appendix 9, which lists banks across the country.

Exhibit 10-1.   Information resources on banks

Where to Find Information on Banks and Their Services
1. Local resources Speak to other business owners or financial managers in your local area. Ask around, for example, at your local chamber of commerce, at Financial Executive Institute chapter meetings, and at meetings and luncheons set up by bankers, accounting firms, or at regional cash management associations.

2. Publications (magazines, newsletters, newspapers)
  • ABA Banking Journal
    Simmons Boardman Publishing
    345 Hudson Street
    New York, NY 10014
    (212) 633-1165

Exhibit 10-1.   *(cont.)*

- American Banker
  One State Street Plaza
  New York, NY 10004
  (212) 943-6700

- Cash Management Digest & Analysis
  Warren, Gorham & Lamont, Inc.
  210 South Street
  Boston, MA 02111
  (800) 950-1216

- CORPORATE CASHFLOW
  Communications Channels, Inc.
  6255 Barfield Road
  Atlanta, GA 30328
  (404) 256-9800

- Corporate Finance
  810 Seventh Avenue
  New York, NY 10019
  (212) 397-2300

- Institutional Investor
  488 Madison Avenue
  New York, NY 10022
  (212) 303-3300

- Journal of Cash Management
  277 Fairfield Road/Suite 331
  Fairfield, NJ 07006
  (201) 575-5740

- The Leahy Newsletter
  P. O. Box 467
  Tustin, CA 92681
  (714) 832-7811

- Pensions & Investment Age
  740 Rush Street
  Chicago, IL 60611
  (312) 649-5200

- Practical Cash Management
  Box 431
  Westport, CT 06881
  (203) 227-1237

Exhibit 10-1. *(cont.)*

- The Treasury Pro™
  277 Fairfield Road/Suite 331
  Fairfield, NJ 07006
  (201) 575-5740

3. Survey organizations

  - American Banker
    One State Street Plaza
    New York, NY 10004
    (212) 943-6700

  - Ernst & Young
    National Cash Management Consulting Practice
    277 Park Avenue
    New York, NY 10172
    (212) 407-1831

  - Greenwich Associates
    Office Park Eight
    Greenwich, CT 06830
    (203) 629-1200

  - NCCMA
    52 Church Hill Road
    Newtown, CT 06470
    (203) 426-3007

  - Phoenix-Hecht
    P.O. Box 13628
    68 T.W. Alexander Drive
    Research Triangle Park, NC 27709
    (919) 541-9339

  - Trans Data Corporation
    994 Old Eagle School Road/Suite 1006
    Wayne, PA 19087
    (800) 876-2990

  - Treasury Strategies Inc.
    309 W. Washington/Suite 1300
    Chicago, IL 60606
    (312) 443-0840

4. Bank officials and vendors
   Meet, call, or have lunch with bankers, bank vendors, and Federal Reserve officials (if you're in one of the 37 Fed head office or branch cities).

Exhibit 10-1.   *(cont.)*

5. Special cash management directories
   - *Pensions & Investment Age* "Cash Services Directory," (November)
   - *Journal of Cash Management* (various issues)
   - *Corporate Finance* (September issue)
   - *NCCMA Membership Handbook and Service Directory* (Annual)
6. Bank safety ratings
   Firms providing an evaluation of bank safety are included in Appendix 8.

Step 3. Send Out a Request for Proposal (RFP)

Send each bank a letter specifying your operating service needs. Request that the bank respond with a written proposal on *exactly* how and at what price it can meet your needs.

For example, if you're looking for a lockbox bank you should do the following:

1. List the number of checks to be processed each month with their approximate dollar volume.

2. Tell the bank exactly how you want it to handle every check, especially the exception items (e.g., checks received with incorrect dollar amounts, without any invoice number identification, or without signatures).

3. Specify how you want to be notified about your daily deposit amount. The method can be phone a call, PC-based information report, telex, or fax.

4. Ask the bank to price out your specific scenario with your volumes and requirements, instead of simply sending you a standard price list of services. In many cases this type of list is difficult to interpret correctly.

5. Ask the bank to guarantee prices for at least a year. You don't want to learn of a price increase one month after you sign up for the service.

6. Ask the bank to send you its response to the *NCCMA/BAI Wholesale Lockbox Questionnaire.* This questionnaire con-

tains every question about lockbox services that you could possibly think of and many more. Contact the NCCMA for a copy at the address in Exhibit 10-1. Most banks have prepared answers to these questions that they can quickly mail back to you. This questionnaire response will provide you with information on the bank's lockbox capabilities, customer base, equipment used, availability and mail times, data transmission options, and many other pertinent facts.

7. After receiving all of the banks' responses, weigh the most important questions and rank the banks overall.

Step 4. Plan Bank Visits

Call the highest-ranking banks and ask them to set a date when you can visit their lockbox operations. Be sure to review each bank's brochures, questionnaire responses, and pricing before you visit and make a list of questions that you want answered. You should use the same approach in selecting any other bank operating service such as controlled disbursement, ACH, or direct deposit of payroll.

Meet the operating personnel, account officer, and account officer's backup and tour all the bank operating areas that pertain to the bank service you need. This may include areas such as the check-processing, data-processing, and transit areas (where direct sends are prepared). Bring along an associate who is familiar with systems or operations to help you assess what you are seeing. If you don't know what you're looking for, you may be wasting both the banker's time and your own.

Step 5. Speak to References

Before making a final selection, obtain 10 references from the bank and call them with specific questions in areas such as quality control, service, response time to inquiries, the bank's ability to customize service, and problems they have encountered. Also, check the bank's ranking compared to other banks in the service you are considering by using a source such as *The Treasury Pro*™. Don't forget to get unsolicited comments from other financial managers.

Requesting a formal bid, meeting with bankers, visiting banks on-site, and calling references is the smart way to pick an operating bank. Don't forget about speaking with financial executives at other companies in your city or in your industry for their insights and recommendations as well. Pick up the phone and call them. Ask pointed questions. Most will be flattered to receive your call.

Key Point.   You must do your homework, otherwise you'll be sorry.

Step 6. Get Your Bank Agreement in Writing

Don't rely on verbal commitments. Understand the terms for charging for services.

Additional Relationship Criteria
Must Be Taken into Account

When selecting a financial institution for both credit and operating services, a more detailed evaluation is needed.

Eleven Key Areas to Cover

Let's review eleven important areas to review in selecting a credit-banking relationship.

Availability of Credit

If your company is selecting a bank for the sole purpose of obtaining bank financing, then you should assess the bank's ability to provide the loan or line of credit when you need it and in the amount that you need.

Get a Written Agreement.   To avoid any problems in this area, thoroughly discuss your specific financing needs, timing, dollar amounts needed, and the repayment schedule with the banker. Obtain the agreement in writing and attach a memorandum to explain any points not included in the bank's standard credit agreement.

It is a terrible situation to find that your bank does not honor its credit line when you're expecting to use it. The media has reported a few instances in which a company went bankrupt because the bank failed to honor its borrowing commitment. Law suits resulted and the bank lost. You don't want to go through this traumatic and potentially financially devastating process. Get your agreements in writing and make sure you understand the circumstances, if any, when your bank can cancel its commitment.

Group Rates for Loans

Small firms can borrow money at unusually low rates by joining together as a group. So far this concept has been used in Seattle and is debuting in Los Angeles and Philadelphia. Here's how it works: Companies that have accounts at the same bank get together and combine their collective checking accounts as a bargaining tool for a better loan deal.

Source: Steven Galante, "Companies Join Forces to Get Reduced Rates on Loans," *The Wall Street Journal,* February 10, 1986, p. 23.

Financial Stability and Health of Bank

Based on the increasing number of bank failures, such as the failures of large commercial banks in Texas and the S & L fiasco, you should carefully assess the financial condition of all financial institutions you are considering for relationships. Your company should have a pre-determined minimum level of financial quality that it is willing to accept. A few years ago when well-known cash management banks in Chicago and Dallas were having financial problems, many financial executives with lockbox accounts in these banks were extremely concerned about the risk of leaving money in these banks overnight. Some firms closed their accounts because the risk was too great. Others stayed the course. Luckily, no problems occurred.

By using a bank rating service such as the ones provided in Appendix 8, you can obtain the critical information on a bank's profitability, asset quality, liquidity, and capital as well as comparisons to the bank's competitors.

Monitor Your Banks Carefully.   Once you select a bank, you should continually monitor the bank's financial health. If you notice a deteriorating financial situation, then you should have a discussion with the account officer or another senior bank officer to determine what, if anything, the bank is doing to improve the situation.

Bank Size

Select a bank that is large enough to service your existing and future needs. For example, the bank should have sufficient capital to execute your wire transfers without hitting its capital limit during the day, because this could delay your transfers. Ensure that the bank has the specialists and a broad array of services to meet your company's growing needs.

Key point.   If you use a local bank or community bank, do not be surprised if the bank is incapable of providing all the services and financing you need. You may have to shop around in your local area, surrounding area, and perhaps in a different state to find a bank that meets your needs. Make sure you find out the bank's legal lending limit so that the bank is able to accommodate your financing needs when you need the money.

Operational Capability

The bank's operating services, such as cash management, should have high quality and be technologically advanced. How do you determine if the bank has sophisticated operating services compared to its competitors? Ask its competitors.

Bank's Reputation.   What do the bank's competitors say about the bank's service? What do industry surveys indicate? Does the bank provide speakers at conventions or at bank-sponsored seminars? What is the expertise and quality of these speakers?

Do bank personnel publish articles in key journals, and are they sought out for interviews? Does the bank have a booth or sponsor activities at major industry conferences? Is the bank's senior management highly thought of by competitors, journalists, and their corporate customers? Is the bank rated highly in the cash management surveys? All these factors will shape the bank's reputation.

Competitive Pricing

Does the bank price its services competitively, or is the pricing much higher than average? Refer to the section in Chapter 11 on bank pricing. If the price is higher than average, is the quality superior? Does the bank accept balance or fee compensation? Does it charge a premium for fee payment? If balances are used, what is the period of time—monthly, quarterly, or yearly—in which the bank measures the required compensation? Are excess balances in one year usable in the next year to offset service costs? How willing is the bank to negotiate its list price? Will it give you a price guarantee for at least a year? Many banks will do both for customers with large volumes of transactions.

Existing Experience

Are you currently using the bank for any operating services? If so, what is the quality of service, the response time on inquiries, and the error rate? Is it willing to customize its service? How technologically sophisticated are its services? Actions speak louder than words.

Budgets

Are the operating department budgets increasing each year? How many people are in the department? Has the service been upgraded recently? What are the plans for the next three years as far as upgrades are concerned?

Quality of Staff

How long has the staff been employed in this specific operating department? How many years of experience does the department manager have? What are the employee pay scales in comparison to other banks in that city? What is the annual employee turnover for the past five years?

Bank Facilities

What is the physical appearance of the premises? What is the quality of the equipment, furniture, and working environment? Are there back-up power supplies in case of a power failure or blackout? Does the bank have contingency plans for malfunctioning equipment and a disaster recovery plan in case of emergencies? Most California banks were very well prepared for the San Francisco–region earthquake on October 13, 1989, and many were up and running within hours of the quake.

Quality Performance

How much experience do the staff members—clerical and supervisory—have? Do they appear to be well trained, based on your tour? What is the annual staff turnover for the past three years? How long has the management been in place? Is there an incentive program used to compensate above-average performance? Is there an annual bonus program in place? Is there a formal quality-control program used to measure quality levels and to improve performance of below-average workers?

Account Officer Performance

Is your account officer providing superior, creative, and innovative service to meet or exceed your needs? Is he or she easily accessible? Does the officer respond quickly to requests and have an adequate backup? Is he or she knowledgeable about your company and industry? If the answers to these questions are negative, then ask for another account officer by contacting the officer's boss.

Manage the Banking Relationship or Else It Will Manage You

In summary, it is important that you manage the banking relationship. Expect high quality service at a competitive price and compensate the banks fairly for the services provided. You should not hesitate to change banks if your existing bank cannot service your banking needs.

Always Have a Backup

Before you change banks, be sure that you have found another bank that can provide the service. You may end up without a bank if you act impulsively. Be extremely careful if there are only a few banks in your city or town from which to choose. As Cordell Hull said, "Never insult an alligator until after you have crossed the river." (*The Great Business Quotations,* Compiled by Rolf B. White, A Dell book, 1986.)

How Does Your Bank Know If You're Adequately Compensating It for the Services That It Provides?

Banks produce a monthly account profitability statement for each business account relationship. This document contains the average balances maintained during the month, the volume of transactions, the bank's cost for providing the services, and the bank's profit or loss on the relationship. Your account officer reviews this profitability statement.

Expect a Call from Your Account Officer

Your account officer may call you if the bank is losing money on your account and you are not compensating the bank with additional balances or fees. He or she may ask you to maintain larger balances or may indicate that the bank will automatically debit your account each month for the balance shortfall. The officer may even tell you to take your business elsewhere, although this is rarely the case.

If you are inadvertently maintaining excess balances, don't expect your account officer to notify you to *reduce* your balances. You should be smart enough to manage your balances more precisely. You could also arrange for the bank to automatically sweep any excess funds into an overnight investment account, if it offers such a service, or to invest the excess funds elsewhere.

How Do You Compensate Your Bank for Services?

It's amazing to me how many intelligent businesspeople tell me that they get their bank services for free. After reviewing the balance levels kept by one retailer, I found that he had average available balances of $125,000, when all he needed to keep to pay for services was $30,000! This situation is more common than you would believe.

When you are dealing with banks, remember what Milton Friedman said: "There's no such thing as a free lunch." Banks would go bankrupt if they foolishly gave away their services. You don't do that and I don't do that, so why should they?

You can compensate your bank in three ways:

1. Balances
2. Fees
3. Combination of balances and fees

Balance Compensation Is Easy to Manage

Balances result from depositing checks, transferring funds from other accounts at your bank or from other banks, and receiving incoming ACH credits or incoming wires from many sources. The bank requires that a certain level of available balances be maintained on average for the month to pay for services. This is sometimes referred to as a compensating, or target balance.

Fee Payment Is Generally the Least Expensive

To pay by fee, the bank will either send you an invoice or automatically debit your account each month for the actual cost of the bank services. If you pay by fee, you are not required to keep any available balances in the account. However, if you deposit any checks or receive any ACH credits or wires, then you will automatically have a build-up of available balances, even if you pull out all your available funds each day. The bank will use these balances to reduce the fee required. To pay by fee, you must budget the funds ahead of time. Some firms do not plan ahead and thus use balance compensation because they didn't approve a budget for bank costs.

Combination of Fees and Balances Is a Sound Approach

Smart firms compensate the bank with a combination of fees and balances. If you use this method, the bank will automatically debit your account or send you an invoice for the balance shortfall, which it will convert into a fee. Keep your balance levels to a minimum by moving out all available funds each day. The remainder of the compensation can be paid for in fees.

Most Banks Are Indifferent to Compensation Method

In most cases, you may choose your method of compensation. Some banks prefer balances, and some prefer fees, but most are indifferent. Others will charge you a premium of 5 percent to 15 percent to pay by fee. About 13 percent of all banks charge a premium for fee payment. The average premium is about 14 percent (Ernst & Young's 1989 *Cash Management Services Survey Results—Executive Summary*).

Is It Cheaper to Pay Your Bank by Fees or Balances?

Fees are less expensive, and we'll see why after reviewing the account analysis statement later in this chapter.

How Do You Know if You're Overcompensating Your Bank?

Simple. If your friendly banker hasn't complained to you lately about your balances or you've not been receiving a monthly account analysis statement, then you're probably paying too much! All kidding aside. You must ask the bank to send you a monthly account analysis statement. As the following sections illustrate, this is not a standard bank statement that provides only ledger balances, debits, and credits.

Most Small Businesses Keep Excess Balances.   Most small businesses, according to recent surveys, keep excess balances in their checking accounts. This is great for their banks, but it is poor cash management. Many small businesses do not receive daily or weekly balance information, but instead rely on their monthly bank statements to check their balance levels.

Unfortunately, this approach is "too little too late" to correct an excess balance position. Few small businesses receive

---

Definition of an Account Analysis Statement

An account analysis statement indicates the banking services used during a month, the bank's charge for each service, the balances maintained in the account, and the balances required to pay for services.

monthly account analysis statements from their banks or even know what the statements are. Most banks provide only their medium and large customers with this document.

How Do You Read an Account Analysis Statement?

Probably with an interpreter! There is no standard format used by most banks, so you have to learn how to read each bank's statement. This task will be easier if you understand what basic information the statements contain. The following provides the information you need. If you have any questions on your statement, ask your bank officer to explain it to you.

Components

The typical account analysis statement (AAS) contains the following data:

- Average ledger balance
- Average float
- Average collected balance
- Bank's reserve requirement (RR)
- Earnings credit rate (ECR)
- Earnings allowance
- Tabulation of all the services used for the month and the total charge for these services
- Balance required for services
- Balances available to support other services
- Balance deficiency

Some banks also include FDIC (Federal Deposit Insurance Corporation) insurance and credit line information.

Let's go over the typical analysis shown in the Exhibit 10-2. Notice the following items on the top portion: the bank's name and address; the name of your account officer; your company's checking account number; the month of the analysis.

Exhibit 10-2.   Account Analysis Statement

ABC National Bank
234 Gulf Boulevard
New City, Michigan 48100

Account Analysis Statement   Analysis period: August 1990

Customer: XYZ Manufacturing Company   Account number: 11223344
111 Bay Boulevard
New City, Michigan 48100

Account officer: Jim Smith (207) 343-5678

Balance position

Average ledger balance	$133,850
Less: average float	−52,007
Average collected balance	81,843
Less: reserve requirement 12 percent	−9,821
Available balance for services	72,022
Collected balances required for services	−366,113
Deficit collected balance	(294,091)

Account earnings

Earnings credit rate (ECR) 7.67 percent	
Earnings allowance	469
Less: cost of services (see below)	−2,385
Additional service cost to be invoiced	(1,916)

Services used during month

Service	Unit price	Volume	Service charge	Collected balance required
Account maintenance	$8.50	1	8.50	$ 1,304
Credits	.10	72	7.20	1,104
Checks deposited	.075	27,755	2,081.65	319,547
FDIC insurance	.065	133	8.64	1,327
Outgoing wires	5.00	6	30.00	4,605
Returned items	1.00	199	199.00	30,548
Balance reporting	2.00	20	40.00	6,140
Special statement	10.00	1	10.00	1,535
Totals			2,385.00	366,113

Average Ledger Balance and Average Float

The average ledger (book) balance for the month is the sum of the closing ledger balance each day divided by the number of calendar days in the month (in this case 31 days). The average float is based on the availability assigned by the bank to your checks. The way it is calculated is similar to the way the ledger balance number is calculated, except the float figures are used.

Reserve Requirement

The reserve requirement of 12 percent is a direct offset of the reserves that banks must keep on deposit at the local Federal Reserve bank to back up their checking account deposits. Banks must keep these reserves, so most simply pass along this charge to their customers. However, your bank is not required to charge you for its cost of reserves. More than 95 percent will.

Collected Balance Required to Pay for Services

After subtracting the reserves, XYZ had an average available balance of $72,022 to pay for services. However, a balance of $366,113 was needed, as indicated in the "Services Used" section of the analysis. Thus, ABC had a balance deficiency of $294,091 for the month.

Account Earnings

Although banks are not permitted to pay interest on corporate checking accounts (except for nonprofit institutions and sole proprietorships), they do provide credit for the balances in the account that can be used to offset the service costs. The most common interest rate used is the three-month Treasury bill rate. This is called the "Earnings Credit Rate" (ECR).

How is the $469 earnings allowance obtained in our example?

$$\text{Earnings Allowance} = \text{average available balances} \times \text{ECR}$$
$$\times \frac{\text{days in a calendar month}}{365}$$

$$= 72,022 \times .0767 \times \frac{31}{365}$$

$$= \$469.16$$

The \$469.16 is the earnings on the \$72,022 over the 31-day month of August. These earnings can be applied against the total cost of services of \$2,385, resulting in a shortfall of \$1,916. The bank would then debit XYZ's account for \$1,916. In this case, the company is paying with a combination of balances and fees.

XYZ's balance was insufficient by \$294,091. Translated into a fee, this amounts to \$1,916. Let's see how this is calculated:

$$\text{Fee} = \text{balance deficiency} \times \left[\text{ECR} \times \frac{31}{365} \right]$$

$$= 294,091 \times [.0767 \times .0849315]$$

$$= \$1,916 \text{ (rounded)}$$

XYZ could have also:

- kept \$366,113 in balances during the month, which would have paid for all the services provided
- kept no balances in the account and paid the fee for services of \$2,385

Services Used during the Month

This section of the analysis statement details all the bank services used during the month. The bank's unit price, the number of transactions the service charge, and the collected balance required are all provided.

In summary, bank services totaled \$2,385 for the month, which was equivalent to \$366,113 in required balances.

**Eleven Common Questions
about Account Analysis Statement (AAS)**

1. How do I receive a monthly account analysis statement? Will the bank automatically send it to me?

You must ask for it! All large banks and regional banks provide AASs to their large and middle-market customers upon request, between one and three weeks after the month ends. Some small community banks may not provide them. Most banks will not send it unless you request it. A few banks send analysis statements to all their customers automatically, but this is usually done for larger corporate accounts or balance-based accounts, not smaller accounts.

Some banks have a policy not to provide AASs to small business accounts. Each bank has its own policy. If your bank provides the analysis only to larger businesses, then ask the bank what size account qualifies you to obtain one. See if you can meet their size criterion without a major effort or increase in balances. Don't be bashful about your need for the analysis and don't necessarily take no for an answer.

2. What happens if I have more than one account at the bank?

You can receive an analysis for each account, as well as a summary or "parent" analysis aggregating all the account information into one analysis. Compensate your bank based on the parent analysis, not the individual accounts.

3. Do all banks have the same account analysis format?

Unfortunately, each bank has developed its own format and terminology. In 1987, the NCCMA developed the "NCCMA Account Analysis Standard" that specifies a suggested standard format and terminology, and banks are slowly beginning to adapt this standard. Banks' cost for software changes can be substantial, though, so the cost has been a deterrent. Contact the NCCMA to obtain this standard.

4. How much will I have to pay for an account analysis?

You should pay zilch. Why should you pay for an invoice? That is what the analysis really is. A small percentage of banks charge for the analysis. Persuade your banker that you would rather *not* pay for an invoice!

5. How does the bank produce the analysis statement?

Most banks use a software program that automatically prints the analysis statements each month. The data on the services provided is obtained from other automated bank systems. About a dozen banks can provide an electronically delivered AAS and send it to your PC. Some small community banks prepare a manual analysis and type in the information. Hopefully, it is accurate.

6. How do I know if the information in the analysis is accurate?

That's a great question. You must keep track of the volume of transactions for each service (e.g., checks deposited, deposit slips, checks paid, incoming and outgoing wire transfers, and so on) as well as your available and ledger balances received each day from your bank for a particular month. If you've just received your first statement, congratulations. But check it out.

Compare your records with the monthly analysis and ask the bank to explain any discrepancies. Each month ensure that the analysis numbers are accurate by spot checking different volumes. You should investigate the accuracy if you notice a large discrepancy in the volume of transactions, the bank's price, or the available balance numbers. Also, compare the AAS balance figures to the sum of the daily balance information provided. They should match.

Be particularly attentive if you see correction fluid on any of the numbers in the bank's computer-generated analysis statement. This means a manual adjustment was made. Find out why it was made. Caveat emptor!

7. If my bank refuses or does not have the capability to send me an account analysis, then what can I do?

You have three choices:

1. Do nothing.
2. Change banks.
3. Manually prepare an analysis with the information you have on transaction volumes and daily balances using the format of Exhibit 10-2. Use standard pricing for services, based on our survey results (see Chapter 11). Base your

ECR on the average T-bill rate for the month being analyzed or use the rate given by another one of your banks.
Then calculate the balance needed for services compared
to the balance you've been keeping. One interesting strategy is to lower your balances until the bank complains or
calls.

8. I use a large bank, but my account officer has never
   mentioned that the bank can provide a monthly analysis
   statement. Why not?

Let's give the banker the benefit of the doubt and say he
or she goofed and forgot to tell you. To be more honest, your
balance levels are probably much higher than the levels required
to pay for the bank services. Account officers may want to tell
you this because their performance is partially measured by the
profitability of each of their accounts.

9. Does the bank use a specific time period to measure my
   balance compensation? In one month I may have excess
   balances, and in another month I may have a balance deficiency.

Yes. Banks use various time frames:

- month
- quarter
- calendar year
- 12-month rolling average

For example, assume your bank is measuring compensation
on a quarterly basis. If your balances for the quarter are below
the level required to pay for services, the bank will either automatically debit your account that month for the deficiency or
send you an invoice.

If you have "excess" balances for the quarter, however, the
bank will not allow you to carry forward the excess to the next
quarter. The bank will keep the earnings on the excess because
you didn't manage the balances very well. Fair is fair.

Therefore, ask your account officer if your bank has a specific
time frame for measuring compensation. If it does, then you
have to manage your balances very carefully if you're paying
the bank in balances, especially if you're near the end of the
compensation period and you have an excess balance position.

10. Do all banks offer a similar ECR?

No, they don't, so shop around. The higher the ECR, the better. However, most banks use some version of the three-month Treasury bill. However, some banks provide their small business customers with a fixed ECR each month ranging from a paltry 1.5 percent to 5 percent, which is not very sporting of them. Guess who is pocketing the difference.

11. Is it cheaper to pay in balances or fees?

It is usually cheaper to pay in fees so that you can use the balances for more rewarding purposes, such as making short-term investments or paying off a loan. Don't forget that 12 percent of your balances are unusable because the bank applies the reserve requirement and subtracts this amount from your available balances. When you pay by fee, this reserve requirement does not enter the picture. Another reason for paying by fees is that you can probably invest the balances elsewhere at a higher rate than the bank's ECR.

How Do You Know What Compensation Your Bank Requires?

Minimum Balance Deception

One local retailer in the Hudson Valley has a business account with a local bank that is a branch of a large New York City bank. The bank informed him when he first opened the account a few years ago that the account should maintain balances of $15,000 to pay for services including checks paid, coin and currency handling, check deposits, and credit card draft processing. In reality only $5,000 would have covered the cost of services, based on my evaluation. Of course, the bank provides only the usual monthly bank statement, not an AAS. The retailer immediately lowered his balance to $5,000 without a peep from the bank.

Most banks will tell small business customers the minimum balance required to avoid per-check charges when the account is opened. Most banks provide a price list for their services and indicate the ECR, if any. A bank will usually automatically debit the account if the balances are insufficient to pay for services, without even asking. Request written notice of price changes. Tell your banker you don't like surprises.

You should determine your target balance levels based on both the volume of services you expect to use during the month and the bank's price for services. Set a target balance that you will manage each day, week, or month. The higher the balances, the more frequently the balance should be monitored to guard against excess balances. By obtaining the AAS every month, you will see how well you're managing the account and how your compensation compares with the required level needed to pay for services.

How Do You Compare Bank Pricing?

Comparing bank pricing is much harder than you might think. Suppose you want to use a bank for zero balance accounts. You've gotten bids from three banks for specific ZBA-related services:

- processing 500 checks a month
- performing a full account reconcilement
- providing next-day notification phone call
- funding the account by an internal transfer

The banks' bids are as follows:

Bank	Monthly price	Reserve requirement	Monthly ECR
A	$325	12 percent	8.45
B	$365	none	8.37
C	$305	12 percent	7.75

Which bank is the least costly, if you want to pay by *fee* only? Obviously, Bank C is the least expensive at $305 per month. Which bank is the least costly if you want to pay by balances?

It's hard to tell unless you compare the price, ECR, and reserve requirement (RR) in a formula:

$$\text{Required balances} = \frac{\text{cost of services} \times (365 / \text{days in month})}{(1 - \text{RR}) \times \text{ECR}}$$

Bank A:

$$\text{Required balances} = \frac{\$325 \times (365/31)}{(1 - .12) \times .0845} = \$51,461$$

Bank B:

$$\text{Required balances} = \frac{\$365 \times (365/31)}{(1 - 0) \times .0837} = \$51,345$$

Bank C:

$$\text{Required balances} = \frac{\$305 \times (365/31)}{(1 - .12) \times .0775} = \$52,656$$

The answer then, is Bank B! Even though the bank had the highest service charges, its competitive ECR and lack of RR made up for the high price. Bank B did not charge for reserves, so the balances were worth 100 percent for compensation, not 88 percent.

Interestingly, Bank C had the highest price based on balance compensation. Why is that? Bank C had the lowest ECR.

When comparing bank pricing use the formula to obtain the "true" cost when planning to pay by balances. Don't guess.

Savings Discovery

A billion dollar household goods manufacturer and distributor maintained 50 bank accounts across the country. Although the firm received monthly AASs, the forms were filed away and not reviewed at all. When the firm's cash manager later made a careful evaluation of these documents, she found that they could be saving $250,000 a year. This savings came after several changes were made:

- elimination of bank accounts with no activity that had $25 monthly account maintenance charges
- elimination of unnecessary services, such as stapling the photocopy of the lockbox check to the envelope
- reduction of balance levels to a specific target level and periodic monitoring of the accounts

Tracking Account Analysis Data
Can Save You Money

Once you receive AASs from each of your banking relationships, you have to decide what to do with them. You should scrutinize them to make sure every piece of information on each line is correct and within a normal range based on month-to-month comparisons. Then you can file them away and forget about them, right? Wrong!

Ongoing Analysis
Is Critical

You should track all the AAS information each month on a spreadsheet program and scan the results each month looking for discrepancies or changes in transaction volume and bank pricing. Only by recording the information in this format will you be able to easily detect variances. Any problems should be immediately brought to the bank's attention for correction.

Every six months look over the AAS file with several goals:

1. Minimizing your balances
2. Avoiding any overdraft charges
3. Adjusting your target balance level, if your service volume has changed
4. Eliminating any extra accounts you keep in which the monthly account maintenance charge is higher than the value of the account
5. Reducing any unnecessary modules in the bank's information reporting service.

You could purchase commercially available AAS software packages usable on a PC that perform a month-to-month comparison, but the cost of these packages ($900 to $5,000) may be too high for your small company and the few bank relationships you have.

Are Small Business Clients Attractive to Bankers?

Small Business Characteristics

According to William C. Knight, vice president at Valley National Bank of Arizona, who spoke at a 1989 American Banker/Bond Buyer conference, there are practical ways for banks to develop increased revenues by targeting small businesses. Knight defines small businesses as those with annual sales under $1 million. He believes that the majority of these businesses are undercapitalized, undermanaged, have weak financial statement quality, and fail to recognize the importance of using outside help in establishing their internal financial controls. Many times the financial aspects of the business are neglected because of lack of knowledge.

Small Business Opportunities Abound

Why should banks want to market to firms with these characteristics? According to Knight, first, the size of the market is huge, meaning there is much opportunity. Second, small businesses have a higher ratio of deposits to credits than larger firms. Lastly, small business borrowers are usually large consumer customers of the bank. This indicates more profit for the bank.

Small Business Needs Are Specific

What do small business owners look for from their banks? Knight believes that they are looking for lending officers who are knowledgeable and interested in their businesses and banking needs. Moreover, they need personal relationships with the officers and assurance that these officers will be there for the long term. They want consistent and stable lending policies. Deposit and cash management services are important to business owners.

Developing a Small Business Image

Banks should sponsor seminars for solving small business problems. Banks should consider the advantages of setting up independent small business centers domiciled in a different section from consumer banking activities. Bank participation in the Small Business Administration and other governmental loan programs is advisable. Calls on businesses by bankers should be targeted because cold calls are ineffective. Bankers should use accountants and lawyers to obtain referrals of satisfied customers for potential leads as bank customers.

Requirements for a Primary Banking Relationship

David Killian, vice president of marketing services at American National Bank in Chicago, targets companies with annual sales between $3 million to $50 million. Killian says, "To build a primary banking relationship with customers at this level, you have to *equally* service their credit and noncredit needs." These services include checking accounts, cash management, funds transfer (international), pension management, and personal financial services for the owner and important executives of closely held businesses.

Source: Reproduced with permission from *Commercial Lender's Alert*, "Tips for Attracting the Small Business Client," May 1989, vol. 19, No. 5, p. 7. "How to Increase Your Share of the Small Business Market," Feb. 1989, Vol. 19, No. 2. Warren, Gorham & Lamont, 210 South Street, Boston, Mass. 02111. Copyright 1989. All rights reserved.

Prepare an Annual Report Card on Your Bank

Your banks should be informed about how they are doing. Why not prepare a report card on each of your banking relationships? That's what more and more companies are doing. You can then discuss the ratings with your banker. In areas where the bank is weak, try to get a commitment that service will improve; otherwise, indicate that you may move the service to another bank.

Certain areas should be included in the report card:

- service quality
- inquiry timeliness
- number of errors and volume of transactions for each separate service (e.g., ZBAs, ACH, lockbox)
- creative solutions to your problems

You shouldn't wait for the end of the year to complain about poor bank service. Each time an incident occurs, bring it to the attention of your account manager or customer service manager. Then make sure the problem is handled to your satisfaction. Perhaps you should think about issuing a monthly or quarterly report card to problem banks.

Banks handle large numbers of transactions each day, so it is likely that errors will occur. However, the percentage of errors is small. Banks that provide retail lockbox services, for example, claim error rates ranging from one in 8,000 transactions to one in 10,000. So, banks are very aware and very concerned about quality, and most do an outstanding job.

Be Prepared for Bank Visits

As your company grows from a small business to a middle-market firm to a larger firm, you will find that more banks will want to meet you to discuss how they can help you. After a while, you may get tired of interviewing banks, other than those you normally use for services and credit.

How can you limit these visits but ensure that you are not inadvertently missing a prime opportunity to learn something that could benefit your company?

Prepare a Cash Management Profile

The key is to prepare a one-page document containing all the information about your existing cash management system and send it to bankers who want to meet you *before* they visit. (Refer to the CASH MAP in Chapter 9, which is a convenient form to use.) Tell the banker that he or she must be prepared to offer practical suggestions on your existing system or ideas on how you can reach your yearly goals.

See Bankers with Interesting Ideas

Using this approach you will avoid bank calls that are boring, unnecessary, and nonproductive. You have more important things to do than to help bankers meet their "calling quotas."

By all means see bankers with whom you are not currently involved. But be selective, prescreen, and then make sure they have something of value to discuss. Some bankers can provide you with invaluable advice and services, be sure that you do not turn away these folks. You'll be well rewarded for your efforts.

11

Survey Results on Bank Cash Management Services

Some Surprising Findings

"Statistics are no substitute for judgment." —Henry Clay

Background on Our Unique Survey

To provide you with current information and insight into cash management services offered by commercial banks to small and midldle-market firms, I surveyed 52 banks across the country. I requested the following information by letter:

1. Brochures on all cash management services offered to this marketplace; and any unique services offered
2. Standard availability schedule used for assigning availability to check deposits received over-the-counter
3. Current "standard" price list for services

Additionally, I asked specific questions regarding the banks' definitions of small and middle-market companies, the differences in the cash management services offered by these banks to small and middle-market firms and to larger companies, and the banks' preferences for balance or fee compensation. I also asked whether the banks normally provided account analysis statements to small and middle-market companies without specific requests for them.

The Response Rate—52 Percent

In total, 52 percent of the 100 contacted banks responded after I followed up the initial request with numerous phone calls and letters. A few of the well-known cash management banks did not want to participate because they did not want to give out their brochures or pricing information or because they did not believe that providing information would help them get new customers. Some said that they participate in too many surveys and do not have the time for another one or that they do not service this marketplace at all.

A listing of the banks responding to our survey is included in Appendix 9 by geographic area. Each bank's name, address, contact person, and phone number are provided for your convenience. The states in each area are provided in Exhibit 11-1.

This chapter provides insights into this survey information. Appendix 10 shows the services that the banks offer in a matrix format. The banks that did not respond to the survey were not included, although they are cash management providers. Remember to obtain information from banks in your local and regional areas when you select a bank for cash management services.

Exhibit 11-1.   States by geographic area

Northeast	Southeast	Central	West
Connecticut	Alabama	Illinois	Arizona
Delaware	Arkansas	Indiana	California
Maine	Florida	Iowa	Colorado
Maryland	Georgia	Michigan	Idaho
Massachussetts	Kentucky	Minnesota	Kansas
New Hampshire	Louisiana	Missouri	Montana
New Jersey	Mississippi	Nebraska	Nevada
New York	North Carolina	North Dakota	New Mexico
Pennsylvania	South Carolina	Ohio	Oregon
Rhode Island	Tennessee	Oklahoma	Utah
Vermont	Texas	South Dakota	Washington
Washington, D.C.	Virginia	Wisconsin	Wyoming
	West Virginia		

Banks' Definitions of Small and Middle-Market Companies Vary

Small Business Definition

Each bank has its own definition of a small business, but seventy-five percent of the respondents defined a small business as a firm with annual sales under $10 million. The specific results are as follows:

Definition of a small company—by annual sales	Number of respondents	Percentage rate
Under $2 million	3	6.25 percent
Under $5 million	9	18.75 percent
Under $10 million	24	50.00 percent
Under $20 million	3	6.25 percent
Under $25 million	3	6.25 percent
Under $50 million	3	6.25 percent
Under $250 million	3	6.25 percent
	48	100.00

Middle-Market Definition

Thirty-six percent of the respondents said they measure the middle market within parameters of $10 million to $100 million in annual sales, but 98 percent indicated that the upper limit is $300 million. About 15 percent of the responding banks use $5 million or below as the beginning measurement for middle market. Here are the results:

Definition of a middle-market company—by annual sales	Number of respondents	Percentage
Under $100 million	18	36 percent
Under $150 million	5	10 percent
Under $200 million	3	6 percent

Under $250 million	3	6 percent
Under $300 million	20	40 percent
Under $750 million	1	2 percent
	50	100

Compensation Preferences Vary by Bank—Most Have No Preference

Banks were asked whether they prefer to receive compensation for services in the form of balances or fees, and if fees are used, whether the banks include a surcharge. Almost 75 percent of the banks surveyed indicated no preference. Twenty-two percent prefer balances, but only 4 percent prefer fees. About 10 percent of the banks said they charge a premium if the customer pays by fees. Typical premiums charged range from 10 percent to 15 percent. (Here's how the premium works: If your firm has service charges of $1,000 for a particular month, then the bank will charge you $1,100 if it uses a 10 percent surcharge.)

Key Point. Choose the compensation method that you prefer, because most banks are indifferent. As you know from the previous discussion on balances and fees, the least costly approach is usually fees only, followed by a combination of fees and balances.

Account Analysis Policy Is Inconsistent

Banks were queried on whether they normally provide account analysis statements to all their small business and middle-market customers. The results were surprising. Only one-third of the responding banks send them out automatically. Forty-five percent of the banks indicated that customers have to request them in order to receive them, and 10 percent of the banks said that the account analysis is sent out at the discretion of the account officer. About 12 percent of the banks do not provide an analysis to small businesses. Some banks did not answer the question directly:

- "Our bank does not create an account analysis statement for all customers. Often, good communications is an adequate substitute for an analysis."
- "[It is] offered to all corporate accounts."
- "[It is] not provided unless they are a loss from a compensation viewpoint."
- "Fee markup evaluated on market by market basis . . . no standard bankwide markup."

Key Point. To get an analysis statement, you must ask for one.

Availability Provided Is Competitive—or Is It?

Most Banks Provide Immediate to Two-day Availability

According to the information provided by the responding banks, almost all banks provide the same availability schedule to their business customers, regardless of company size. Small businesses supposedly receive the same availability as the $1 billion company bank clients. Banks provide availability on deposited checks of zero to two days, based on the bank's internal deadline for pre-encoded work.

Certain Banks Give Consumer Availability to Businesses

Based on my personal travels, I found that some Boston and New York City banks provide small business accounts not with the corporate availability schedule, but rather with the *consumer* availability schedule. As we know, the consumer schedule shows availability of one to five days and sometimes more, depending on the bank. Certain banks in other cities may not be providing their business customers with the fastest availability. You should check this out wherever you bank.

Key Point.   Check your schedule now. You should be receiving availability of zero to two days, and if you are not you should speak to your bank officer to see how you can get it. Be persistent.

Most Services Offered to Small Companies Are Not Unique

More than 95 percent of all bank respondents offer specialized cash management services or different pricing only to their large corporate customers (e.g., those with annual sales over $250 million). This is not surprising because the sophistication and needs of different-sized companies are diverse. Keep in mind, though, that certain banks *only* market to middle-market and smaller businesses. Many banks urge small business customers to select the services that best meet their needs. Sometimes this involves using the bare minimum capabilities of a particular product. For example, when small companies select a bank's information reporting service, they may select only the previous day's balance reports, debits, and credits for one account. Other options such as same-day reporting, wire transfer initiation, ACH initiation, and historical information may not be chosen.

Appendix 10 provides a listing of the typical cash management services provided to small and mid-sized companies, as well as to their large clients, by the responding banks. Use this listing to compare your existing bank's services to these banks' services. Your bank may not be offering you all the services that you need. Ask your bank and others for a complete set of brochures and prices to compare them.

Special Services Offered Are Mostly PC-based

Certain banks offer services specifically designed for small business and middle-market customers. These services include specially designed information reporting systems provided by surveyed banks including Marine Midland Bank, Deposit Guaranty National Bank, Riggs National Bank of Washington D.C., First Union National Bank of Florida, First Union National Bank of North Carolina, Chemical Banking Corp., Wells Fargo Bank, and Worthen Bank & Trust Company. Norwest Banks of Minnesota has developed a PC-initiated tax deposit product and a PC-ACH initiator. Other surveyed banks offering PC-initiation include Commerce Bancshares Inc., Continental Bank, First Interstate Bank of California, First National Bank of Maryland, Citizen's & Southern National Bank, Sovran Bank, and Sun Bank.

Bank Pricing Varies across the Country

Price is one of the critical elements in selecting banks for cash management services. Of course, don't neglect the bank's ability to provide high quality service.

To provide you with a general guideline for comparing bank prices, my survey included a review of the standard bank pricing. The banks were classified into four geographic regions—Northeast, Southeast, Central, and West—as were shown in Exhibit 11-1.

Additional Source Used for Pricing

In addition to using the price lists provided by banks in the survey, I used supplementary pricing data for 1989 to ensure a fair representation across all regions. I used the *1989 Bank Pricing Program* Third Quarter—Quarterly Report prepared by Trans Data Corporation. Details about this survey are provided in Exhibit 11-2.

Ten Pricing Caveats—Read These Carefully

Before discussing bank pricing, let's consider a few important points about the pricing data:

1. The pricing data were gathered from early 1989 to mid-1989.

2. Current prices may have increased since the data was collected. Banks tend to adjust prices annually. However pricing increases rarely exceed 5 percent.

3. These prices are "averages." That means that all the prices for each product were gathered, summed, and divided by the number of banks involved. Bank prices from my survey that were abnormally low or high were not included in the calculations.

4. Some banks provide customized pricing for your company's needs. Volume discounts on various services are available from many banks based on the number of transactions processed.

5. Pricing varies between regions of the country, within states, and even within cities.

6. The prices should be used not as a negotiating tool, but as a reference point.

7. Specific prices for banks are not shown. Banks prefer to keep prices confidential because prices change periodically and because many banks customize prices.

8. Although "information reporting" is a popular product, it was not included in our results because of the difficulty in determining a standard reference point. Banks inclusion and exclusion of numerous modules and reports makes a comparison difficult for determining the monthly maintenance charge.

9. Very few banks have different price schedules for small businesses and middle-market firms and for large corporations.

10. Ten percent of the banks did not provide pricing data because they thought it was confidential or because they custom price most services.

Bank Pricing for Selected Services

Standard Check Services

The most commonly offered bank cash management–related services are highlighted in this analysis. Remember, these prices are representative of average pricing. A specific bank's price may vary widely, in either direction from the average numbers.

- **Account maintenance**. This is the average monthly fixed charge for maintaining a standard business checking account:

Northeast	Southeast	Central	West
$15.28	$10.61	$15.07	$11.19

- **Debit/credit posting**. The per-item charge for posting a debit or credit to an account is as follows:

	Northeast	Southeast	Central	West
Debit	$0.44	$0.13	$0.15	$0.12
Credit	$0.54	$0.20	$0.45	$0.44

- **Deposit ticket**. This is the charge for depositing a batch of checks using one deposit slip to list all the checks.

Northeast	Southeast	Central	West
$0.68	$0.41	$0.80	$1.25

- **Check deposited**. This is the per-check price for processing a pre-encoded check and an unencoded check. A pre-encoded check has the dollar amount MICR printed by the depositor. An unencoded check has no dollar amount encoded prior to deposit.

	Northeast	Southeast	Central	West
Pre-encoded	$0.07	$0.06	$0.06	$0.05
Unencoded	$0.12	$0.08	$0.08	$0.09

- **On-us check.** This is a check deposited on the same bank where the check is drawn (Banks did not distinguish between pre-encoded and unencoded).

Northeast	Southeast	Central	West
$0.06	$0.06	$0.06	$0.05

- **Return of deposited check.** This is a deposited check that is returned to depositor for any number of reasons (e.g., closed account, insufficient funds).

Northeast	Southeast	Central	West
$3.27	$2.36	$2.13	$2.29

- **Check paid.** This is a charge for posting a check to a regular business checking account.

Northeast	Southeast	Central	West
$0.17	$0.13	$0.17	$0.12

- **Stop payment.** This charge is for the customer's instruction to stop a check from being paid on the account.

Northeast	Southeast	Central	West
$13.63	$13.07	$12.96	$10.50

Wholesale Lockbox

The charges include the following:

- *Maintenance.* Monthly fixed charge for a lockbox account at bank. (Note: Some banks require a minimum monthly charge rather than charge a fixed amount.)
- *Per-item charge.* Per-check base price for lockbox processing. (Typically does *not* include a photocopy charge or other customized requirements.)

Service	Northeast	Southeast	Central	West
Maintenance	$81.80	$61.25	$73.33	$140.00
Per-check deposited	0.42	0.28	0.27	0.38

Controlled Disbursement

The following changes were considered:

- *Account maintenance.* Fixed monthly charge for maintaining a single controlled disbursement account. (Note: Some banks require a minimum monthly charge rather than a fixed fee.)
- *Per-item charge.* Per-check price for posting to controlled disbursement account.
- *Notification.* Monthly charge for receiving daily notification of check-clearing totals.

| Service | Charge | | | |
	Northeast	Southeast	Central	West
Maintenance	$115.00	$99.64	$128.52	$117.97
Per-check paid	0.13	0.13	0.16	0.15
Notification	75.00	59.07	48.33	74.91

Account Reconcilement

These are fixed monthly charges for reconciling a disbursement account. Two common types of reconcilement are full and partial. Services include the following:

- *Full reconcilement.* Bank provides complete reconcilement service based on issue tape provided by the customer
- *Partial reconcilement.* Bank provides customer with a paid tape and customer typically performs reconcilement inhouse
- *A/R check paid.* Per-check charge for processing
- *Check-sorting.* Per-check charge for sorting checks in a specified order before presenting to customer.

Service	Charge			
	Northeast	Southeast	Central	West
Full reconcilement	$84.50	$60.62	$45.20	$100.97
Partial reconcilement	57.40	38.67	27.50	70.57
Check paid	0.07	0.05	0.06	0.07
Check sorted	0.04	0.03	0.03	0.04

Concentration Services

- **ACH Debit/credit.** This is the per-item charge for an ACH debit or credit.

Service	Charge			
	Northeast	Southeast	Central	West
Debit	$0.13	$0.10	$0.11	$0.11
Credit	0.13	0.09	0.08	0.11

- **ACH/DTC concentration.** Per item cost of concentrating funds using an automated Depository Transfer Check or an ACH.

Service	Northeast	Southeast	Central	West
DTC	$0.54	$0.84	$0.32	$0.77
ACH	0.23	0.20	0.27	0.28

- **Incoming/outcoming wire Transfer.** Per item cost of receiving an incoming funds transfer and sending an outgoing funds transfer.

	Northeast	Southeast	Central	West
Incoming	$5.98	$6.26	$5.47	$9.16
Outgoing	9.57	7.50	8.19	9.36

Summary of Lowest and Highest Priced Regions

Average prices vary significantly across the country. Individual bank charges vary as well. In general the lowest prices are found in the Southeast and Central regions, and the highest prices are in the Northeast and Western regions.

Service	Lowest priced region	Highest priced region
Account maintenance	Southeast	Northeast
Debit/credit posting	Southeast	Northeast
Deposit ticket	Southeast	Central
Check deposited		
Pre-encoded	West	Northeast
Unencoded	Southeast	Northeast
On-us check	West	Northeast
Return of deposited check	Central	Northeast
Check paid	West	Northeast
Stop payment	West	Northeast
Wholesale lockbox		
Maintenance	Southeast	West
Per-check deposited	Central	Northeast
Controlled disbursement		
Account maintenance	Southeast	Central
Per-check paid	Northeast	Central
Notification	Central	Northeast
Account reconcilement		
Full reconcilement	Central	West
Partial reconcilement	Central	West
Check paid	Southeast	Northeast
Check sorted	Central	Northeast/West
ACH		
Debit	Southeast	Northeast
Credit	Central	Northeast
Concentration		
ACH	Southeast	West
DTC	Central	Southeast
Wires		
Incoming	Central	West
Outgoing	Southeast	Northeast

Exhibit 11-2.   Additional source used for bank pricing

The additional source of pricing used was:

1989 Bank Pricing Program
Third Quarter, Quarterly Report
Prepared by Trans Data Corporation
994 Old Eagle School Road, Suite 1006
Wayne, PA 19087
(215) 341-9650 or (800) 876-2999
Contact: Beth A. Ritchey, Research Associate

The *1989 Bank Pricing Program* surveyed prices at almost 150 banks, based on *specific scenarios* rather than on the bank's price list. For example, a typical scenario would be a study of the bank's pricing for a wholesale lockbox with 400 checks, check photocopies, daily deposit notification, and outgoing wire.

Pricing is displayed separately by four geographic regions, and a national average is given.

12

More Surveys Provide More Insight

The More You Know, the Better Prepared You Will Be

"If you understand everything, you must be misinformed."
—Japanese Proverb

This chapter will review the principal findings of four major small business studies and two middle-market studies. The small business studies focused on the relationship of small businesses to their financial institutions and studied the banking services used. The middle-market studies, on the other hand, focused on use of cash management services and calling-officer solicitation program. These studies are presented in the second section of this chapter.

Small Business Surveys

Most small business owners are unaware of how other businesses deal with banks, how perceptions vary among bank users, and how banks service their customers, so reviewing these studies will provide you with significant insights and help you understand and deal with your bankers. Moreover, you can see how your situation compares to other firms of a similar size.

Small Business and Banks:
The United States

The first study, entitled *Small Business and Banks: The United States*, was published in 1988 by NFIB Foundation, an affiliate of the National Federation of Independent Business that is based in Washington D. C. It was written by William J. Dennis, Jr., William C. Dunkelberg, and Jeffrey S. Van Hulle. You can obtain the complete report by writing to the NFIB at 600 Maryland Avenue S. W., Suite 700, Washington, D.C., 20024, or by calling the office at (202) 554-9000.

This most recent survey is part of a continuing research project by the NFIB Foundation. The project began in 1980 and the survey has been replicated in 1982, 1984, and 1987. Its purpose is to track and better understand the relationship between small businesses and commercial banks. The study focuses on the financing aspects of businesses and their banks. It gives many interesting insights, however, on the bank-corporate relationship, the small business owners' perceptions of their bankers, the banks' shortcomings, and the bank's pricing policies.

Demographics

This most recent survey, conducted in November 1987, elicited 1,921 responses from a universe of 7,970 geographically stratified small businesses. Respondent businesses represented 10 industry groups and usually employed fewer than 50 people. Their annual gross sales were distributed in nine ranges, with the lowest range spanning from zero to $75,000 and the highest at $4.5 million or more.

The Small Business View of Banks

Banks are a very important source of cash and liquidity for businesses. However, small businesses have conflicting opinions about their banking relationships. An overwhelming number of small businesses are extremely concerned about interest rates charged by banks for their debt servicing. They believe they are paying excess interest rates compared to the banks' "best customers" (large corporations).

Bank collateral requirements for loans are particularly onerous to new businesses, even more burdensome than interest rates. Credit availability is a big problem for almost 20 percent of all businesses. Refer to Exhibit 12-1 for business owners' most important concerns with banks.

Bank Fees Are Nebulous and Bewildering

Interestingly, the survey indicates that nonborrowers are twice as concerned about bank fees than borrowers. Bank service charges have recently become an important issue with small businesses. The problem stems from a lack of accessible information that allows small businesses to measure and compare fees. Additionally, the large number and variety of fees make the charges hard to understand. Also, some businesses are unaware of all their service charges. Many firms believe their fees are fixed, but others negotiate better deals.

Business owners have great difficulty shopping intelligently for bank services because banks do not clearly and simply explain their fee structures. Moreover, it may take a large amount of time and expense for the business owner to obtain the needed information.

Exhibit 12-1. Important concerns with current banking practices

Most critical concern	Borrowers	Nonborrowers
Interest rates	33 percent	22 percent
Collateral requirements	19	15
Credit availability	13	15
Fees/charges	8	17
Account officer competence	5	3
Loan processing speed	3	3
Other	3	4
No concerns	13	19
No answer	3	2
Total	100	100

Most Businesses Use Loans

Forty-two percent of the respondents have a bank line of credit. Forty-five percent have term loans, and 20 percent have both. The larger the firms' annual revenues, the higher the percentage of companies that use some type of bank borrowing. For example, only 19 percent of firms with sales under $75,000 use a bank line of credit, compared to 84 percent of the firms with sales of $4.5 million or more.

Banks Are Not Fulfilling the Major Needs of Their Customers with a High Level of Satisfaction

The *most important factor* to business owners in the banking relationship is how they are treated as individuals—the amount of personal attention they receive. Other important criteria are their ability to obtain a loan when needed, quick access to a loan officer, and quick loan decisions. Unfortunately, business owners needs are not being met with a high level of satisfaction. For the most part, banks are doing an acceptable job rather than an outstanding job. Exhibit 12-2

Exhibit 12-2.   Bank fullfillment of customer needs—top six attributes

Bank attribute	Needs		Fullfillment of needs	
	Very important	Not important	Good	Poor
Knows you/your business	68 percent	4 percent	44 percent	16 percent
Reliable source of credit	65	5	50	11
Speedy decisions/ service	57	3	38	13
Access to loan officer	57	7	50	7
Cheapest money available	49	10	16	23
Knows local market	42	14	38	9

shows the extreme ratings for the top six needed bank attributes and for the fullment of these needs. According to this survey, banks are not very good at offering the best deals, providing account officers that know the business owners' industries, and providing helpful advice and suggestions.

Service Fees Are Important

Eleven percent of the respondents ranked fees as their most important problem with their banks. Almost 40 percent of the firms reported that they paid higher-than-usual bank fees in the past year. By a margin of seven to one, the firms that faced increases in fees believed that they were not receiving any increase in quality. Until business owners become more familiar with the ways banks charge for services, they should ask banks to provide them with complete information on their fee structure. Also, business owners should monitor and compare prices at banks where they do business.

Banks have a responsibility to provide their customers with varied services at a high level of quality. Banks have to understand that customers in different business categories prefer different volumes of services. In particular, the attributes that small businesses want are not being provided at the fulfillment level desired.

Bank Size Affects Service

Small business owners are looking for the same bank attributes, regardless of bank size. Of the survey respondents, 29 percent use small banks, 33 percent use medium-sized banks, and 32 percent use large banks. Six percent didn't answer the question.

Small banks reportedly provided certain services better than large banks:

- More personal attention
- More account officer stability
- Faster decisions on loans and faster access to account officers

- Higher levels of customer satisfaction (83 percent) than larger banks (75 percent satisfaction)
- Slower increase in bank fees
- More reliable source of credit

Larger banks, however, consistently offered loans at *lower rates* than smaller banks. Also, over the past three years, small banks have tightened up more on their criteria for loans than have the larger banks. Small business owners have severe restrictions on their options for bank credit. These restrictions are geographic. The smallest business owners must deal with a local bank and must usually compromise on the attributes they consider most important. Better pricing on loans may be attainable at large banks in distant cities. This geographic disparity causes the business owners to settle for a less-than-optimal bank.

Other Study Observations

The following were observed in this *Small Business and Banks: The United States* study:

- Business owners are particularly concerned about the person handling their accounts—they want stability and a banker who understands their business and needs.
- Bankers are slowly beginning to understand the importance of small businesses to their banks.
- Sixty-five percent of the businesses are borrowers, and 35 percent to 50 percent are regular borrowers.
- Position stability in account officers is positively related to owners' feelings about the bank.
- Fifty-five percent of those who rated their bank "poor" on credit availability shopped for another bank.
- Bank switching also occurs for other major reasons: slow decisions on credit requests; limited access to account officer; bank an unreliable source of credit; fewer services; less capable personnel; poor continuity of account officers; and too restrictive lending criteria.

- In the past three years, two-thirds of the respondents did not shop for a new bank mainly because they think they have nothing to gain.
- Of the 35 percent that did shop for another bank, 42 percent switched banks.
- Increased banking competition brought about by deregulation has failed to provide small businesses with more of the type of services that they desire or with reasonable interest rates on loans.
- Since 1980 there is no evidence to suggest that the needs of small businesses are being met with better or higher quality service.
- Only 60 percent of the small business loan applicants were satisfied with their banks.
- Services provided by banks may not be the ones that the business owner wants. The creation of specialized banks for small businesses, rather than typical consumer branches, may be a solution.

Advice to Bankers

To market to small businesses successfully, bankers must understand several facts:

- More small business customers are lost by banks than gained.
- Small businesses start small and grow. They cannot spring up at the size that banks define as their small business market.
- A large percentage of small businesses in the country have sales below $500,000. Banks are probably not marketing heavily to this group unless this size of business falls into their individual target markets.
- Banks attempt to attract the larger, well-established end of the small business market from their competitors, but a smarter strategy would be to nurture embryonic businesses into larger businesses.

- Account officer turnover is a problem for small business owners as well as for banks. Because personnel turnover is a bank problem, the bank must take steps to increase the stability of the client-account officer relationship; otherwise, they drive small business customers away. Small businesses want personal attention above all else.

- Opening specialized small business banks to serve the needs of the small business marketplace may be a savvy idea. The existing use of consumer branches for business accounts is not working very well.

Small Business Financial Relationships 1989

The second and more recent study is entitled *Small Business Financial Relationships 1989*. It was prepared by the Banking Group of the Trans Data Corporation, a research firm based in Wayne, Pennsylvania. Trans Data is a research affiliate of American Banker/Bond Buyer. This study focused on the attitudes and opinions of small businesses and their use of specific bank products. The complete study can be purchased from the Trans Data Corporation, 994 Old Eagle School Road, Wayne, Pennsylvania 19087. The phone numbers are (800) 876-2999 or (215) 341-9650.

Demographics

The data for this study was collected by a nationwide telephone survey of 523 small businesses conducted during March and April 1989. A random stratified sample of companies was obtained from Dun & Bradstreet files, using three distinct annual sales categories:

- $500,000 to $999,999 (smallest companies)
- $1.0 million to $1.9 million (medium-size)
- $2.0 million to $5.0 million (larger)

The designations in parentheses indicate how these firms will be referred to as we discuss the study findings.

Companies were selected from seven major industry classifications, and the data was broken down into five geographic regions. About 28 percent of the firms were sole proprietorships, 9 percent were partnerships, and the remaining 63 percent were privately held corporations. The average firm had 16.5 employees and annual sales of $1.7 million.

Banking Services

Checking Accounts

According to the survey, almost 100 percent of all small businesses use standard commercial bank checking accounts. Checking account balances rise as a company's size increases. The smallest firms with sales less than $1 million had average monthly balances of $22,000. This is low compared to $57,000 for firms with sales up to $2 million, and $77,000 for firms with sales between $2 million to $5 million.

About 44 percent of the businesses use night depository services, more for convenience than for cash management. As expected, retailers (53 percent) and wholesalers (51 percent) are heavy users of this service. Coin and currency are needed by 25 percent of the businesses, with retailers as the heaviest users (42 percent). Firms with a high volume of cash transactions need this service. Thirty-six percent of the firms using this service said they do not pay for it. Twenty-nine percent prefer to pay for this service based on the time spent on the order, however, and 21 percent preferred being billed on a per-item basis.

Account Reconcilement and Lockbox Use Varies

Account reconcilement is used by 27 percent of the firms, and 49 percent receive their checks in serial number order from their banks. Lockbox services are used infrequently by respondents. Only 4 percent use lockboxes and 3 percent have future plans to use the service. It appears that some business owners cannot cope with the idea of receiving their customer remittances indirectly.

Wire Transfer Usage Is Steady

Wire transfers are the most heavily used cash management service. Thirty-five percent of the firms use the service, especially business services companies. The size of the firm is directly related to the usage. For example, only 22 percent of the smallest firms use wires, compared to 42 percent of the larger firms. Sixty-one percent of wires are used to pay vendors, and 30 percent are used to move funds from one bank account to another bank. Small businesses use wires because of the security issue with large payments, not because they are effective cash management tools. Interestingly, wire transfer frequency is low: About 40 percent of the users send wires only once a month, and 30 percent of the users initiate wires three or more times a month. The heaviest users are retailers and wholesalers, with 23 percent of each group initiating wires five or more times a month.

Information Reporting
Has Limited Use

Only 10 percent of the small businesses use daily balance reporting, and 3 percent plan to start the service within a year. Almost 15 percent of the larger companies use the service, compared to 8 percent of the smallest firms. Of the users, 54 percent call the bank for the information, 16 percent of the firms have the bank call them, and 22 percent use a computer to obtain the information.

The larger firms prefer phoning the bank (67 percent) to using a computer (15 percent) to obtain the daily information. This may be so because some banks may not charge for the phone call information report. Companies will continue to use the phone until banks price this service to discourage phone usage. Over 27 percent of the smallest firms and 33 percent of the medium-sized firms use computers. Only 8 percent of the firms receive daily debit and credit detail reporting, but 12 percent of the larger firms receive it.

Electronic Funds Transfer Products Are Rarely Used

Company use of direct deposit of payroll is only 8 percent, with 3 percent planning to use it within a year. Higher usage (13 percent) is found in the larger companies. This limited use may be a result of the small number of employees (averaging fewer than 20 full-timers) at firms this size. Corporate-to-corporate trade payments are used by barely 4 percent of all respondents. The highest usage is among wholesalers with sales above $1 million (8 percent).

Short-Term Investments Are Popular

Approximately 43 percent of the respondents make short-term investments. The larger the company the more the use increases. In order of frequency, respondents use money market deposit accounts (65 percent) bank savings accounts (34 percent), CDs (Certificates of Deposit) or Repos (Repurchase Agreements) (25 percent), and commercial paper (11 percent). Only 12 percent of the firms invest daily, but 11 percent invest weekly, 33 percent invest monthly, and 43 percent invest less often than once a month. Slightly more than 40 percent of the companies have their bank automatically sweep funds from a checking account into a short-term investment account.

Of those firms that invest, the average investment rises as company size increases. The smallest firms invest $30,000 a month, compared to $97,000 for the medium-sized firms and $150,000 for the largest firms surveyed.

Borrowing Is Popular

Sixty-two percent of the surveyed firms borrow money, use a credit line, or use leasing or letters of credit. The use of borrowing is directly related to company size. More than 80 percent of the firms using credit obtained it from a bank, 30 percent from a leasing firm, and 12 percent from a commercial finance company. The most common uses for credit are:

Uses	Percent of Users
Equipment financing	54.7 percent
Financing of inventory/ accounts receivable	41.9
Plant/building expansion	13.4
New plant/building	12.1
Working capital	10.6

(Multiple uses of credit are also possible.)

For the firms that borrow, the average monthly debt rises as the company size increases. The smallest firms average a monthly debt of $52,000 compared to $101,000 for the medium-sized firms and $168,000 for the largest firms.

Bank Satisfaction/Dissatisfaction

Small businesses have relationships with an average of 1.7 banks. Ninety-seven percent of business deposits are kept at commercial banks. One-third of all businesses significantly increased the number of bank deposits they made at their major bank in 1989. Almost 50 percent of respondents were very satisfied with their primary bank, and 29 percent were somewhat satisfied. Areas of highest satisfaction were courtesy of branch personnel, branch locations, quality of service, and range of services available. High levels of dissatisfaction were for fees and charges, interest rates paid on loans, and banks' unwillingness to provide unsecured loans. About 25 percent of the businesses were dissatisfied or very dissatisfied with banks.

Bank Contact

Fifty-six percent of the business owners are visited by a bank representative from their major bank. Visits increase as company size expands. For example, 39 percent of the smallest firms were visited compared to 66 percent of the larger firms. Half the firms prefer personal visits to phone calls from their bankers, 25 percent prefer phone contact, and 20 percent have no preference.

Just over 20 percent of businesses visit their banks daily, and 40 percent are there once a week or more. Only 2 percent of businesses use "business only" branches compared to the 97 percent that use regular consumer branches.

Bank Problem Resolution

One-third of the respondents had a problem or complaint with their bank. Ninety-six percent brought the problem to the attention of the bank, but 40 percent were unsuccessful in resolving it satisfactorily. The smallest firms had the highest percentage of unresolved problems. As a result of the problems, 11 percent of the firms closed their account and another 11 percent stopped doing business with the bank entirely.

Other Observations

- Business owners find cash management services difficult to understand and the terminology confusing. Although the services are fairly straightforward and are understood by the business owners, the technical details on implementing the service from the bank's perspective can create unnecessary complexity that frustrates the potential buyer.
- 60 percent of the firms strongly agree that "the new financial services available today are confusing."
- 42 percent of the firms somewhat disagree with the statement that "I regard myself as more financially sophisticated than other businessmen."

Small Business Speaks Out:
Companies Rate Their Banks

Background

The third major survey was prepared by the staff of the *American Banker/Bond Buyer* and is entitled *Small Business Speaks Out: Companies Rate Their Banks*. This report views financial services organizations from the perspective of small businesses, which are defined as companies with sales ranging between $1 million to $20 million a year. The complete survey can be purchased for $50 from the American Banker Surveys, One State Street Plaza, New York, NY, 10004. You can also call (800) 221-1809 or if you are in New York, (212) 943-8677.

Demographics

Trans Data Corporation, a financial research affiliate of the *American Banker/Bond Buyer*, conducted telephone interviews in January and February 1989 for this survey. The 408 respondents were business owners or officers who had responsibility for choosing financial services firms. The firms surveyed were divided into categories according to annual sales ranges: $1 million to $4.9 million, and $5 million to $20 million. Additionally, geographic breakdowns were made into four regions—Northeast, North Central, South, and West. There were seven industry classifications including a category for other types of firms.

Overview

Small businesses use as few banks as possible, but use a local bank as their major bank. Thus, community banks and banks with branches are the most heavily patronized. Almost 40 percent of the respondents use one bank or thrift, 31 percent use two institutions, 25 percent use three to five institutions, and 5 percent use six or more. Companies typically stay with their institution for a long period, averaging 14.5 years with the major bank. The average age of the surveyed companies was 25.

Financial Guidance Is Needed

Businesses indicated that banks could offer more help in providing financial guidance, particularly for loan applications. Bankers theorize that the small business owners or officers may know their business very well but aren't well schooled in financial matters.

Cross-selling Other Services and Employees

Respondents believe that banks are missing a significant cross-selling opportunity by not selling business *and* personal banking relationships. Almost 62 percent of the respondents use the same bank for their personal and business requirements.

Many banks realize that for a business relationship to be profitable, other services must be used in addition to loans. Moreover, small business employees are becoming the target market for aggressive banks for such services as direct deposit of payroll and on-premises banking that offers check cashing privileges. Interestingly, 80 percent of the business owners who use the bank for both personal and business accounts indicate that their banks haven't solicited their employees' personal financial accounts.

Financing Needs

Today the community banks and in-state regionals control the financing of small businesses. Almost 90 percent of the 408 respondents use either community or in-state regionals as their principal banks. Ninety-eight percent of the firms surveyed use a commercial bank for their business accounts. Bankers should not be complacent because increased competition from other banks and other financial institutions can whittle away their supposedly strong relationships with customers.

Another recent study mentioned in this report indicates that 33 percent of the firms with annual sales between $1 million and $15 million are thinking about changing their major banking relationship. Other service providers that are used by respondents besides banks are finance companies (35 percent) and thrifts (20 percent). Moreover, 28 percent of the small businesses surveyed use investment banks or brokerage firms for certain services. Almost 80 percent of the firms did not expect their banking relationships to grow over the next two years.

Banks Must Learn about Their Customers' Businesses

A large majority of banks do not fully realize the tremendous opportunity they have in the small business market. Banks can provide this market with many more services than they are now offering.

Small businesses want personal attention and excellent service. Almost 45 percent of the firms rate their bank service as excellent, 36 percent rate it as above average, 10 percent rate it average, and 6 percent rate it poor. Over 50 percent of the respondents say they are receiving high quality service, quick responses on requests, and good service from bank personnel. Unfortunately, 20 percent of all the firms indicated on the survey that their primary bank has an average knowledge of their business. Another 18 percent think their bank's knowledge is either below average or poor. The knowledge becomes important when firms apply for loans. About 20 percent of the firms believe their loan requests were rejected because the bank did not understand their business requirements.

It's Hard for a Bank to Lose a Customer, But It Does Happen!

Small business owners stick with their banks despite bad service, as long as their loan needs are met. Bankers may call it loyalty, but business owners call it money. Of all surveyed companies, the *top consideration in selecting a bank is the availability of financing.* Companies usually won't shop for new banks if their credit needs are fulfilled and they are treated fairly by their bank. Many small businesses indicate that the human element is a very important factor in the relationship equation.

Smart banks assign a backup account officer to each account to avoid problems if the original officer moves on.

Banks should focus on providing small business customers with high quality service and responsiveness to their most critical needs. By setting up small business departments, smart bankers are showing their interest in businesses this size. Bankers have to realize that to keep their clients, they must cater to clients' needs. It is not surprising that almost 60 percent of the firms that say they receive good service also say that their banks have small business departments. Why does a small business go to a particular bank? The survey indicated that 30 percent had had a previous relationship with that bank, and 22 percent found a local branch that was convenient.

Electronic Cash Management Services to the Rescue

One way for banks to increase their deposits is to sell electronic cash management services to the small business market. About one-third of the companies with sales below $5 million that were surveyed indicated that they might use a computer to obtain transaction and balance information from their banks. A higher percentage of the larger companies expressed a similar interest. Some of the more aggressive banks offer specific miniversions of their large corporate market balance reporting systems to the small business segment and have increased sales.

"The Future of Small Business Banking"

Introduction

Arthur J. L. Lucey, President of Denver-based Alexander Lucey Inc., has surveyed the banking needs of small businesses in 21 regional markets for his specific bank clients over the past few years. He discussed the results of his surveys in a session entitled "The Future of Small Business Banking" at the

1989 annual convention of the American Bankers Association. Mr. Lucey can be reached at 600 17th Street, No. 1605S, Denver, Colorado, 80202, or by phone at (303) 825–1665.

Lucey believes that the banking needs of small businesses are unique and that the opportunities for community banks are attractive. Yet most businesses are underserved by banks: Community banks have been neglecting this growing market.

Demographics

Small businesses, as defined by Lucey, are firms with annual sales between $1 million and $10 million. Each year, he noted, 650,000 companies are started, but only 3 percent ever reach $1 million in sales. The average small business in his survey was eight years old and was not in a start-up mode. The respondents were owners, presidents, or top managers of their firms. Almost two-thirds were active managers in their privately-held companies. Half the firms had 15 or fewer employees. Lucey found that small businesses represent a major source of deposits to banks and that they will make loans at the prime rate plus a few percentage points. They are seasonal borrowers.

Formalized Survey Procedure Was Used

The survey process was handled in a standard way in each of the 21 markets. About 80 percent of the questions were similar from market to market. Lucey developed the questionnaire using bank management interviews, calling officer and support personnel focus groups, and prior experience. Different levels of bank personnel were interviewed including calling officers, coin dispensing persons, and back-office personnel to obtain a wide range of viewpoints. Bank marketing, training, and sales support material were also reviewed. Small business executives were taught how to shop for bank services by visiting a number of banks and asking a lot of questions, including at the bank requesting the survey.

Small businesses were selected for interviews based on sampling from lists such as the Dun & Bradstreet list. The interviewers were executives, not unskilled personnel. They performed 250 to 300 30-minute interviews with the selected small businesses. The results of the survey were presented to the requesting banks in an interactive mode along with recommendations.

Small Business Myths

According to Lucey, the following are commonly held beliefs that must be changed:

1. *Community banks have a lock on small business.* Nothing is further from the truth. Actually, larger banks are making significant marketing inroads. For example, in Florida only 20 percent of the small businesses use a community bank. Brokers and finance companies are educating small businesses on other available services. Fewer than 50 percent of the companies are called on individually by their bank president.

2. *Serving the small business market is easy.* Actually, small banks can't provide all the types of services that their small business customers need. Maybe the community banker should refer the customer to other financial institutions for certain services without losing the customer's patronage entirely.

3. *The small business market is fat, dumb, and happy.* This is wrong, because each company has different needs. Small businesses have specific needs, as Exhibit 12-3 indicates.

Most Frequent Services Used

Most small businesses use a business checking account, and almost 50 percent use a secured loan, make short-term investments, and execute a line of credit. Interestingly, 55 percent use nonbanks for investments. Exhibit 12-4 delineates the major financial services used by small businesses.

Exhibit 12-3. The most important factors in a banking relationship

Factor	Percent
Personalized, flexible services	65
Convenient location	31
High caliber, interested account officer	18
Bank well run	17
Bank loans available when needed	16
Long-term relationship	15
Accurate service	13
Attentive top management	13
Wide range of services available	8
Competitive loan pricing	5
Friend at bank	2

Frequency of Bank Calls Is Low

More than 80 percent of the respondents have a specific account officer at their bank. About 66 percent have never received competitive calls from another bank's account officer, and about 20 percent have cash balances over $100,000. Of those who borrow, most borrow less than $500,000. Although 35 percent of the firms borrow from their bank and use three to four banking services, almost 34 percent of the companies

Exhibit 12-4. Financial services used by small businesses

Service	Percent
Business checking	99
Business secured loan	47
Short-term investments/money market	45
Line of credit	44
Business savings account	29
Business unsecured loan	23
Letter of credit	18
Mortgage loan	14
Payroll services	12
Night deposit	7
Pension/profit sharing/thrift/IRA	6
Computer-based accounting services	3

never receive a call from their account officer. Another 20 percent were called less than twice a year.

Small businesses are heavily influenced by the responsiveness and interest in their business shown by account officers. Account officers play a major role in the relationship of the business to the company, and it is not surprising to find that the **account officer is 3.2 times more important** to small businesses than the bank itself. The most important account officer characteristics from the small business owner's perspective are listed in Exhibit 12-5.

Small Businesses Have Unmet Needs

Small businesses, on average, use 1.33 banks. About half of small business owners and executives use the same bank for their business and personal banking needs. The business banking relationship was established first 43 percent of the time, the personal banking relationship was first 18 percent of the time, and both began at the same time in 13 percent of these cases. Banks can obtain the personal banking business of owners and employees if they go after it.

Respondents expressed interest in investment management, pensions, profit sharing, mutual funds, and international services that aren't offered by the banking community. Just over

Exhibit 12-5. The most important account officer qualities

Quality	Percent
Responsive to my needs	41
Interested in satisfying my needs	36
Understands my business/banking needs	35
Available when needed	31
Knows business, financial, and economic conditions	27
Friendly, easy to get along with	17
Keeps in touch with me	16
Able to get loans approved quickly	13
Corrects errors promptly and efficiently	9
Mature, seasoned professional banker	6
Has detailed knowledge of bank's products	5

33 percent said that their accountant was 16 times more important to them as their financial advisor than their bankers. About 62 percent don't remember any financial institution advertising directed to the business community. If called on, the majority would prefer phone calls. Personal calls rank second.

Why Do Banks Lose Customers?

Community banks have an excellent chance to obtain new customers, because 65 percent of the respondents would probably change banks if their existing bank made too many errors and had high service charges. However, small businesses are generally loyal to their financial institution. The key reasons why businesses change institutions are shown in Exhibit 12-6.

My Conclusions

After reading the key findings of these enlightening surveys, you should now be more knowledgeable about banking relationships. Although each study had different survey respondents and occured in different time periods, the three studies came out with surprisingly similar results. Personal

Exhibit 12-6. Reasons to change financial institutions

Problems with bank	Percent of respondents who would consequently change banks
Frequent errors	49
High service charges	40
Disinterested account officer	35
Bank unwilling to extend credit	33
Too much turnover	19
Better loan price elsewhere	18
Better officer at another institution	16
Other institution offers full services	10
Friend at key position at another institution	8
Current bank too small	6

service, fair interest rates on loans, quick response to credit needs, and high quality service keep coming through loud and clear as the key requirements of small businesses.

What Action Do You Take Now?

Now that you know what to expect from your bank, what are you going to do about it? If you are fortunate enough to have a bank that provides you with high quality services and a fairly priced credit line, then be grateful and pray that it continues. However, if this is not the case, then you have four distinct options:

1. Sit back and do nothing, hoping the situation will somehow improve.
2. Decide that you must take immediate action and berate your banker in person at your next encounter.
3. Plan a strategy to work with your banker to improve the situation.
4. Meet with other banks and move your business elsewhere.

The first option is fine if you are not an aggressive, bottom-line-oriented person. However, if you own your business or are a major player in your firm, I doubt that this option suits you. I do not recommend this option.

Option 2 is acceptable if you have another bank in the wings; otherwise, you are looking for more trouble than you have now. So stay calm. You could do one of the following instead:

- Become more assertive, in a pleasant manner, and diplomatically persuade your bank that it is in its best interest to improve its service on an ongoing basis. Remind your banker that you have other alternatives (make sure you do in case he or she calls your bluff) if the bank will not or cannot provide you with the services that you need.
- Criticize the bank, but make sure that you provide *specific detailed information*. Remember, neither you nor your bankers are perfect, but continual errors are unacceptable.

You can be sure that your local banker's ears will perk up when you casually mention your recent meeting with a competitor down the street or an out-of-state behemoth. You may find that your banker suddenly begins to realize the importance of your relationship to his or her institution, especially if your company is prospering and growing rapidly with increasing profits every year.

The third option should be considered. One way to approach the problem is to use other bank customers to help point out the bank's shortcomings. For example, suggest that your bank invite a group of its business customers to lunch to discuss areas of common interest and concern and to explain what the bank is doing to meet customers' needs. Volunteer to get the ball rolling and organize the luncheon. This option can work out well.

Only consider Option 4 if your existing bank refuses to change. Don't be bashful about meeting with other local, regional, or large multinational U.S. and foreign banks to see what they have to offer. You may find out something very useful that can save you money or help solve a problem that your local bank may not have the interest or capability to solve.

Middle-Market Surveys

This section focuses on two surveys of the middle market, both conducted and published in 1989 by Trans Data Corporation. TDC defines the middle market as firms with annual sales between $5 million and $250 million. The first study is entitled *1989 Corporate Cash Management Survey Results*, and it concentrates on the middle-market use of the following cash management products:

- Wire Transfer
- Lockbox
- ACH
- Disbursement (check-based)
- Electronic Data Interchange (EDI)

- Information reporting and treasury automation
- Short-term investments

Phone interviews with 533 randomly selected companies from across the country formed the sample used for this study. The companies were segmented into three groups by sales size:

- $5 million to $19.9 million (smallest)
- $20 million to $49.9 million (medium)
- $50 million to $250 million (large)

When referring to companies in these groups in our synopsis, we will use the terms in parentheses rather than repeating the dollar ranges.

Overview

Seventy-five percent of all firms use more than one bank for financial services, but only 35 percent use more than one bank for cash management services. Eight out of ten firms use the same number of cash management banks as they did two years ago. Almost 90 percent report that they use the same major bank for cash management and other financial services.

To the surveyed companies, the most important factors in selecting a new cash management bank are customer servicing, variety of services, pricing, availability of credit, and location. Besides these factors, the bank's service quality is mentioned more often than pricing as a critical evaluation factor. Most firms want one servicing contact at their bank for cash management needs, rather than numerous bank personnel.

The cash management products used most frequently by the surveyed firms are shown in Exhibit 12-7.

Wire Transfer Demand Is Stable

Use of wires is directly related to company size. Slightly more than 50 percent of the smallest firms use wires, compared to

Exhibit 12-7   Top five cash management services companies use. ©1989, Trans Data Corporation.

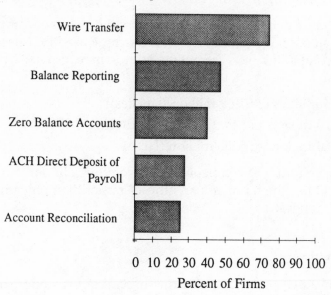

almost 80 percent of medium-sized firms and 93 percent of the larger firms. Wire transfer volume is also sales-related with the smallest firms initiating nine wires a month, medium firms initiating 17 wires, and large firms initiating 26 wires. Wires are used mainly for disbursing (38 percent), concentrating (31 percent), and collecting funds (29 percent). They are initiated by telephone in 72 percent of the firms.

Lockbox Service Demand Remains Steady

About 25 percent of all the respondents use lockboxes, with usage dependent on sales. Ten percent of the smallest firms and 43 percent of the largest firms use lockboxes. Manufacturing firms have the highest usage, at almost 50 percent. Of the firms using lockboxes, 70 percent use wholesale lockboxes and 40 percent use retail. Some firms use both. Most firms that use wholesale lockbox banks use only one (78 percent). Seventy-one percent of the firms using retail lockboxes use one bank, and 28 percent use two to four banks. Lockbox *networks* are only used by 7 percent of all firms.

ACH Service Demand Also Remains Stable

Demand for direct deposit of payroll has remained fairly stable at 30 percent of all firms, compared to prior surveys. Usage of the service is directly related to sales size: Only 18 percent of the smallest firms use the service, compared to 38 percent of the largest firms and 26 percent of medium-sized firms.

ACH concentration usage remains low at 15 percent of all firms (5 percent of the smaller firms and 24 percent of the larger companies). ACH preauthorized debits are used by only 5 percent of all firms. ACH corporate-to-corporate payment usage has grown from 4 percent in 1986 and 1987 to 10 percent beginning in 1988. Lack of knowledge seems to be one reason why its use is low (see Exhibit 12-8). Interestingly, 4 percent

Exhibit 12-8. Reasons why companies do not use corporate ACH services (for companies that do not use corporate-to-corporate ACH services). ©1989, Trans Data Corporation

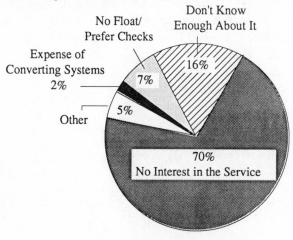

Percent of Firms Not
Using Corporate ACH

of the firms that use the service indicate it is their primary payment method.

The methods used by firms to initiate ACH payments vary: magnetic tape (42 percent), phone (28 percent), paper (16 percent), and PC transmission or diskette (12 percent). The large firms expressed a relatively high degree of interest in using automated means (26 percent); but the smallest firms showed only a minor interest (4 percent). Receipt of ACH payments is mostly handled by automated means (53 percent) or paper (36 percent).

EDI Usage Remains Low

Usage of EDI in 1989 by reponding firms was 11 percent, 1 percent higher than it was a year earlier. The reasons for lack of interest in EDI are shown in Exhibit 12-9.

Disbursement Services

Controlled Disbursement Is Becoming More Popular

Overall, 17 percent of all firms surveyed use controlled disbursement. As with most other services, the larger firms are heavier users. In this case, 30 percent of the large firms, 17 percent of the medium-sized firms, and 7 percent of the small firms use controlled disbursement. Phone calls are used most often (60 percent), to obtain check-clearing notification, followed by automated method (PCs) at 40 percent.

Account Reconciliation Is Steady and Check Safekeeping Gets Mixed Reviews

Account reconciliation is used by 29 percent of all firms. The distribution of usage by company size is shown in Exhibit 12-10.

Middle-market firms have not embraced bank check-safekeeping services. Only 6 percent of these firms use the

Exhibit 12-9. The reasons companies cite for not using EDI and corporate ACH (among firms that do not use the services). ©1989, Trans Data Corporation

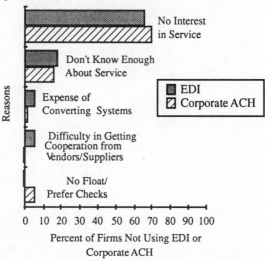

Percent of Firms Not Using EDI or
Corporate ACH

service, and again company size plays an important part in its usefulness.

Zero Balance Accounts (ZBAs) Are Favored, but Coin and Currency Services Have Limited Demand

Just over 40 percent of all firms use ZBAs. Almost 60 percent of the larger firms use ZBAs compared to 20 percent of the smaller firms. Only 2 percent of all firms use bank coin and currency processing services. This service is typically used by companies with high volumes of cash transactions, such as retailers.

Information Reporting Is Popular

Daily balance information is received by almost half of the surveyed companies. Although 66 percent of the large firms

Exhibit 12-10.   Usage of account reconciliation plans (ARP), by sales size. ©1989,
Trans Data Corporation

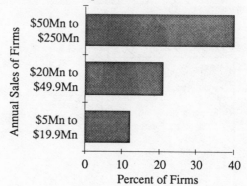

receive it, only 26 percent of the smaller firms do. Of those
firms that obtain information daily, 36 percent receive both
previous-day and same-day information, 45 percent receive
only previous-day, and 19 percent receive only current-day.
The methods by which companies receive their information is
illustrated in Exhibit 12-11.

Exhibit 12-11. Methods by which companies
receive daily information about account balances
(for companies that receive daily information about
account balances). ©1989, Trans Data Corporation

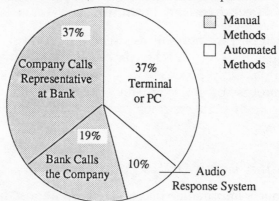

Percent of Firms Using Information Reporting

A small number of firms used information other than balances as well as other modules:

Information/Initiation	*Percent of Users*
Detailed debits and credits	14%
Wire transfer initiation	8
Same day lockbox balance	6
Same day controlled disbursement clearings	6
Stop payment initiation	3

Short-Term Investments Are Popular

The magnitude of short-term investments rises as a firm's sales rises. The smallest firms invested $58,000 in an average month, medium-sized firms invested $1.3 million, and the larger firms invested $2.5 million. Over 50 percent of the firms made investments. Twice as many larger firms use overnight "sweep" accounts as smaller businesses. On average, one-third of all the firms used "sweep" accounts.

1989 Corporate Solicitation and Calling Officer Effectiveness Survey Results

This study was also performed by Trans Data Corporation. It was based on telephone interviews with 526 randomly selected middle-market firms from across the country with sales between $5 million and $250 million. The focus of this study was to examine how banks call on their client relationships and to determine how effective those efforts were. The sample was divided into three classifications based on annual sales and exactly paralleled the previous study.

Overview

The average number of commercial banks used by middle-market firms was three in 1989. This is a decline from five banks in 1987 and 1988. The smallest firms used an average of two banks, and the larger firms used four banks. Respondents use an average of four other nonbank financial service firms with leasing firms, brokerage firms, and insurance firms the most heavily used.

When middle-market firms build up a financial services relationship, the main reason is to obtain credit (27 percent), followed by company growth (25 percent), personalized attention (13 percent), and variety of services (12 percent). Conversely, the major reason given by firms for dropping or decreasing a relationship is poor quality of service and poor customer servicing (18 percent and 21 percent, respectively).

Calling Efforts

Middle-market firms are called upon more by their existing nonbank financial service providers (seven times a year) than commercial banks (six times). This difference is even more apparent when these service providers call on prospective clients. Here, banks call an average of four times a year compared to 23 times a year by nonbank providers.

The number of calls received by firms is directly related to their sales size. The small firms are called upon four times a year; the large firms receive eight calls. Interestingly, 35 percent of the small firms never get called on by their bank, compared to 28 percent for middle-sized firms and 21 percent for the large firms. Companies reactions to calling efforts are illustrated in Exhibit 12-12.

Solicitation Methods
and Their Effectiveness

Calling efforts by existing banking relationships are focused on in-person visits (55 percent), followed by telephone contact (36 percent), and personalized mailings (8 percent). Banks pursuing new relationships use phone calls more frequently (50 percent), followed by in-person visits (31 percent) and personalized mailings (21 percent). Nonbank financial providers use phone contact (60 percent) and personalized mailings (27 percent) more than in-person visits.

Exhibit 12-12.   How companies feel about the amount of solicitation they receive from commercial banks versus other financial service organizations. ©1989, Trans Data Corporation

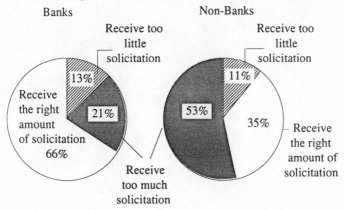

Percent of Firms

Surprisingly, *middle-market firms prefer personalized mailings and telephone contact* by 36 percent and 34 percent, respectively. However, 28 percent still prefer in-person visits. About 25 percent of the firms signed up with a financial service provider after receiving a solicitation within the past year. It is interesting that 64 percent of the respondents that began a new business relationship based their decision on an in-person visit. Twenty-seven percent based it on telephone solicitation, and ten percent on personalized mailings. The reasons given for deciding to start a new relationship are shown in Exhibit 12-13.

Overall Effectiveness of Calling Officers

By a wide margin of 74 percent, middle-market firms see commercial banks having more effective calling officers than any other financial services vendor. The important factors in evaluating calling officers from the perspective of the respondents are shown in Exhibit 12-14.

Exhibit 12-13.   The reasons companies decided to establish new business as a result of solicitation. ©1989, Trans
Data Corporation

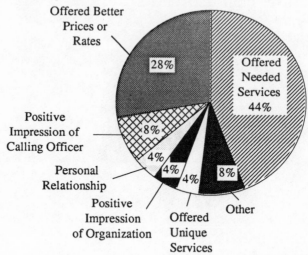

Percent of Firms Establishing New Business
in the Last Year as a Result of Solicitation

Exhibit 12-14.   Factors perceived as important in rating calling
officer performance. ©1989, Trans Data Corporation

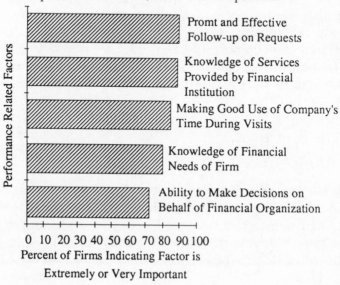

My Conclusions

Middle-market firms are much more frequent users of cash management services than small businesses. This makes sense, because larger firms have greater needs for credit and bank services. Not surprisingly, the criteria specified by middle-market firms for selecting a new bank and the important characteristics mentioned by small businesses for maintaining existing bank relationships are similar:

- Personalized or customized service
- Availability of credit
- Fair pricing
- Quality of service
- Variety of services offered

Company Size Doesn't Matter

In essence, company size does not appear to change the criteria used to select or stay with banks. Of course, there are variations in needs of a $500,000 company and a $50 million firm, but the underlying requirements are constant.

Banks Need to Service the Market

Bankers are slowly beginning to realize the critical importance of calling on and servicing small and middle-market firms with more tailored products and more personalized attention. Yet the bankers have a long way to go to satisfy the specific needs of this mushrooming marketplace. The bankers should realize, if they haven't already, that this market segment is the fastest growing and most dynamic of all segments.

Bankers Must Nurture Small Businesses

By using a more frequent and targeted calling program, run by knowledgeable personnel, bankers can obtain significant business relationships over the long-term. Savvy bankers are not neglecting the smallest firms, those with sales under $5 million, because some of these firms may eventually have sales of $10 million to $100 million. Once a banking relationship is established, companies would rather not change banks. But if their main bank neglects them, takes unfair advantage of them, or has significant service problems, then the bank deserves to lose the business.

Bankers Need Long-Term Perspective

The large corporate market (sales above $250 million) is over-banked, but new market segments such as small and middle-market firms are ideally suited for bank marketers, that can meet the needs of these companies. New businesses are incorporating at the rate of over 650,000 a year, the market for banking services will always be expanding. Of course, banks may not make much of a profit on individual small business accounts, but if banks have enough of them and if they provide good service, they will have built a solid profit center that will keep expanding. Thus, bankers must take a long-term perspective if they expect to participate successfully in this market place.

13

Interviews with Three Experienced Bankers

Everyone Has a Different View of the World

"Too often the American dream is interrupted by the Japanese alarm clock." —Anonymous

---

To find out what experienced bankers think about the opportunties for small and middle-market firms, I interviewed three bankers across the country that have visited hundreds of middle-market firms and small businesses. Here are their insights.

Interview Number One: Keith D. Kulper

I first interviewed Keith D. Kulper, Vice President—Group Manager, Cash Management Division of Midlantic Bank of Edison, New Jersey. Midlantic defines the middle market as companies with sales of $15 million to $100 million. When companies exceed $100 million they begin to act like large corporations that have regional and international needs. The following is a condensed version of Mr. Kulper's responses to my questions.

Cash Flows Tracked Closely

Most middle-market companies are very aware of their cash flow. Because they have a small margin of error in their cash flow, they really focus on it. Typically the president or owner of the firm is very close to the cash management function. The cash management techniques can actually put a spin on how the whole company is managed, as it goes through its different stages of growth.

In-house Seminars Provide Marketing Opportunities

Companies obtain information on cash management on the fly. Ninety percent do not have a plan on how to find out about cash management. That's why Midlantic provides specially designed seminars. These seminars are excellent marketing opportunities for Midlantic, and our bank is very upfront with the firms on why they should be using Midlantic. Our president and chairman usually attend the cocktail reception after the seminar.

Midlantic plans to hold seven or more seminars (two and a half hours each) a year for middle-market companies to learn cash management basis. We like to use current examples of cash management systems to illustrate out point. We then review our vision of the future of cash management and review issues (outside banking) that can affect this planning process such as advances in PCs.

ACH Initiation and EDI Are Not Popular

Common products used by the middle market include whole-sale lockbox, controlled disbursement, information reporting (information and transaction details), and investments. ACH initiation is not that meaningful to this market. EDI is considered "Star Wars"—forget it for now. It's important, though, for this marketplace to be aware of what's going on in EDI, but EDI aspects are very limited for now, since they are much more contained in the inner workings of the company itself. The banking aspects are minimal.

This marketplace benefits from the technology and systems work that is done for the large corporate market because it is so applicable to this market. Everybody has a PC.

Most Firms Have
Astute Managers

Most middle-market company managers are very astute and truly have no time for boondoggles or time-wasting activities. It's a common misconception that middle-market companies are unsophisticated about cash management. In reality, the managers of these firms are extremely practical-minded and as such, readily understand that cash management techniques can have an immediate positive impact on the company's bottom line.

Flow Chart the Cash Management
System First

When we call on a company we look at their present cash management system. We help the customer analyze their system by placing the information provided on our specially designed form. This may be the first time that the company has done this type of exercise, making it very enlightening for many companies. We try to provide the customer with a picture of what is currently done, how it is done, and at what cost. We try to be sensitive in what we say so that our ideas will be meaningful to the customer, and as such we avoid a canned approach. Too much packaging puts scales on their eyes—we are trying to be helpful, after all.

For example, a $5 million to $15 million company may be very concerned about bank debt and how to keep debt as low as possible. If the company makes mistakes in cost accounting and in the prices it establishes for the services it uses, it could find itself bankrupt. If it takes on too much or too little debt or is backward in its views toward technology, this could also result in business failure.

Once a company grows to $15 million or perhaps $30 million, the owner becomes more distant from the administrative and operational aspects of the business and is usually much more focused on sales and production. Effective treasury management is viewed as a necessary aspect of the business.

Banks Must Provide Value to Customers

Middle-market firms are extremely dependent on banks for capital infusion, and consequently their bank relationships can become very close. If the bank loses sight of its real purpose, which is to provide financial services and products of most value to the company, and instead focuses on protecting its balance position or worrying about what happened yesterday as opposed to where the relationship is headed, then the banker can actually be part of the problem of the company's ability to grow. Many potential users may be blocked from using a product because their bankers are afraid, uninformed, or greedy.

It's the same thing on the corporate side. If the corporation doesn't want to listen and is locked into the status quo, then the company can be left behind. Interestingly, smaller clients can be more apt to listen to our ideas than larger companies, because they tend to be less structured.

Account Stability Is Paramount

The stability of the account officer relationship is very important to companies. Entrepreneurs get very upset if their account officer is changed. Their voice on the loan committee is the account officer, so a change can kill the relationship. Midlantic gets a great deal of middle-market business because of account officer turnover at other banks. It also gets business because other banks have denied companies loans or because their service levels are just not acceptable.

Bank Pricing Views

Bank pricing to all markets is becoming a key issue, just as it is in any market that begins to mature (like calculators or PCs). Bank cash management services are being viewed more and more as a commodity with little difference between offerers.

Some of the bank cash management pricing practices (when banks are desperate for market share) are clearly counter productive. No cost analysis work is done, yet they think their spreads on loan business will be sufficient to have a positive affect on bank profitability. These banks eventually get restructured, acquired, or become insolvent over the long run.

Bank Selection Criteria

The three most important factors that a middle market company looks for in a bank relationship are the following:

1. A company wants a banker who will take time to listen and understand what the customer is all about, where the company's going and where the company wants to be.

2. A bank should understand the objectives and goals of the company, help the firm achieve them, and teach it to network to others that provide important information or contacts.

3. Banks who are tough do not permit entrepreneurs to bamboozle them with overly wishful thinking.

Human nature doesn't change, and technology can come and go, but people who are trying to advance themselves need a lot of useful information. A bank can play an important role in this process if it remembers that it's there to provide capital and services to make that company grow and that it should know when to say no.

Midlantic gets in (most times) when our competition is asleep. It's the people on the account and their relationship management that's important. We run lean and can't afford to be sleepy.

The Future Is Limitless

The future for Midlantic with middle-market firms is limit-less. There are a myriad of prospects that we haven't seen yet because our focus in cash management was on the large corporate market. That's where all the action has been. Now we focus on both markets.

Interview Number Two: Karl Ostby

My second interview was with Karl Ostby, Vice President of Norwest Bank Minnesota, N.A. Norwest defines the small business market as companies with sales below $10 million. The middle market is defined as companies with sales of $10 million to $250 million. Here are his comments.

Education Is Needed—Not Selling

Most small and medium-sized firms are not as knowledgeable in cash management as their larger counterparts. For these companies, Norwest uses an educational process as opposed to direct selling. There is a heavy element of the consultative approach, and different skills are required.

The cash management products that small businesses most often use are balance reporting, lockboxes, touch-tone tax deposits, serialized statements, and special handling of return items. Some controlled disbursement is sold to the $20 million to $50 million firms. These firms are looking for either early notification of check clearings or some additional check-clearing float.

Small Business Focus Began
Two Years Ago

About two years ago, Norwest Cash Management began focus-ing on the small business segment in order to build volume on electronic PC-based products. The bank has a large fixed expense, so this is a great way of lowering the unit cost.

Norwest wants to develop relationships with these small companies now and grow up with them. There is a lot of opportunity there: This year 30 percent of new sales will be with small businesses. We've greatly exceeded our intial expectations.

Internal Training is Vital

The training of business account officers is critical to our sales in this marketplace. We can't afford to make a lot of individual sales calls, because the average sale to a company is small, Norwest believes that prequalifying a call is important and that it helps the account officer close the sale.

The approach we use to sell a large number of small businesses on our PC-based ACH product is interesting. Basically, we provide one-half–day training sessions at the bank on how to use PCs with our product. Rarely does a company not buy the service after seeing how easy it is to use in our training class. In the future, small businesses will make much greater use of PCs, and they will be looking for more banking applications to use.

Same Product Line Offered to All Firms

Norwest hasn't modified its cash management product line or its pricing at all. It sells the same products to the large corporate market and to the middle and small markets. One product that has been a big hit in the small business market is the touch-tone tax deposit service, which handles withholding tax payments electronically. After only a three-week introduction, 300 customers signed up.

PC-based Products Are a Smash with Small Businesses

We're also working on a PC-based account reconcilement product. Firms will be mailed their account reconcilements with software on a disk that they can then use to interface to their business accounting system. Other PC products we're looking at are on-line investing and advances and paydowns on lines of credit. These two products will provide our bank with significant back-office savings. To come up with ideas for new products, we use input from our sales force, our small business bankers, and our customers.

Key Factors in Selecting a Major Bank

Ostby indicated that in selecting a bank, a company should use the following criteria:

1. The account officer and cash management salesperson must be good. After all, banking is a people business.

2. The bank's size is important. The bigger the better.

3. The bank's reputation should be excellent.

4. Find out whether the bank cares about small companies or is focused on the larger-sized companies. Smart banks should work hard to position themselves as being concerned and caring about the small business market.

We haven't found that the price for services is a big issue. Of course, it is a big concern on the borrowing side. It is the most visible way to evaluate a loan. It's hard, however, for a company to compare pricing with other banks for cash management services.

Why Are Relationships Lost?

Norwest loses relationships because of three main reasons:

1. We didn't pay attention to the firm's needs

2. Our pricing was not competitive on a large piece of business.

3. We asked a company to leave because of credit reasons.

Small Businesses Are Ideal Customers

Our sales staff love to work with small businesses since they can build a nice network of business banker account officers, if they train them well. Remember that we have over 200 banking offices in four Federal Reserve Districts. The customers are astonished at what our electronic products can do. At this time, we don't see a lot of competition on our PC products. We differentiate ourselves by our strong electronic capability and quality of service.

Interview Number Three: A West Coast Banker

My third interview was with a west coast banker who preferred to remain anonymous. The individual's bank defines the small business and middle-market companies with sales below $250 million. The bank has surveyed the small and medium-sized business marketplace in California to determine strategy and product focus. Currently, the major banks competing in this marketplace are Wells Fargo, Security Pacific, Bank of America, and First Interstate. Japan is also a formidable competitor. The penetration of the Japanese is apparent, because they control 30 percent of the banking assets collectively in California. The banker's responses to my questions are summarized in the following section.

Middle-Market Attributes

In surveys, we found that middle-market firms at $50 million in sales and below have specific attributes:

1. They have a full-time CFO who is not usually a specialist in bank relations or cash management. Firms with sales below $50 million and especially below $25 million have three primary concerns: their own day-to-day operations, their business survival, and the continued growth of their business.

2. They don't have much time to manage their bank relationships. Typically, these firms use only one or two banks.

3. They are looking for these critical elements from their banks:

   • Credit and access to credit

   • Basic, effortless banking that is as simple as possible

   • Operating services that reduce their day-to-day job pressures and services that will strengthen their relationship with the bank

4. They look for two qualities in their checking account services:

   • Accounts that can be tied to a revolving line of credit

   • Accounts that offer a sweep capability into an investment account

5. They are looking for their bank to offer personal banking services to their employees and family members

The $25 million companies and below are limited users of PCs. They may use PCs for word processing, but not for treasury functions. An educational process is needed to explain cash management uses of this technology. The higher end of the middle market is fairly knowledgeable about cash management. Based upon my own calling experience, people feel comfortable with what works. They will use technology if they can be convinced of the benefits they will realize through its application.

Bank Relationships Are Stable

Once a bank is selected, a company does not want to change. Inertia sets in. A company will put up with a lot. Changing banks is a time-consuming and difficult process. The more services the company has with the bank, the more difficult it is to move. Small companies pull out of relationships for credit reasons more than any other single reason. The smaller the firm, the more critical are its credit needs. As a company grows, quality of bank services becomes another important criterion. This marketplace wants top quality service, but it wants to pay the lowest price.

Companies change banks for various reasons. Lower middle-market firms look for high-quality service and competitive pricing. Larger middle-market firms look at the overall pricing for credit and services and look for a variety of services to meet their needs. Small companies' need for credit is foremost.

The Future Is Bright

In my view there are opportunities galore in the small and middle market, especially in California. There is a lot of risk, if banks aren't careful, but huge amounts of operational services can be sold. There is a void in cash management knowledge in the marketplace. Many times, people don't understand what they need, what's available or how to use a bank service to their best advantage. However, banks have to do their credit analysis homework to make sure that they are marketing to companies whose credit qualities meet pre-established standards. Banks want quality credits, not problems.

What I see happening in the future is that the large corporate market will keep shrinking because of mergers and acquisitions and LBOs. If a company we do business with disappears and then its banking relationships are consolidated, the we're out—the business is lost. The growth market left for banks is the small and middle-market firms. This market is not well understood by most banks. The ones who take time to study this market and offer pricing and services to address its special needs will reap enormous amounts of long-term new business.

14

Prepare for the Future—
It Will Be Here Soon

What Will Banking Look Like
in the Future?

"There is nothing permanent except change."
—Heraclitus (501 BC)

"You can never plan the future from the past"
—Edmund Burke (1791)

Future Scan: Banking Deregulation
Is Coming

Banking deregulation and interstate banking, when they come to pass, will have a positive impact on your banking relationships. Banks are currently not permitted to engage in investment banking and provide banking services simultaneously because of the antiquated Glass-Steagall Act (Banking Act of 1933).

In mid-1989, the Federal Reserve slowly chipped away at the wall separating banking and investment activities by allowing four large banks—Citicorp, Bankers Trust, Chase Manhattan, and J. P. Morgan—limited powers to underwrite corporate debt with certain restrictions. These restrictions included requirements that each bank set up a separate subsidiary to handle the underwriting and that underwriting be limited to 5 percent of the bank's revenues. The Fed also intends to allow banks to underwrite stocks this year.

250

Banks other than the well-known investment banks on Wall Street may soon be able to handle your financing. This increase in competition from aggressive commercial banks will provide you with more competitive and creative financing alternatives in the 1990s.

Interstate Banking Will Be Here by 1995

True interstate banking in the United States does not exist. It is moving at a fragmented pace. Each state has its own regulations that determine which banks can acquire new banks in that state. For example, on January 1, 1991, California will allow reciprocal banking nationwide. Currently, only banks in the 12th Federal Reserve district can acquire California banks. New York, however, has permitted out-of-state banks to acquire New York banks on a reciprocal basis since 1982.

Many other states permit only banks in nearby states the right to buy banks in their states. Unlike Canada, whose laws allow its six large banks to have countrywide branches, the United States has an antiquated banking law, the Banking Act of 1933, which the large U. S. banks are' trying to repeal.

Your company would greatly benefit from nationwide banking: You could deal with fewer banks, obtain more clout by providing a bank with more business, and reduce your overall banking costs. Interstate banking is inevitable.

Competitive Banking Environment Will Accelerate

According to Walter B. Wriston, "National borders have already become porous—news, data, and capital move across them on fiber-optic cables, satellite transponders and via channels all across the electromagnetic spectrum" ("A New Kind of Free Speech," *Forbes* Dec. 14, 1987, p. 264).

Today's banking environment is extremely competitive. Even though there are 13,700 commercial banks in the country, the majority of deposits are concentrated in the 100 largest banks. These banks also provide the panoply of services that most companies require.

Competition for corporate business is not limited to U.S. banks. Foreign banks offer loans at rates below their U.S. competitors' rates, and third-party vendors offer information and check-processing services. Large corporate conglomerates and financial companies offer investment, banklike, and ancillary services without restrictive banking legislation affecting their ability to offer more products and services than banks can offer.

The restrictions that keep banks from engaging in interstate banking and selling securities has further eroded the banks' ability to compete effectively and fairly in the marketplace. Thus, foreign banks and financial companies have stepped in to give a much broader array of services available to them than ever before. From your perspective, this competition provides you with an opportunity to shop around for services. This has caused banks to reassess their product offerings and develop new and enhanced products to retain their existing customer base.

Technological Advancements Will Continue

Advances in technology and information processing will also have a major impact on your banking relationships and on your business operations. As banks buy faster and more sophisticated computers and systems that can obtain instantaneous information on a worldwide basis, you will have to keep abreast of these changes. You will have to decide whether the cost of obtaining an avalanche of available information is justified by its usefulness in improving decision making, financial data accuracy, and bottom-line profits.

The incredible advances in PC sophistication—speed, capability, ease of use, and positive price/performance ratio—can provide your company with productivity and cash flow savings. Therefore, you and all your employees should become computer literate. Make sure that you can use word processing, spreadsheet, graphics, and database programs to handle your information needs.

Use of Expert Systems Will Mushroom

In the last few years, a handful of banks, corporations, and management consulting firms have been experimenting and implementing so-called "expert systems," which are developments in a branch of artificial intelligence. An expert system clones the expertise of an individual or group of individuals in a specific field and translates this knowledge base into a computer software program in a rule-based approach. An expert system thinks intelligently and can reason in some cases. These systems have already been developed for diagnosing illnesses, locating oil in the ground, analyzing handwriting samples for personality traits, training students in various disciplines, evaluating insurance portfolios, determining a person's eligibility for Medicaid, and planning corporate finances.

Use of Expert Systems in Financial Applications Is Underway

In the area of finance, systems have been developed in financial planning, portfolio management, option and stock trading, credit scoring and evaluation, insurance underwriting, and tax preparation. Security Pacific National Bank has developed applications in foreign exchange trading, real estate appraisals, commercial and retail loan applications, credit card fraud detection, branch operations processing, and telex processing.

Future financial applications for expert systems for small and medium-sized businesses that can be used on powerful PCs could include the following:

- Cash forecasting and budgeting
- Cash position calculation and daily monitoring

- Automated investment management
- Inventory, accounts receivable, and accounts payable management
- Financial decision making
- Bank evaluation, selection, and quality control measurement
- Automated account analysis statement analyzer

Keep abreast of this important field by reading business publications and start looking for applications that will help you save time and money.

Conclusion

Congratulations! You've finally reached the end of this money-making journey. Actually, it is only the beginning. Why? Because it is up to you to turn the ideas and suggestions presented here into bottom-line profits for your company. If you put this book aside without taking steps to improve your cash management and banking systems, then you have wasted your valuable time and robbed your company of its potential for improved cash flow.

Thirty Ways to Improve Your Cash Flow

Step back for a minute and consider the 30 ways you've learned to improve your cash flow. You've learned how to:

1. Evaluate your existing cash management system and techniques.
2. Select banks based on pricing, quality, and service.
3. Interpret bank availability schedules and fight for immediate to 2 day availability on your deposited checks.
4. Speed up your invoice process and your check collection process.
5. Decide on your accounts payable policy.

6. Evaluate whether to take a discount or to offer a discount.

7. Minimize check float on customer checks.

8. Choose whether you want to maximize check-clearing float on disbursement checks.

9. Avoid or minimize bad debts.

10. Review each step of the inventory process.

11. Pay your employees using direct deposit instead of paper checks.

12. Use lockboxes to minimize mail, processing, and availability float.

13. Evaluate an internal versus external retail lockbox provider.

14. Concentrate your funds in the least costly manner.

15. Obtain balance and deposit-reporting information.

16. Use zero-balance, controlled, or remote disbursement accounts.

17. Use account reconcilement services.

18. Use drafts to control certain types of disbursements more tightly, such as sales staff reimbursement.

19. Use lockbox and disbursement model studies to select optimal cities for collecting and disbursing funds.

20. Select specific lockbox and disbursement banks.

21. Understand the risks involved in using nonrepetitive wire transfers.

22. Use the CASH MAP to show you whether your cash management system needs improvement.

23. Read and use the account analysis statement to cut your bank costs.

24. Better manage your banking relationships.

25. Analyze whether to compensate your banks by fees.

26. Use the general pricing provided for specific bank services across the country as a guide in shopping for bank services.

27. Understand how bankers perceive the banking relationship.
28. Select a bank with a good credit rating.
29. Review the cash management services offered by 52 banks.
30. Find additional information on treasury workstations, financial and investment books, and software.

Now is the time to take action. Do it now!

Remember to call me at (914) 783-1231 if you need help. I look forward to hearing from you. Keep in mind what J. Paul Getty said: "There is no feeling like the feeling of success."

The success of your business depends on your ability to maximize your cash flow. Start today, you'll be happy you did.

Appendix 1

Federal Reserve System Offices

Fed District	Head Office	Branch Offices	Regional Check-Processing Centers
1	Boston		Lewiston Windsor Locks
2	New York	Buffalo	Cranford Jericho Utica
3	Philadelphia		
4	Cleveland	Cincinnati Pittsburgh	Columbus
5	Richmond	Baltimore Charlotte	
6	Atlanta	Birmingham Jacksonville Miami Nashville New Orleans	Columbia, SC
7	Chicago	Detroit	Des Moines Indianapolis Milwaukee
8	St. Louis	Little Rock Louisville Memphis	Charleston, WV
9	Minneapolis	Helena	
10	Kansas City	Denver Oklahoma City Omaha	

Fed District	Head Office	Branch Offices	Regional Check-Processing Centers
11	Dallas	El Paso Houston San Antonio	
12	San Francisco	Los Angeles Portland Salt Lake City Seattle	

Appendix 2

Bank Availability Deadline Example

Assume that you are depositing six checks at your bank's teller window at 2 P.M. Monday. Your company has not dollar amount encoded the checks before depositing them to ABC National in downtown New York City. The checks were drawn on the banks in the following Fed districts:

Deposited Check Routing Code	Check Amount	Bank Availability Assignment	Bank Deadline*
0210 (New York)	$ 4,000	0	7 A.M.
0210 (ABC National)	5,000	0	3 P.M.
0711 (Chicago RCPC)	15,000	1	5 P.M.
0421 (Cincinnati RCPC)	50,000	1	1 P.M.
0610 (Atlanta)	8,000	1	10 P.M.
0611 (Atlanta RCPC)	6,000	1	3 P.M.
1210 (San Francisco)	2,000	1	5 P.M.

* Deadline refers to *fully* encoded checks. Assume it takes two hours for a check deposited at teller's window to reach the encoding department.

The availability you'd receive on each check is provided as follows:

Deposited Check Routing Code	Check Amount	Bank Availability Provided	Bank Deadline
0210 (New York)	$ 4,000	1	missed
0210 (ABC National)	5,000	1	missed
0711 (Chicago RCPC)	15,000	1	made
0421 (Cincinnati RCPC)	50,000	2	missed
0610 (Atlanta)	8,000	1	made
0611 (Atlanta RCPC)	6,000	2	missed
1210 (San Francisco)	2,000	1	made

Four checks missed the deadlines. The New York City check was not deposited by 7 A.M. today, and therefore, you received next-day availability instead of immediate availability.

Although deposited one hour before the deadline the on-us check (drawn coincidentally on your bank ABC National) was not dollar amount encoded. Therefore, the bank added two more hours to its deposit time resulting in a 4 P.M. deposit time that missed the deadline for immediate funds by one hour.

The Cincinnati check had a 1 P.M. deadline for next-day availability. Since that deadline was missed, you received two-day availability.

Finally, the Atlanta RCPC check missed the one day availability deadline because it was not dollar amount encoded.

Guidelines to Meet Bank Deadlines

To meet bank deadlines, you must know when they are and then take specific actions to meet them.

- Make your daily deposit as early as possible so that any deadline between 11 A.M. and 1 P.M. can be met.

- Dollar encode your checks prior to depositing them with a MICR encoder (e.g., portable or used workstation model). Determine the cost-benefit of buying or leasing this equipment compared to the gain in availability and reduction in bank charges. Banks charge a few cents less for dollar encoded checks.

- Change deposit banks if the availability deadlines are later or more favorable, and if the move is practical.

- Have all customers send their checks directly to a lockbox banks. Since these banks operate around-the-clock six or seven days a week, your checks will make more deadlines. (See discussion of lockbox banking in Chapter 5.)

In our example, how much would you be losing by missing these deadlines? Assuming the funds could be invested at an 8 percent annual interest rate, we calculate the opportunity loss as follows:

Check	Days Lost	Check Dollar Amount
New York check	one	$ 4,000
ABC National check	one	5,000
Cincinnati check	one	50,000
Atlanta RCPC check	one	6,000
Total		$65,000

Calculation: Float loss = days lost × principal
× daily interest/360

1 × $65,000 × .08/360

= $14.43

Appendix 3

Cost-Benefit Analysis of a Direct-Send Program

To determine whether to use a direct send to another bank, a bank has to analyze the costs and float benefits. For example, let's make the following assumptions:

- Chase Manhattan Bank (New York City) has received 125 checks valued at $5 million drawn on the Bank of America (San Francisco). The checks are ready for dispatch at 7 A.M.
- The New York Fed's deadline for the checks for next-day availability is 4 A.M.
- The Fed's price per check is 5.2 cents plus $4.50 for the bundle of checks (called a cash letter).
- A direct send to Bank of America will cost $75 with availability the next day if the checks are received by 3 P.M. California time.

Analysis

The Fed's deadline of 4 A.M. is too late to make for next-day availability. Delivering checks to the Fed would result in receiving availability in two days and the Fed's processing cost would be $11[(.052 × 125) + 4.50].

Using a direct send would provide availability of one day, compared to two days from the Fed. The availability gain from the direct send is $1,111 ($5 million × 1 day × .08/360). The cost of the courier is $75. Therefore, the benefit of the direct send is $1,036 ($1,111 − 75). The net loss of using the Fed is $1,122 ($1,111 + 11).

Chase would break even on the direct send even if the courier cost $1,111! As you can see, the dollar value of the checks plays as critical a role in the decision as does the Fed's next-day availability deadline does.

Appendix 4

Composition of Checks Issued

The Federal Reserve Bank of Atlanta analyzed the composition of check volume in the United States in 1979 and provided the following results:

- Consumer-initiated (55%)

  Pay bills (25%)
  Pay retailers (18%)
  Obtain cash (7%)
  Other uses (5%)

- Corporate-initiated (40%)

  Pay other businesses (20%)
  Pay payroll (10%)
  Pay dividends/pension (10%)

- Government-initiated (5%)

The statistics have probably shifted in the past decade. The percentage of consumer-initiated checks has decreased due to the growth of credit card payments for retail purchases and the increase in ATM usage for obtaining cash.

The percentage of checks issued by corporations for payroll has probably diminished as more companies offer direct deposit of payroll. Likewise, the government's check writing has greatly diminished because of its policy to pay employees, beneficiaries, and vendors electronically through the ACH and FedWire systems.

Appendix 5

Phoenix-Hecht Postal Survey Subscribers (January 1, 1990)

American Security Bank
Ameritrust
Amsouth
Bank of America
Bank of Boston
Bank of California
Bank of New England
Bank of New York
Bank of Oklahoma
Bank One, Ohio
Bank One, Texas
Bankers Trust
Barnett Banks
Boatmen's Bancshares
Boston Safe Deposit & Trust
Cash Tech Consulting
Central Bank of Denver
Chase Lincoln First Bank
Chase Manhattan Bank
Chemical Bank
Citibank
Citizens & Southern National
   Bank
Comerica
Commerce Bank (Kansas City)
Connecticut Bank & Trust
Connecticut National Bank
Continental Bank (Chicago)
Continental Bank (Philadelphia)
Crestar Bank
Equitable Bank (Baltimore)
Ernst & Young
Fidelity Bank (Philadelphia)

Fifth Third Bank (Cincinnati)
First American Banks (Virginia)
First Bank Minnesota
First National Bank of Chicago
First City Banks (Texas)
First Fidelity (Newark)
First Interstate Banks
First National Bank of
   Louisville
First National Bank of Maryland
First Pennsylvania Bank
First Tennessee Bank
First Union National Bank
First Wachovia
First Wisconsin National Bank
Frost Bank
Harris Trust and Savings Bank
Huntington National Bank
Indiana National Bank
La Salle National Bank
Liberty National Bank (Louisville)
Manufacturers Hanover Trust
Manufacturers National Bank of Detroit
Marine Midland Bank
Marshall & Ilsley Bank
Maryland National Bank
Mellon
Mercantile Bank (St. Louis)
Merchants National Bank & Trust
   (Indianapolis)
Merchants National Bank (Iowa)
Meridian Bank
Midlantic National Bank

National Bank of Commerce
(Memphis)
National Bank of Detroit
National City Bank (Cleveland)
National Westminister Bank USA
Nationwide Remittance Center
NCNB National Bank
NCNB Texas National Bank
Northern Trust
Norwest Bank Minnesota
Philadelphia National Bank
PNC Financial
Provident Bank (Cincinnati)
Riggs National Bank
Security Pacific National Bank
Shawmut
Signet Bank
Society National Bank

South Carolina National Bank
Southeast Bank
Sovran Bank
Star Bank
State Street Bank & Trust
SunBank
Team Bank (Fort Worth)
Texas Commerce Bank
Third National Bank in Nashville
Trust Company Bank
U. S. National Bank of Oregon
United Bank of Denver
United Jersey Bank
United Missouri Bank
Valley National Bank of
Arizona
Wells Fargo Bank

Source: Reprinted with permission of Phoenix-Hecht

Appendix 6

Retail Lockbox Third-Party Providers

Alpha Beta Data Services
1501 Wilshire Boulevard
Los Angeles, CA 90017

Contact: Linda Ferrentino
Vice President Marketing & Sales
(213) 413-3282

CashFlex
420 Kuller Road
Clifton, NJ 07013

Contact: Joseph Proto
Vice President
(201) 772-0500

**EDS Retail Remittance
Processing Services**
26533 Evergreen
Southfield, MI 48086

Contact: Jeffrey Harvey
National Marketing Manager
(313) 262-7674

National Processing Company
1231 Durrett Lane
Louisville, KY 40285

Contact: James Strozdas
Vice President
(502) 364-2264

NRC-Express Payment Network
7926 Jones Branch Drive, Suite 500
McLean, VA 22102-3390

Contact: Donna Ray-Belcher
Director of Marketing
(703) 827-5090

Sears Payment Systems, Inc.
2500 Lake Cook Road
Riverwoods, IL 60015

Contact: Robert Archer
Vice President-Sales
(312) 405-3700

Appendix 7

Treasury Workstation Providers

ADS Systems
(a division of ADS Associates, Inc.)
Product name: RESOURCE
23586 Calabasas Road
Calabasas, CA 91302

Contact: Barry Bolger
(818) 347-9100

Chemical Banking Corporation
Product name: ChemLink II
55 Water Street, 7th Floor
New York, NY 10041

Contact: Peter Ramsey
Vice President
Middle Market Sales
(212) 309-5334

**DuPont Information Engineering
    Associates**
Product name: Treasury Information
    Management System (TIMS)
Nemours Building FD, Suite 9451
Wilmington, DE 19848

Contact: Richard P. Hairsine
(800) 638-4637

Gateway Systems, Inc.
Product name: Gateway Treasury
    System
1000 Hart Road
Barrington, IL 60010

Contact: Orazio Manzi-Fe Pater
President
(312) 381-6674

ICMS International
Product name: ICMS
1150 Bayhill Drive, Suite 121
San Bruno, CA 94066

Contact: Robert Wills
President
(415) 583-7909

**MH Financial Management
    Systems, Inc.**
Product name: Interplex Financial
    Manager
140 East 45th Street
New York, NY 10017

Contact: James P. Witkins
President
(212) 808-0264

Mellon Bank, N.A.
Product name: Telecash
  Microcomputer Option
3403 Three Mellon Bank Center
Pittsburgh, PA 15259-0001

Contact: Robert W. Stasik
Senior Vice President
(412) 234-1126

Wells Fargo Bank
Product name: Micro Express II
420 Montgomery Street
San Francisco, CA 94163

Contact: David Kurrasch
Vice President
(415) 396-7777

Appendix 8

Bank Safety
Rating Services

Firms that analyze financial condition of banks are listed. Each offers numerous reports and services that are too detailed to review here. Some firms analyze financial institutions other than commercial banks.

Cates Consulting Analysts, Inc.
40 Broad Street
New York, NY 10004
(212) 968-9200

Keefe BankWatch
Two World Trade Center
New York, NY 10048
(212) 323-8300

Moody's Investors Service
99 Church Street
New York, NY 10007
(212) 553-7181

Sheshunoff Information Services, Inc.
505 Barton Springs Road
Austin, TX 78704
(512) 472-2244
(800) 456-2340

Standard & Poor's
25 Broadway
New York, NY 10004
(212) 208-8000

Weiss Research, Inc.
Financial Safety Division
2200 N. Florida Mango Road
West Palm Beach, FL 33409
(407) 684-8100

VERIBANC, Inc.
P.O. Box 2963
Woburn, MA 01888
(617) 245-8370
(800) 442-2657

Appendix 9

Bank Survey Participants

Northeast Banks

Bank of Boston
Cash Management Division
Mail Stop 01-17-08
100 Federal Street
Boston, MA 02110

Contact: Susan M. Rugnetta
Cash Management
Division Executive
(617) 434-3780

Bank of Delaware
(affiliate of PNC Financial)
222 Delaware Avenue
P.O. Box 791
Wilmington, DE 19899

Contact: Kirsten K. Schell
Cash Management Sales
Consultant
(302) 429-2257

Bank of New York
101 Barclay Street
New York, NY 10286

Contact: Kenneth J. Soldwedel
Senior Vice President
(212) 815-6300

Chemical Banking Corporation
55 Water Street
New York, NY 10041

Contact: Peter Ramsey
Vice President
Middle Market Sales
(212) 309-5334

Citibank Cash Management
641 Lexington Avenue
6th Floor Zone 1
New York, NY 10043

Contact: Robert Taaffe
National Sales Manager
(212) 486-3445

Connecticut National Bank
One Landmark Square
P.O. Box 1454
Stamford, CT 06904-1454

Contact: Pamela M. Drouin
Vice President
(203) 358-6190

First Fidelity Bank, N.A.,
  New Jersey
550 Broad Street
Newark, NJ 07102

Contact: Robert L. Verderame
Senior Vice President
(201) 565-3387

First National Bank
of Maryland
25 S. Charles Street
P.O. Box 1506
Baltimore, MD 21203

Contact: Mark Furst
Vice President
(301) 244-4790

First New York Bank
for Business
111 East 57th Street
New York, NY 10022

Contact: Bernard Miluzzo
Commercial Services Manager
(212) 310-0654

Manufacturers Hanover
Trust Company
270 Park Avenue
New York, NY 10017

Contact: Michael Curran
Vice President
Director Sales and Marketing
(212) 286-6000

Marine Midland Bank, N.A.
One Marine Midland Center
Buffalo, NY 14203

Contact: Frances T. Carter
Vice President
Manager Sales and Marketing
(212) 912-2114

Mellon Bank, N.A.
Global Cash Management
Mellon Bank Center
Pittsburgh, PA 15259-0001

Contact: Juliann Kwasneski
Assistant Vice President
Market and Product Support Manager
(412) 234-1126

Meridian Bancorp, Inc.
35 North 6th Street
P.O. Box 1102
Reading, PA 19603

Contact: Janet C. Anderson
Assistant Vice President
Corporate Market Management
(215) 320-3528

Midlantic National Bank
Metro Park Plaza
P.O. Box 600
Edison, NJ 08818

Contact: Keith D. Kulper
Vice President
(201) 321-8214

National Westminster Bank USA
175 Water Street
New York, NY 10038

Contact: Saul E. Jones, Jr.
Vice President
(212) 602-2708

People's Bank
Cash Management Services
850 Main Street
Bridgeport, CT 06604

Contact: John Stophel, CCM
Vice President
(203) 338-6625

Philadelphia National Bank
A CoreStates Bank
FC 8-11-20
P.O. Box 7618
Philadelphia, PA 19101-7618

Contact: Cindy Yasinski
Vice President
(215) 973-5627

Pittsburgh National Bank   Contact: George R. Seifert
(an affiliate of PNC Financial)   Vice President
Fifth and Wood Streets   (412) 762-4996
Pittsburgh, PA 15265

The Riggs National Bank   Contact: Janice L. Sprague
of Washington D.C.   Senior Vice President
Cash Management Division   (202) 835-6313
808 17th Street, N.W.
Washington, D.C. 20006-3950

Southeast Banks

Citizens Fidelity Bank   Contact: Frank Cushman
& Trust Company   Vice President
Citizens Plaza   Manager of Cash Management Services
Louisville, KY 40296   (502) 581-4971

The Citizens & Southern   Contact: Robert M. Stegall
National Bank   Senior Vice President
P.O. Box 4899   (404) 581-3672
Atlanta, GA 30342-4899

Deposit Guaranty   Contact: Lee Ann Bargery
National Bank   Assistant President
P.O. Box 1200   (601) 960-6027
Jackson, MI 39215-1200

First National Bank   Contact: Janice E. Ostrand
of Commerce   Vice President & Manager
210 Baronne Street   (504) 582-7453
P.O. Box 60279
New Orleans, LA 70160-0279

First Tennessee Bank, N.A.   Contact: Ken Youngblood
Box 84   Senior Vice President
Memphis, TN 38101   Manager, Corporate Products Division
                                      (901) 523-4066

First Union National Bank   Contact: Ray Breault
of Florida   Senior Vice President
8653 Baypine Road, Suite 100   (904) 361-4491
Jacksonville, FL 32216

First Union National Bank   Contact: Christina C. Black
of Georgia   Vice President
55 Park Place   (404) 827-7961
Atlanta, GA 30303

**First Union National Bank
of North Carolina**
301 South College Street
Charlotte, NC 28288

Contact: Catherine A. Bates
Assistant Vice President
(704) 374-3227

**First Union National Bank
of South Carolina**
One Shelter Centre
P.O. Box 1329
Greenville, SC 29602

Contact: C. Sims Propst
Vice President
(803) 255-8055

**First Union National Bank
of Tennessee**
P.O. Box 3377
Nashville, TN 37219-0377

Contact: Lynn Evans
Cash Management Officer
(615) 271-1572

**Liberty National Bank
and Trust Company**
Cash Management Department
P.O. Box 32500
Louisville, KY 40232

Contact: John Sweeney
Senior Vice President
(502) 566-2491

NCNB National Bank
NCNB Plaza
Charlotte, NC 28255

Contact: Johnnie B. Quinn
Vice President
(704) 374-8447

NCNB Texas
P.O. Box 831000
Dallas, TX 75283-1000

Contact: Shirley J. Gilmer
Senior Vice President
(214) 508-2587

Signet Bank/Virginia
20 North Eighth Street
P.O. Box 25970
Richmond, VA 23260

Contact: T. Diane Lett
Product Market Analyst
(804) 771-7770

Southeast Bank, N.A.
One Southeast Financial Center
MS 1197
Miami, FL 33131

Contact: Donald R. Cochran
Vice President
Corporate Services
(305) 375-6692

**Sovran Bank/
Central South**
One Commerce Place
Nashville, TN 37219

Contact: Stephen L. Page, CCM
Cash Management Officer
Product Management
(615) 749-4311

Sovran Bank, N.A.
Sovran Center
12th & Main Streets
P.O. Box 27025
Richmond, VA 23261-7025

Contact: Michael W. Paulette
Senior Vice President
(804) 788-2424

Sun Bank, N.A.
P.O. Box 3833
Orlando, FL 32897

Contact: Letitia B. Gavin
Senior Vice President
and Sales Manager
(407) 237-4977

Third National Bank
201 Fourth Avenue North
P.O. Box 305110
Nashville, TN 37230-5110

Contact: Anna R. Morrow
Cash Management Representative
(615) 748-5020

Worthen Bank &
  Trust Company, N.A.
Worthen Bank Building
P.O. Box 1681
Little Rock, AK 72203

Contact: Donald J. Cook
Senior Vice President
Corporate Services Division
(501) 378-1678

Central Banks

Central National Bank
  and Trust Company of Enid
Box 3448
Enid, OK 73702

Contact: Charlene Smyly
Vice President
(405) 233-3535 ext. 336

Central Trust Company, N.A.
201 East Fifth Street
Cincinnati, OH 45202-4117

Contact: Ray D. Mallory
Vice President
(513) 651-8687

Commerce Bancshares Inc.
1000 Walnut Street
Kansas City, MO 64105

Contact: Teresa Rouse
Vice President
(816) 234-2429

Continental Bank
231 South LaSalle Street
Chicago, IL 60697

Contact: Patricia P. Scanlon
Vice President
(312) 828-4691

First Banks
First Bank Place
Minneapolis, MN 55480

Contact: Elizabeth R. Dienst
Assistant Vice President
Cash Management Group
(612) 370-4563

First Chicago
1 First National Plaza
Suite 0196
Chicago, IL 60670

Contact: Scott E. Bates
Senior Vice President
(312) 732-8038

Harris Trust and
  Savings Bank
Financial Services Group
111 West Monroe Street
P.O. Box 755
Chicago, IL 60690-0755

Contact: Thomas L. Kesman
Vice President
(312) 461-7663

National Bank of Detroit
611 Woodward Avenue
Detroit, MI 48226

Contact: Ronald W. Eppler
Corporate Cash Management Department
(313) 225-4157

Norwest Bank Minnesota, N.A.
Norwest Center
Sixth and Marquette
Minneapolis, MN 55479-0001

Contact: Jane O'Connor, CCM
Vice President/Manager
(612) 667-7419

Western Banks

**First Interstate Bank
  of California**
Cash Management Sales
1200 West 7th Street, G5-80
Los Angeles, CA 90017

Contact: Hans Heim, CCM
Vice President
(213) 239-5133

**First National Bank
  in Albuquerque**
40 First Plaza
Albuquerque, NM 87102

Contact: Ann R. Losee
Assistant Vice President
Corporate Cash Management
(505) 765-4849

**First Security Bank
  of Utah, N.A.**
15 East 100 South
Salt Lake City, UT 84111

Contact: Chris Feinauer
Cash Management Officer
(801) 350-5163

Security Pacific Bank
Treasury Management Services
The Sequor Group Inc.
333 S. Hope Street
Los Angeles, CA 90071

Contact: Karen M. Taylor
Vice President
(213) 345-7019

Wells Fargo Bank
595 Market Street, 15th Floor
San Francisco, CA 94163

Contact: David P. Kurrasch
Vice President
Cash Management Division
(415) 396-7777

Appendix 10

Surveyed Banks

NORTHEAST BANKS	Collection				Disbursement			ACH	EFT		EDI	Info.	Inv.
	Wholesale lockbox	Retail lockbox	Lockbox network	Return item lockbox	Zero balance accounts	Controlled disbursement	Account reconciliation	ACH	Wire transfer	Corporate trade payment	Electronic Data Interchange	Balance reporting	SWEEP accounts
Bank of Boston	✓		✓	✓	✓	✓	✓	✓	✓	✓		✓	✓
Bank of Delaware (an affiliate of PNC Financial Corporation)	✓	✓		✓	✓	✓	✓	✓	✓	✓		✓	✓
Bank of New York	✓		✓		✓	✓	✓	✓	✓	✓	✓	✓	✓
Chemical Banking Corporation	✓	✓	✓		✓	✓	✓	✓	✓	✓	✓	✓	✓
Citibank	✓	✓	✓	✓	✓	✓	✓	✓	✓	✓	✓	✓	✓
Connecticut National Bank	✓	✓			✓	✓	✓	✓	✓			✓	✓
First National Bank of Maryland	✓	✓		✓	✓	✓	✓	✓	✓	✓		✓	✓
First Fidelity Bank, N.A., New Jersey	✓			✓	✓	✓	✓	✓	✓	✓		✓	✓
First New York Bank for Business	✓	✓			✓	✓	✓	✓	✓				
Manufacturers Hanover Trust Company	✓		✓	✓	✓	✓	✓	✓	✓	✓	✓	✓	✓
Mellon Bank N.A.	✓	✓	✓	✓	✓	✓	✓	✓	✓	✓	✓	✓	✓
Meridian Bancorp, Inc.	✓	✓	✓	✓	✓	✓	✓	✓	✓	✓	✓	✓	✓
Marine Midland Bank, N.A.	✓		✓		✓	✓	✓	✓	✓	✓			
Midlantic National Bank	✓	✓	✓		✓	✓	✓	✓	✓		✓		
National Westminster Bank USA	✓				✓	✓	✓	✓	✓	✓	✓		
People's Bank	✓	✓			✓	✓	✓	✓	✓				
Philadelphia National Bank (a CoreStates bank)	✓	✓	✓	✓	✓	✓	✓	✓	✓	✓	✓	✓	✓
Pittsburgh National Bank (an affiliate of PNC Financial Corporation)	✓	✓	✓	✓	✓	✓	✓	✓	✓	✓	✓	✓	✓
The Riggs National Bank of Washington D.C.	✓	✓	✓	✓	✓	✓	✓	✓	✓	✓	✓	✓	✓

Services Offered

SOUTHEAST BANKS	Collection				Disbursement			ACH	EFT		EDI	Info.	Inv.
	Wholesale lockbox	Retail lockbox	Lockbox network	Return lockbox item	Zero balance accounts	Controlled disbursement	Account reconciliation	ACH	Wire transfer	Corporate trade payment	Electronic Data Interchange	Balance reporting	SWEEP accounts
Citizens Fidelity Bank & Trust Company (an affiliate of PNC Financial Corporation)	✓				✓	✓	✓	✓	✓		✓	✓	
The Citizens & Southern National Bank	✓	✓	✓		✓	✓	✓	✓	✓	✓	✓	✓	
Deposit Guaranty National Bank	✓				✓	✓	✓	✓	✓		✓		
First National Bank of Commerce	✓	✓	✓		✓	✓	✓	✓			✓	✓	
First Tennessee Bank, N.A.	✓			✓	✓	✓	✓	✓	✓		✓		
First Union National Bank of Florida	✓				✓	✓	✓	✓	✓		✓	✓	
First Union National Bank of Georgia	✓				✓	✓	✓	✓	✓		✓	✓	
First Union National Bank of North Carolina	✓				✓	✓	✓	✓	✓		✓	✓	
First Union National Bank of South Carolina	✓				✓	✓	✓	✓	✓		✓	✓	
First Union National Bank of Tennessee	✓	✓			✓	✓	✓	✓	✓		✓	✓	
Liberty National Bank and Trust Company	✓	✓			✓	✓	✓	✓	✓		✓	✓	
NCNB National Bank	✓	✓	✓	✓	✓	✓	✓	✓	✓		✓	✓	
NCNB Texas	✓	✓	✓	✓	✓	✓	✓	✓	✓		✓		
Signet Bank/Virginia	✓	✓		✓	✓	✓	✓	✓	✓		✓	✓	
Southeast Bank, N.A.	✓	✓	✓		✓	✓	✓	✓	✓		✓	✓	
Sovran Bank/Central South	✓	✓	✓		✓	✓	✓	✓	✓		✓	✓	
Sovran Bank, N.A.	✓	✓	✓		✓	✓	✓	✓	✓		✓		
Sun Bank, N.A.	✓	✓			✓	✓	✓	✓	✓		✓	✓	
Third National Bank	✓				✓	✓	✓	✓	✓			✓	
Worthen Bank & Trust Company, N.A.	✓	✓			✓	✓	✓	✓	✓		✓	✓	

Services Offered

	Collection					Disbursement		ACH	EFT		EDI	Info.	Inv.
	Wholesale lockbox	Retail lockbox	Lockbox network	Return item lockbox	Zero balance accounts	Controlled disbursement	Account reconciliation	ACH	Wire transfer	Corporate trade payment	Electronic Data Interchange	Balance reporting	SWEEP accounts
CENTRAL BANKS													
Central National Bank	✓	✓				✓	✓	✓	✓	✓	✓		
Central Trust (an affiliate of PNC Financial Corporation)	✓	✓			✓	✓	✓	✓	✓	✓	✓	✓	
Commerce Bancshares Inc.	✓	✓	✓		✓	✓	✓	✓	✓	✓	✓		
Continental Bank	✓	✓			✓	✓	✓	✓	✓	✓	✓	✓	
First Banks	✓	✓		✓	✓	✓	✓	✓	✓		✓	✓	
First Chicago	✓	✓	✓	✓	✓	✓	✓	✓	✓	✓	✓	✓	
Harris Trust and Savings Bank	✓	✓	✓		✓	✓	✓	✓	✓	✓	✓	✓	
National Bank of Detroit	✓	✓			✓	✓	✓	✓	✓	✓	✓		
Norwest Banks Minnesota, N.A.	✓	✓			✓	✓	✓	✓	✓	✓	✓	✓	
WESTERN BANKS													
First Interstate Bank of California	✓	✓	✓		✓	✓	✓	✓	✓	✓	✓	✓	
First National Bank in Albuquerque	✓	✓			✓	✓	✓	✓	✓		✓		
First Security Bank of Utah, N.A.	✓	✓			✓	✓	✓	✓	✓	✓	✓	✓	
Security Pacific Bank	✓	✓			✓	✓	✓	✓	✓		✓	✓	
Wells Fargo Bank	✓							✓	✓		✓		

Note: Banks may have added return item lockbox and EDI since this was prepared.

279

Appendix 11

Financial and Investment Books

Financing

Entrepreneurial Finance: Taking Control of Your Financial Decision Making by Robert Ronstadt. Published in 1988 by Lord Publishing, Inc. $16.95 (softcover), $32.95 (hardcover).

This comprehensive and easy-to-read book provides insightful information on starting a business or expanding an existing one. It shows you how to identify and implement applicable financial strategies. (See Appendix 12 for Ronstadt's financial software program.)

Borrowing

Business Loans: A Guide to Money Sources & How to Approach Them Successfully by Rick Stephan Hayes. Revised and updated. Published in 1989 by John Wiley and Sons. $17.95

The Complete Small Business Loan Kit by Consumer Loan Foundation. Published in 1990 by Bob Adams, Inc., 260 Center Street, Holbrook, MA 02343. $12.95

How to Borrow Money from a Banker, by Roger Bel Air. Published in 1988 by AMACOM. (518) 891-1500 $17.95

This clearly written, detailed guide offers rules to help business owners raise money and take the mystery out of the bank loan approval process.

Raising Money: Venture Funding & How to Get It by Ron Merrill and Gaylord Nichols. Published in 1990 by AMACOM. (518) 891-1500. $24.95

This book shows entrepreneurs how to raise venture capital. Included are the business plans presented for critique of almost 50 companies at the CalTech/MIT Enterprise Forum. Sample documents are also provided.

The Small Business Guide to Borrowing Money by Richard L. Rubin and Philip Goldberg. Published by McGraw-Hill in 1980. $38.95

This book includes every major public and private financing source available from both inside and outside normal channels. The preparation for the loan application is also covered.

Financial Matters

Beyond IBM by Lou Mobley and Kate McKeown. Published in 1988 by McGraw-Hill. $18.95

Based on IBM's development, Chapters 10 and 11 on *the total financial system* and *financial strategy,* respectively, offer a crash course in understanding finance. The Mobley Matrix is explained, which offers a discussion on the interrelationship between the income statement and the balance sheet in producing the cash statement. It provides cash information critical to managing your business.

For more information on the book or the Mobley Matrix contact:

McKeown & Company, Inc.
P.O. Box 39155
Washington, D.C. 20016
(800) 772-1990
Contact: Kate McKeown

Collection Strategies and Techniques by R.D. "Rusty" Rutherford. Published in 1985 by National Association of Credit Management, Publishing Division, 520 Eighth Avenue, New York, NY 10018. $19.95

The Entrepreneur & Small Business Problem Solver (second edition) by William A. Cohen. Published by John Wiley in 1990. $24.95

Financial Management for Small Business by Edward Rausch. Published by AMACOM in 1982. $9.95

The Guide to Understanding Financial Statements by S.B. Costales. Published by McGraw-Hill in 1979. $26.50

Financial statements and how they work are clearly explained. No previous accounting or financial background is necessary.

How to Control Accounts Receivable for Greater Profits—A Dun & Bradstreet Small Business Handbook.

How to Start, Finance and Manage Your Own Business by Joseph R. Mancuso. Published by Prentice Hall, New York. $14.95

Turnaround: Avoid Bankruptcy and Revitalize Your Company by Edmond P. Freiermuth. Published in 1989 by Liberty House, a division of TAB BOOKS Inc., Blue Ridge Summit, PA 17294-0214. $14.95

This is geared to help small business owners and managers to achieve a fast and successful business turnaround, or avoid the necessity for one.

Up Your Cash Flow by Harvey A. Goldstein. Published in 1986 by Granville Publications, 10960 Wileshire Boulevard, Suite 826, Los Angeles, CA 90024. $12.95

Business Plans

Business Plan for Startups by University of North Dakota. Published by Lord Publishing, Inc., 8A Pleasant Street, South Natick, MA 01760, (800) 525-5673. $29.95

Organized in 19 chapters with appendices, references, and a glossary, this book covers the steps in developing a comprehensive business plan.

Business Plans That Win $$$: Lessons from the MIT Enterprise Forum by Stanley R. Rich and David E. Gumpert. Published in 1987 by Harper & Row, New York. $9.95

Miscellaneous Topics

How to Set up Your Own SMALL BUSINESS by Max Fallek. Published by American Institute of Small Business, 7515 Wayzata Boulevard, Suite 201, Minneapolis, MN 55426, (800) 328-2906. $149.95

Two volume text on all aspects of setting up and operating a small business.

Legal Handbook for Small Business (revised edition) by Marc J. Lane. Published in 1989 by AMACOM, (518) 891-1500. $18.95

This handbook provides crucial legal information for running a small business efficiently and profitably. Chapters on tax regulations, accounting procedures, credit law, and hiring practices are offered with many useful checklists, figures, and forms.

Small Business Matters: Topics, Procedures, and Strategies by Mary Frech McVicker. Published in 1988 by Chilton Book Company, Radnor, PA. $14.95

Basic information needed by the owner or manager of a small- or medium-sized business is provided. Part 3 of the book covers the basics in accounting and finance.

Short-Term Investments

Corporate Investments Manual: Short- and Intermediate-Term Fixed-Income Securities by Alan G. Seidner. Published in 1989 by Warren, Gorham & Lamont, Inc., 210 South Street, Boston, MA 02111, (800) 950-1216. $98

This book contains a wealth of information for anyone interested in investing in the fixed-income securities market. Checklists, forms, flow charts, and other useful material are provided with a glossary, suggested readings, and index.

The Dow Jones-Irwin Guide to Bond and Money Market Investments by Frank J. Fabozzi. Published in 1987 by Dow Jones-Irwin, Homewood, IL, (800) 634-3966. $29.95

The Money Market (3rd edition) by Marcia Stigum. Published in 1990 by Dow Jones-Irwin, Homewood, IL. $62.50

Stocks, Bonds, Options, Futures: Investments and Their Markets by The Staff of the New York Institute of Finance and edited by Stuart R. Veale. Published in 1987 by New York Institute of Finance, 70 Pine Street, New York, NY 10270-0003, (212) 344-2900. $24.95

This is an easy to read basic textbook on the securities markets. Investment fundamentals and the different markets are covered.

Appendix 12

Financial Software Programs

This listing does not denote any endorsement. It is recommended that you obtain available brochures and demo disks, taking advantage of free trial periods and asking for references.

Accounting Packages for IBM PC and Compatibles

ACCPAC Easy Quick Start Accounting Pak 1.01

This is an entry-level program with an accounting training disk and payroll module. It has rudimentary accounts receivable and payables. No help screens are offered. Cost: $169

ACCPAC Bedford Integrated Accounting 3.25

Suitable for larger small businesses and businesses with a full-time bookkeeper. Data is exportable to Lotus® 1-2-3® and many word processors. Cost: $249
Computer Associates International, Inc.
1240 MacKay Drive
San Jose, CA 95131
(800) 531-5236

ACT 1

A general ledger, accounts receivable and payable, inventory, order entry, and payroll are included in this program. Cost: $179.50. 30 day money back guarantee

Cougar Mountain Software
2609 Kootenai
Box 6886
Boise, ID
(208) 344-2540

AXS Accounting Solutions Level 2 1.1
This is a useful program for businesses with under 10 employees. offering a general ledger and accounts payable and receivable. Cost: $140

Computer Trends, Inc.
116 E. Washington
Ann Arbor, MI 48104
(313) 662-4430

DacEasy Accounting 4.0

Aimed at accrual rather than cash accounting, this program has a general ledger and accounts payable and receivable. It is more useful to larger small businesses, and is good for a larger firm with a full-time accountant. Cost: $150

DacEasy, Inc.
17950 Preston Road, Suite 800
Dallas, TX 75252
(214) 248-0205
(800) 877-8088

4-in-1 Basic Accounting
Real World Accounting Series

This comprehensive entry-level package has a general ledger, accounts payable and receivable, and payroll. It is more difficult to install and learn than most, but it is a good program. Cost: $249.95

RealWorld Corporation
282 Loudon Road
P.O. Box 2051
Concord, NH 03302-9985
(800) 678-6336

One-Write Plus Accounting 2.05

This can be easily used with no prior accounting knowledge, and it includes accounts receivable and payable. The payroll module is $149 extra. Only 30 days of free telephone support are included, but the documentation is easy to understand. Cost: $299

Great American Software, Inc.
9 Columbia Drive
Amherst, NH 03031
(800) 528-5015

Peachtree Complete II 4.21

Includes extensive manuals and accounting primer, general ledger, accounts receivable and payable, inventory, payroll, and job costing. Cost: $199

Peachtree Software, Inc.
1505 Pavilion Place
Norcross, GA 30093
(404) 564-5800
(800) 247-3224

RAMbase Accounting

This program contains accounts receivable and payable, inventory control, and check book reconciliation, and it produces over 100 reports. Cost: $149. Unconditional 30-day guarantee

Ram Base Systems, Inc.
22749 Highway 18, Suite B-3
Apple Valley, CA 92307
(619) 247-4224

TAS Books 2.0

This higher-priced package with excellent capabilities comes with a general ledger, accounts receivable and payable, and payroll and inventory control. Cost: $399

Business Tools, Inc.
15395 S.E. 30th Place, Suite 310
Bellevue, WA 98007
(206) 644-2015

Cash Flow Software

Cash Flow Analysis

This program provides cash flow projections. It requires no programming knowledge. The user inputs data into eight categories: total sales, cost of goods sold, general and administrative expense, long-term debt, other cash receipts, inventory-buildup/reduction, capital expenditures, and income tax. The program allows changes in assumptions and provides a complete array of reports. Cost: $495. Free demonstration disk available. 30-day money back guarantee

Superior Software
16055 Ventura Boulevard, Suite 725
Encino, CA 91436
(818) 990-1135 (In California)
(800) 421-3264 (Outside California)

The Mobley Matrix

This is a financial management system including *Beyond IBM*, Mobley Matrix Guide to Finance, audio tapes, videotape, software, and an installation/reference/user's manual. Cost: $895. 30-day money back guarantee

McKeown & Company, Inc.
P.O. Box 39155
Washington, D.C. 20016
(800) 772-1990

Ronstadt's Financials™

This software program was developed in conjunction with Ronstadt's book, *Entrepreneurial Finance: Taking Control of Your Financial Decision Making.* It provides sound financial information useful for beginning or expanding a business. Business planning, budgeting, new venture analysis, financing presentations, and cash flow planning are covered. Included are a technical support package, both $5\frac{1}{4}$" and $3\frac{1}{2}$" diskettes, and one of eight customizable industry specific models. Cost: $245

Lord Publishing, Inc.
8A Pleasant Street
South Natick, MA 01760
(508) 651-9955
(800) 525-5673

Up Your Cash Flow Software

Contained in this program are automatically prepared spreadsheets for business plan financial data, profit and loss forecast/budget, and payroll analysis (by employee). Cost: $129.95. Also Macintosh II software

Granville Publications Software
10960 Wilshire Boulevard, Suite 826
Los Angeles, CA 90024
(800) 873-7789

Business Plan Software

BizPlanBuilder

This business plan developer software runs under a Lotus® 1-2-3®-compatible spreadsheet on PCs and under Excel® or Multiplan® on the Macintosh versions. Cost: $99. IBM PC and Macintosh versions

Tools for Sales
13335 Wildcrest Drive
Los Altos, CA 94022
(415) 941-9191
(800) 442-7373

Business Plan Toolkit
Financial Forecasting Toolkit

Templates for business planning and financial forecasting are contained in this program. Cost: $69.95 to $99.95. IBM PC and Macintosh versions.

Palo Alto Software
260 Sheridan Avenue, Suite 219
Palo Alto, CA 94306
(415) 325-3190
(800) 336-5544

How to Write a Business Plan

The program provides hands-on exercises in writing a business plan, including profit and loss statements, balance sheets, and cash flow statements. Cost: $125. IBM PC and Macintosh versions

American Institute of Small Business (AISB)
7515 Wayzata Boulevard, Suite 201
Minneapolis, MN 55426
(612) 545-7001
(800) 328-2906

The AISB also sells an $85 hard copy publication entitled "How to Write a Business Plan Project Kit." It includes examples and a sample case study.

The Pro Forma 1—Planning the Business Venture
A business plan technique is built on Lotus® 1-2-3® and Microsoft Excel® spreadsheets, and either package is needed to use this software. Cost: $199. IBM PC and Macintosh versions

The Company Co.
333 North
Alpine, UT
(801) 756-2774

Venture—The Entrepreneur's Handbook

The handbook includes Business Plan Builder and a word processor, spreadsheet, file manager, and general ledger with a check writer. Cost: $349

Star Software Systems
363 Van Ness Way
Torrance, CA 90501
(213) 533-1190
(800) 242-7827

Appendix 13

Other Useful Resources

National Automated Clearing House Association (NACHA)

NACHA publishes booklets and brochures on ACH applications, rules and regulations, and a monthly newsletter.
For further information contact NACHA at:
607 Herndon Parkway
Suite 200
Herndon, VA 22070
(703) 742-9090
(703) 787-0996 (fax)

National Corporate Cash Management Association (NCCMA)

NCCMA is a national organization representing over 5,000 cash management professionals. It provides programs for continuing education, professional certification—Certified Cash Manager (CCM), industry standards, government relations, publications, and conducts an annual conference.
For further information contact the NCCMA at:
52 Church Hill Road
Newtown, CT 06470
(203) 426-3007

Electronic Data Interchange (EDI)

One to Get Ready: How to Prepare Your Company for EDI by Bernell K. Stone. Published by The CoreStates Banks in 1988.
To obtain a complimentary copy of this 112-page book call CoreStates at (800) 544-6310. This book contains a thorough explanation of the concepts, uses, strategies, and transaction details of EDI.

EDI Software (nonbank software for small and middle market firms)

InTouch*EDI PC Software

InTouch*EDI software allows your firm to communicate with any trading partner using the ANSI X12 format to exchange business documents such as purchase orders and invoices. An electronic desk that functions like an office desk is needed to use the software. Pull-down menus, mouse support, and color make the system easy to learn and operate. A toll-free hotline is provided for questions.

Cost: $900 per unit (software license fee). After first year, $8 monthly maintenance. Other fees for transactions. Compatibility: IBM PC/ XT/ AT or PS/ 2. Demonstration disk available.

For more information contact:

Harbinger*EDI Services
1800 Century Place, Suite 340
Atlanta, GA 30345
(404) 320-1636

Check Writing Software (nonbank software)

CheckFree

CheckFree is a checkless checkwriting service. A modem attached to a 256K IBM PC or compatible is needed. Payment information entered on a formatted screen includes the payee's name, check amount, and date to be paid. Payments are processed through the Federal Reserve system. It has a built-in automated check register. A bank statement provides information on each transaction.

Cost: $49.95 software; $9 month for 20 checks; $3 month for increments of 10 checks.

For more information contact:

CheckFree Technologies, Inc.
P.O. Box 897
Columbus, OH 43216
(614) 898-6000

Index